Advance Praise for *You Should Test That!*

If you want to create massive advancements in your business and drive more sales, you have to read You Should Test That!.

    —Neil Patel, Co-Founder of KISSmetrics, Crazy Egg, and Quicksprout

In a world where you can test everything, why are companies testing nothing? Maybe that's being too harsh, but it's true. In You Should Test That! *Chris doesn't just talk about what you should test, but how to think about your marketing in a very smart and strategic way. Too many brands are wasting too much money on marketing without doing the strategic testing first.* You Should Test That! *screams, "You should buy this book!"*

    —Mitch Joel, President of Twist Image & Author, Blogger, Podcaster of *Six Pixels of Separation*

Chris Goward does a fantastic job of explaining not just effective testing techniques, but also the strategic value testing can deliver to your entire marketing program. This well-illustrated guide to all aspects of testing is a must-read for anyone responsible for marketing decision-making.

    —Roger Dooley, author of *Brainfluence*

With You Should Test That!, *Goward has delivered a well-researched and insightful exploration of the latest conversion optimization principles and techniques in a practical and enjoyable book that pushes the boundaries of the art and science of optimized marketing. A definite must-read that ought to be required reading for anyone serious about optimization.*

    —Brett Tabke, Founder and CEO, Pubcon, the premier optimization and new media conferences

Everyone knows about A/B testing and wants to do it, but not many are doing it regularly. Why? Chris Goward has written an excellent book to answer this precise question where he urges businesses to create internal testing and optimization champions to drive business success. And to corroborate his message, Chris deploys his years of experience in the industry to show successful case studies, discuss his proven LIFT model, and analyze scientific techniques and all-too-essential rules-of-thumb. You Should Test That! *is a fantastic book that covers testing and optimization from many different angles. I highly recommend it!*

    —Paras Chopra, CEO of Visual Website Optimizer

Chris Goward discusses a proven, scientific approach to experimentation with clarity and simplicity—while not losing the conceptual depth this topic deserves. This book at times is a primer in modern online marketing and an advanced study for hypothesis-based testing at others. A wonderfully written text—the very best on this topic I can find!
    —RAJU MALHOTRA, Director, Microsoft Corp.

Read this book, and you will profit. Chris Goward gets it. I know. I've stalked him for years. His LIFT framework was the missing piece of my CRO puzzle leading to millions of dollars in additional sales for our small family business over the past few years.

If you're a competitor of mine, I'm just kidding. CRO is just a fad. Your shopping cart is just fine. Don't change a thing.
    —ROB SNELL, Gun Dog Supply

You Should Test That! *is a thorough and irreverent guide for website testing. The wealth of case studies and various testing recipes provides any marketer with plenty of ideas from day one. I particularly liked Chapter 13, which talks about how to make testing a broader discipline throughout the entire organization.*

Let's face it, we need to move from an era of "Which button is better?" to also go after questions like "What part of our product's value prop is most compelling?" or "How should we acquire new customers?" The good news is we can use a lot of the fundamentals and best practices developed over the years in website testing and apply it much more broadly to lean marketing and entrepreneurial management practices in general.
    —TOM LEUNG, CEO of Yabbly and former Sr. Product Manager for Google Website Optimizer

Wow! This is packed full of stuff you can use today. So many business books have a couple of good ideas and are padded out with fluff. This is jammed with good ideas from start to finish, debunking myths in a humorous and practical way and giving you the tools you need to make more money online.
    —CHARLES NICHOLLS, Founder, SeeWhy

The days of marketing online just for the sake of being present are long gone. Stakeholders at all corporate levels now demand optimized campaigns, making clear the value proposition and return on investment. You Should Test That! *reveals deep online testing secrets that fuel some of the most effective companies in the world.*

Read this book, or read about it somewhere else.
    —MARTY WEINTRAUB, author of *Killer Facebook Ads* and CEO, aimClear

Chris Goward knows the secret to business: listen to your gut, and then test what it says. This book is a must read for understanding why scientific testing is the key to continuous improvement in your organization.

—JACKIE HUBA, author of *Creating Customer Evangelists and Citizen Marketers*

Chris Goward is the Nate Silver of conversion optimization—smart, entertaining, and a step ahead of everyone else. If you want to be prepared for the future of online marketing, read his book.

—LANCE LOVEDAY, Co-author, *Web Design for ROI* and CEO, Closed Loop

What I really liked about this book was the thorough data-driven approach to helping you make informed decisions of what to do with your website. Packed with 15 real-world case studies, Chris writes a non-technical book that is full of practical tips for building a culture of business decisions through tested insights. In other words, getting data and its sibling testing optimization out of a silo and integrated into the blood stream of your organization.

—BRIAN CLIFTON, author of *Advanced Web Metrics with Google Analytics*

I thoroughly enjoyed the unique perspective Chris is taking in his book when talking about conversion rate optimization. It's an eye-opener! Also, the great number of case studies in the book makes the message even more convincing. As an entrepreneur, I did find something new in this approach.

—ANN SMARTY, Founder, SEOSmarty.com

Chris is a highly regarded conversion expert who has produced a wonderful book that makes a complex process easy to understand. It covers many of the organizational barriers to change and how to get support for changes to the website. It also covers what you need to know about managing and implementing your conversion project. I recommend this book to anybody wanting to improve their conversion success.

—BRUCE CLAY, coauthor of *Search Engine Optimization All-in-One For Dummies* and President, Bruce Clay, Inc.

What I like about Chris's approach is that he can be both tactical and strategic. On the one hand, you can use this book to ensure your website isn't a slacker. But on the other, you can also use it on a broader level, to guide decisions based less on gut, and more on real insight.

—ANN HANDLEY, co-author of *Content Rules* and Chief Content Officer, MarketingProfs

Marketing has changed fundamentally with the rapid growth of the online channel, to the point that "close enough" and "gut feel" are mostly working their way out of marketers' vernacular. Chris Goward's new book is an important manifesto for today's digital marketers that want to continue to push lead and conversion performance while also aiming for the holy grail of outstanding user experience. He describes that testing is so much more than simply "conversion optimization," and makes solid arguments for the value of adopting a data-driven iterative testing model. I would recommend that this book be read not only by marketing executives and strategists, but also by the analysts that are collecting and evaluating business performance data.

    —CHRIS BOGGS, Digital Marketing Strategist with over 13 years of experience, currently serving as the Chairman of SEMPO.org

In his book You Should Test That! *Chris Goward preaches the importance of clarity, among other things, and he takes his own advice. Goward is unambiguous and unyielding as he guides us to tests that give clear direction toward online success. Yet, he successfully weaves scientific rigor into intuition and creativity. The chapter on creating an optimized value proposition should be required reading in business schools. His Optimization Manifesto sums it up perfectly: "We believe in art and science."*

    —BRIAN MASSEY, Conversion Scientist and author of *Your Customer Creation Equation*

Testing and data changed the way we market at Grasshopper, starting with conversion optimization, we built a culture around data and marketing optimization that now has gone into all parts of the organization. Data has optimized everything we do, resulting in increased revenue and profit. Every Founder and Marketer should read this book.

    —DAVID HAUSER, Cofounder of Grasshopper, Chargify, PopSurvey, and Angel Investor

Before the Web, non-targeted advertising ruled and creative people dominated marketing. But as Chris Goward shows, the Web allows for infinite data analysis, driving success to those who test. Guess what? The quants are now the most important people on your marketing team.

    —DAVID MEERMAN SCOTT, bestselling author of *The New Rules of Marketing and PR*

Website optimization has long been one of the easiest ways to improve your conversion rate, but how and what to test is always in contention. What has never been in contention among the best testers, however, is that your tests should be structured and scientific. You Should Test That! *provides an easy to understand framework for testing, and lots of excellent ideas for how to optimize toward specific goals. A much needed comprehensive approach to testing that doesn't exist today.*

    —JESSE NICHOLS, Agency Partnerships, Google Analytics

Chris Goward's book You Should Test That! *presents a compelling marketing manifesto to test everything—gut instincts, market research best practices, experts' advice—for continuous improvement. Testing works, and as the author's manifesto states, "testing is the crucible for decision-making,"—profitable decision making. This book details a clear, actionable explanation of the science and art of getting more revenue generating actions from the same amount of visitors.*

Using a top-notch roster of case studies, Chris Goward talks us through just how real companies increased conversions and revenue doing so. His book is a thoroughly persuasive argument for creating a data driven culture at your company and a road map for being an effective evangelist for it. How to gain senior-level buy-in for testing. How to involve other departments. Interactive tools to tie results to revenue.

—ANNE F. KENNEDY, International Search & Social Marketing Strategist, and author *Global Search Engine Marketing: Fine-tuning Your International Search Engine Results*

Understanding marketing testing, website optimization, search traffic improvement, usability testing and all the rest are simply part of being a marketer these days. But this book is also about marketing; branding, messaging, persuasion, etc. And once you have those under your belt, you are well on your way to strategic marketing optimization.

—JIM STERNE, Founder, eMetrics Summit and Chairman, Digital Analytics Association

All businesses create content today...but only a handful test their web content. You Should Test That! *will help you set up a culture of testing in your organization that will deliver bottom line results. Heck, since you're spending so much on your content, why don't you check to see if it actually is working for you. Read this book...then share it with your entire marketing team.*

—JOE PULIZZI, Founder, Content Marketing Institute and author of *Managing Content Marketing: The Real-World Guide for Creating Passionate Subscribers to Your Brand*

Testing is, without a doubt, one of the most effective ways to improve digital customer experiences, yet it remains an untapped resource for most organizations. Chris' book offers a definitive guide on how to approach testing to develop a systematic program that will elevate your business tomorrow and for years to come. This book is a must have for the modern digital marketer's bookshelf.

—JOHN LOVETT, Senior Partner, Web Analytics Demystified and President, Digital Analytics Association

You Should Test That! *provides the most comprehensive framework for testing and optimization that I've seen. Chris not only goes far deeper into strategies that deliver results than most but makes the business case as well. A must-read for anyone looking to optimize their digital marketing results.*

—JONATHAN MENDEZ, CEO, Yieldbot

It is a misnomer that creative types abhor any left-brain stimulation. In fact, the best right-brain thinkers feed on data that informs, inspires, and empowers them. This book outlines the converged path between art and science and how data, optimization and analytics can produce the ultimate 1–2 punch: sales and experience.

—JOSEPH JAFFE, author of *Flip the Funnel*

Analytics is amazing. But all the data and analysis in the world doesn't mean anything unless you take action. And in the online world that means testing.

But many people are scared to test. They don't understand the process and think it's too complicated or risky. And they very rarely know where to start. Chris does a great job of presenting an easy to understand framework that will help anyone in the online space get started with testing. Once you start testing you'll come to understand testing as a way to better understand your user and not just a way to improve conversion rate.

—JUSTIN CUTRONI, author of *Google Analytics*, coauthor of *Performance Marketing with Google Analytics*, and blogger at cutroni.com/blog

Continuous website conversion data is essential to all aspects of online success—if it ain't tested, don't fix it! Chris Goward gets it and delivers the "how-to's" that will get you results.

—KEN JURINA, President & CEO, Top Draw Inc.

Buy this book right now if you are interested in turning your website into a conversion generating machine. While countless books exist that cover a multitude of strategies for generating traffic to your website, few exist that actually help you close the deal once a visitor arrives. This how-to guide on conversion optimization by Chris Goward unveils proven strategies and scientific methods to help you optimize your website and drive more conversions; it represents one of the best investments you can make to make more money by closing more deals.

—KRISTOPHER B. JONES, Chairman, Internet Marketing Ninjas and best-selling author of *Search Engine Optimization: Your Guide to Effective Internet Marketing*

I really, really wish I'd written this book—*picture sad face*—it's the clearest definition of the what, how and why of conversion rate optimization I've read. Best of all, it's a unique approach. After reading about 100 marketing books and only learning one thing from each, it's exciting to come across a book that makes you smarter after every chapter.

—OLI GARDNER, Co-founder & Creative Director, Unbounce.com

Wow, this is some of the best content I have read in the optimization world in a long time! It provides a very solid strategic framework but at the same time breaks it into practical steps people can immediately turn into action in their conversion optimization efforts. I really liked the flow, the examples, how close it was to the day-to-day experiences and challenges we have. This strategy works for Dell to continuously improve our online sales. All business managers, marketers and conversion optimizers should read this and give copies to their teams.

—NAZLI YUZAK, Sr. Digital Optimization Consultant, Dell.com

You Should Test That! *cuts through the myths of universal best practice and exposes the common mistakes even the experts make when developing a testing program, and offers a comprehensive, data-driven methodology for high impact testing. If you want to move from testing practitioner to strategist, "You Should Read This."*

—LINDA BUSTOS, director of ecommerce research, Elastic Path Software, getelastic.com

Online testing is rapidly evolving from a standalone activity to a core discipline within leading online Enterprises. Today's Enterprises are requiring an integrated range of optimization techniques, including testing, to deliver the most relevant, engaging and consistent customer experience for every prospect and customer across every channel. This book is perfectly timed with the market and will show the reader how to get the most out of testing and optimization.

—MARK SIMPSON, Founder and President of Maxymiser

Changes in conversion rates can significantly increase company's bottom line. This is obviously powerful and Chris does an awesome job distilling information & making conversion concepts easy to grasp & understand. You Should Test That! *is a must read for anyone looking to take their conversion optimization efforts to the next level.*

—MONA ELESSEILY, VP Online Marketing Strategy, Page Zero Media

For everyone who has suspected there's more to successful conversion optimization than the latest "Quick Wins" list, this book is for you. You Should Test That! *outlines a clear, powerful approach to improving your website's bottom line.*

— SANDRA NIEHAUS, Co-author, *Web Design for ROI* and VP of User Experience at Closed Loop

When marketers complain that they don't know what's working, they're really complaining that they don't know how to figure it out. The fact is that we're past the dark ages of digital, and that there are robust methods for understanding and improving marketing performance.

You Should Test That! *does a lot more than just give advice from on high...it explains what to test, and how to test it, in clear language. Just as important, the book is an excellent guide for where to spend precious testing resources (and where not to) because time is marketing's most precious, nonrenewable resource.*

Readers of most business books finish with the knowledge of what they should be doing, but quickly run up against the realities of how to get it done. When you've finished You Should Test That!*, you'll be armed not just with the belief in an importance of testing and optimization, but with the mental tools to accomplish them.*

— STEFAN TORNQUIST, VP Research, Econsultancy US

Powerful conversion advice from an industry luminary.

— STEPHAN SPENCER, Co-Author of *The Art of SEO* and Author of *Google Power Search*

Landing page optimization is often the most poorly executed discipline of digital marketing, yet can be one of the biggest payoffs. Read this book to learn how to go beyond the basics, get a graduate degree, and become a strategic marketing optimization ninja.

— ERIC ENGE, Co-Author of *The Art of SEO* and CEO of Stone Temple Consulting

You Should Test That!

You Should Test That!

Conversion Optimization for More Leads, Sales and Profit or The Art and Science of Optimized Marketing

Chris Goward

WILEY

John Wiley & Sons, Inc.

Senior Acquisitions Editor: WILLEM KNIBBE
Development Editor: JIM COMPTON
Technical Editor: BRENDAN REGAN
Production Editor: CHRISTINE O'CONNOR
Copy Editor: TIFFANY TAYLOR
Editorial Manager: PETE GAUGHAN
Production Manager: TIM TATE
Vice President and Executive Group Publisher: RICHARD SWADLEY
Vice President and Publisher: NEIL EDDE
Book Designer: FRANZ BAUMHACKL
Compositors: CODY GATES, CRAIG JOHNSON, KATE KAMINSKI, HAPPENSTANCE TYPE-O-RAMA
Proofreader: LOUISE WATSON, WORD ONE NEW YORK
Indexer: NANCY GUENTHER
Project Coordinator, Cover: KATHERINE CROCKER
Cover Design: JOHN WILEY & SONS, INC.

Copyright © 2013 by John Wiley & Sons, Inc., Indianapolis, Indiana

Published simultaneously in Canada

ISBN: 978-1-118-30130-2

ISBN: 978-1-118-33415-7 (ebk.)

ISBN: 978-1-118-46383-3 (ebk.)

ISBN: 978-1-118-33528-4 (ebk.)

Library of Congress Control Number: 2012951871

Dear Reader,

Thank you for choosing *You Should Test That!: Conversion Optimization for More Leads, Sales and Profit or The Art and Science of Optimized Marketing*. This book is part of a family of premium-quality Sybex books, all of which are written by outstanding authors who combine practical experience with a gift for teaching.

Sybex was founded in 1976. More than 30 years later, we're still committed to producing consistently exceptional books. With each of our titles, we're working hard to set a new standard for the industry. From the paper we print on to the authors we work with, our goal is to bring you the best books available.

I hope you see all that reflected in these pages. I'd be very interested to hear your comments and get your feedback on how we're doing. Feel free to let me know what you think about this or any other Sybex book by sending me an email at nedde@wiley.com. If you think you've found a technical error in this book, please visit http://sybex .custhelp.com. Customer feedback is critical to our efforts at Sybex.

Best regards,

Neil Edde
Vice President and Publisher
Sybex, an Imprint of Wiley

To Danica, Medo, and Shalom. You. Rock.

Acknowledgments

I'm thankful.

Thankful for the limitless (so far) supply of support my wife, Danica, has given me over the years and especially the past few months as I've developed this content, grown WiderFunnel, and overcome obstacles. She never fails to give before I know what I need.

I'm thankful for my joyous, encouraging, and loving daughters, Medo and Shalom, who have given many Skype hugs as I travel the world promoting and refining the concepts in this book.

I'm thankful to the conversion heroes at WiderFunnel for delivering awesome results for our clients with or without me in the office.

I'm thankful for the WiderFunnel clients who have allowed us to learn these marketing-optimization principles using their web traffic and share a few of the test results with the world.

I'm thankful to the many conference organizers and business leaders who have repeatedly invited me back to speak to their audiences about these ideas and fine-tune the message over the years.

I'm thankful to Willem Knibbe, senior acquisitions editor, for sharing my vision and advocating for this book. Thanks also to Pete Gaughan, editorial manager; Jim Compton, developmental editor; Brendan Regan, my technical editor; and the rest of the Sybex team for giving me support and teaching me the process as a teething author.

I'm thankful for my CEO mastermind group, PX6, for your advice and support through the challenges: Tom, Claudia, Paul, Maurice, Jill, Greg, Diane, Geoff, and Mike. You've been lifelines and valued mentors to me—each of you.

I'm thankful for an extended network of parents, sisters, brothers, and friends who always show up when we need support and truly provide a safe village to raise our family. You give me the freedom to take on ambitious projects like this.

I'm thankful to have some thoughts that some people seem to want to read.

I'm thankful that you've decided to read this book.

About the Author

Chris Goward was one of the first people to look at online content and say, "You Should Test That!" From that revelation he founded WiderFunnel—the full-service marketing-optimization agency that pioneered landing-page and conversion-rate optimization methods for companies such as Google, Electronic Arts, Iron Mountain, and BabyAge.com.

Chris is a top-rated speaker and keynote at conferences and seminars globally, like Search Engine Strategies, PubCon, Search Marketing Expo, European Conversion Summit, eMetrics, and Conversion Conference, where he evangelizes how marketers should test and gain insights about their messages and websites.

Chris began his first digital marketing consultancy in 1994, and he has led online and offline response strategies for ad agencies DDB, TBWA, and Cossette. He developed the LIFT Model and Kaizen Method in response to the traditional agencies' flawed mentality: "*Win industry awards regardless of client results.*" Today, his marketing-optimization system is helping some of the world's most successful websites lift their leads, sales, and revenue by double- and triple-digit percentages.

An entrepreneur at heart, Chris has also launched numerous businesses since his early childhood candy bar arbitrage venture, including the Rockit Roller human-powered scooter, a graphic design and signage company, an online jewelry business with his wife, and a web design consultancy. He is currently a founding member of the Global Conversion Alliance and is an advisor to startups like Unbounce.com. *Marketing Magazine* named him a "Top 30 Under 30" in 2004.

When Chris is not planning conversion strategies for WiderFunnel's clients or on the road speaking, he can be found hitting the ski slopes with his wife and daughters, cheering on the Vancouver Canucks, or trying to grow parsley in his office.

Contents

Foreword: Be Super Awesome

A few days into my first job on the web, over a decade ago, our senior most executive said to me: "Our product is so good that we should replace all the text, images and links on our home page with one giant red button that says 'start now.' People will just love the product and will convert into paying customers. No need to show them previews, explain the problem it solves, have a product recommendation engine. Just one big red button."

In that one instant I became a fan of experimentation!

I realized that there was no way I could say no to the idea. I was simply not that important (and our salary differential was too big!). My only option was to figure out how to show the executive that we respected his idea, tried it and measure the results.

We jury rigged our CMS to split traffic that landed on the home page to go to two different pages (giant red button and no giant red button). Data collection was painful (log file parsing!). Computation of statistical significance was crude (ok Excel, still works!). The result was surprising. To the HiPPO—because the red button performed miserably. To me as well—I realized this is all it took to let your actual customers pick good ideas.

A lot has happened since that early foray. We have a ton of options when it comes to doing A/B testing. We have tools that make it ever easier to deliver the sexy magic of multivariate testing. An increasing number of people are discovering the exhilarating thrill of controlled experimentation—what a magnificent way to answer questions we thus far thought were unanswerable.

Yet experimentation sadly remains less used than it should be. Tools are not the problem anymore—too many and at all price points. Senior leaders are less of a problem every day—they are starting to see the benefits and career enhancing potential. The problem is that experimentation requires a unique mental model. It requires a systematic approach. It requires a distinct analytical rigor. It requires the love of process excellence.

The problem is you, your employees, me, and our peers in digital marketing.

That's where Chris rides in to save the day. In 13 chapters, he systematically takes us on a journey from the very first basic steps of testing and experimentation, to making a strong and compelling case for conversion optimization, to the critical sections of prioritization of the many opportunities in front of us and executing our experiments.

My favorite parts of the book are the ones that address the core reasons experimentation is not an all-subsuming part of our digital existence. Chapter 4 introduces us to the LIFT model (this is not going to let you down as you imagine scaling your testing program!), and Chapters 5 through 10 gently hold your hand and provide specific guidance on each element of the model. Any excuse you could come up with to save yourself from being awesome will be gone by this point.

And since just having the knowledge is not sufficient, the 15 real world case studies included will allow you to tell stories to your management team: stories that will inspire them to permit you to unleash your wings and go save the day (and then the next day and then the day after) for your business. Regardless of what your company's size is. Regardless of where you are on the digital evolutionary cycle.

Buy the book. Be super awesome. Then email Chris and thank him.

Good luck!

AVINASH KAUSHIK

Author: *Web Analytics 2.0, Web Analytics: An Hour A Day*

www.kaushik.net/avinash

Introduction

Anybody can say charming things and try to please and to flatter, but a true friend always says unpleasant things, and does not mind giving pain. Indeed, if he is a really true friend he prefers it, for he knows that then he is doing good.

—*Oscar Wilde*

The discipline that I call strategic marketing optimization can change your business and dramatically increase your profits. This book will tell you how.

You have your own opinions about your marketing, perhaps strong ones. Others in your organization may hold differing beliefs. I may have another view entirely.

Which is right? How do you decide whose perspective to take?

Some organizations use a consensus approach where everyone needs to agree before action is taken. Others crown their opinion leaders based on experience, title, or personality. But is the group's decision always best? Are leaders always right?

No. Opinions are flawed. They are distorted by skewed perspectives, unrelated experience, personal biases, and outdated notions. Yet people believe very strongly in them, despite evidence. As the scientist Peter Medawar said, "The intensity of a conviction that a hypothesis is true has no bearing over whether it is true or not."

Today, it's easier than ever to stop debates over whose opinion should win. By scientifically testing marketing approaches, you can gain insights that improve your marketing and business results. Businesses that have embraced split testing in their culture and processes are leading their industries. Others are missing out on this powerful strategy. Some are distracted by the latest unproven marketing trend, social application, or technology. The "shiny new things" can be appealing, but those who fall for distractions are doomed to a downward spiral of false hopes.

I'll be straight with you. Developing a rigorous optimization process that delivers results isn't easy. It takes creativity, perseverance, and discipline to get the best results. My goal for this book is to inspire you to be a conversion champion who will evangelize these concepts in your organization and commit to a rigorous approach to continuous improvement. I can promise you that it will be worth the effort.

By reading this, you will learn the processes, frameworks, and tactics that we at WiderFunnel are using to help businesses win. We have refined this optimization system with some of the world's most successful e-commerce, lead-generation, and affiliate companies like eBay, Google, Shutterfly, SAP, ABB, Citrix, Electronic Arts, and many more. Through dozens of example and case studies of real test results, you will see how you can adopt a similar process in your organization, for whatever products, services, and ideas you need to sell.

In the end, I hope your response to debates and opinions will be to say, "**You Should Test That!**"

Who Should Read This Book

This book is intended to inspire and equip corporate marketers, web directors, product managers, business owners, web analysts, advertisers, affiliate marketers, agencies, and business strategists:

Are you responsible for improving results at your company? This book will tell you how to gain key insights about your customers that can impact your entire organization.

Do you influence or control your marketing messages? This book will show you how to test your value-proposition messages and find out what propels your prospects to action.

Do you want to get more leads, sales, and profit from the same website traffic volume you currently have? This book will show you how to dramatically lift your sales without spending more on advertising.

Do you manage landing pages? This book will show you how conversion optimization will lift your conversion rates and revenue.

Does your company have a website? This book will show you how to create a website that generates more business and has great design, all while avoiding the risks of a website redesign.

Do you manage a company or division? This book will inspire your entire marketing team to use the principles and techniques of scientific marketing to make better decisions and achieve industry-leading results.

Everyone who wants to improve your marketing results: **You Should Read This!**

What's Inside

Here is what to expect in each chapter:

Chapter 1, "Why You Should Test That," shows why testing and optimization are important for your success, the traditional website redesign is broken, and so-called "best practices" are not best.

Chapter 2, "What Is Conversion Optimization?" introduces the scientific testing method, dispels common myths of conversion optimization, and shows how to align your business goals with your website conversion goals. A case study in this chapter shows how a multi-test conversion-optimization strategy improved website content engagement for a tourism organization.

Chapter 3, "Prioritize Testing Opportunities," gets into practical steps to prioritize your testing opportunities using the PIE Framework to organize your web analytics and heuristic analysis and offers an affiliate marketing case-study example.

Chapter 4, "Create Hypotheses with the LIFT™ Model," defines the LIFT Model heuristic analysis framework and introduces the following six chapters that show how to use that framework to develop great test hypotheses.

Chapter 5, "Optimize Your Value Proposition," digs into the concept of the value-proposition equation and how to test all aspects of your tangible features and intangible benefits and costs. A case study with Electronic Arts demonstrates how a conversion-optimization strategy doubled the game registration conversion rate for *The Sims 3*.

Chapter 6, "Optimize for Relevance," shows how to optimize the four aspects of relevance—source, target audience, navigation, and competitive—and includes an e-commerce case study of a dramatic home page redesign test and another multivariate test case study.

Chapter 7, "Optimize for Clarity," gives guidelines and examples for enhancing the clarity of your information hierarchy, design, call to action, and copywriting, with three case studies, including a landing-page test for SAP.

Chapter 8, "Optimize for Anxiety," shows how to turn anxiety in your favor and reduce your prospects' concerns about privacy, usability, effort, and fulfillment. An e-commerce case study shows a 42 percent increase in revenue per visitor.

Chapter 9, "Optimize for Distraction," gives many examples of how distraction factors can reduce conversion rates, and how you can test to fix them.

Chapter 10, "Optimize for Urgency," will help you test the effects of internal and external urgency and make sure your test results are valid in any season.

Chapter 11, "Test Your Hypotheses," wraps up the hypothesis-development chapters and shows how to build a strong testing plan with the right goals, test areas, test types, and hypotheses isolations. The chapter also includes a case study and tips on how to get great test results.

Chapter 12, "Analyze Your Test Results," gives guidelines for monitoring tests and analyzing them for reliable results and marketing insights.

Chapter 13, "Strategic Marketing Optimization," is your call to action to become your organization's SMO champion and advocate a culture of continuous improvement.

The Color of Conversion includes 16 color pages with click heatmaps, examples of clarity and distraction, and screenshots from select split test case studies.

> **Note:** You can download all the files and resources mentioned in the book from `www.sybex.com/go/youshouldtestthat` or at `YouShouldTestThat.com`, where you can also join discussions and find additional resources.

How to Contact the Author

I welcome feedback from you about this book or any of my work. You can reach me at author@chrisgoward.com and on Twitter at @chrisgoward. For more information about my work, you should check out the world's best marketing optimization agency (which I also founded) at WiderFunnel.com.

Sybex strives to keep you supplied with the latest tools and information you need for your work. Please check their website at `www.sybex.com/go/youshouldtestthat`, where we'll post additional content and updates that supplement this book, should the need arise.

1

Why You Should Test That

Almost everything that distinguishes the modern world from earlier centuries is attributable to science, which achieved its most spectacular triumphs in the seventeenth century.

—Bertrand Russell

What is optimization? The word *optimization* has become extremely popular in digital marketing in recent years, which has led to some confusion as well as a plethora of acronyms.

There's conversion-rate optimization (CRO), also known as conversion optimization (CO); landing-page optimization (LPO), which is really a subset of CRO; marketing optimization (MO); business process optimization (BPO); search engine optimization (SEO); website optimization (WSO); social media optimization (SMO); and now, apparently, video search engine optimization (VSEO) and more!

In Internet marketing circles, conversion-rate optimization is too often confused with SEO. I think the repeated use of *optimization* makes sense, but it can also be distracting. If we were in the business of pancake optimization, we would probably be pursuing the perfect pancake, right? Likewise, conversion-rate optimization is the pursuit of the optimal conversion rate, not a higher search-engine ranking or any other type of optimization or efficiency.

For the purpose of this book, we'll define conversion-rate optimization (or conversion optimization) as *the science and art of getting more revenue-generating actions from the same number of visitors*. If that goal sounds good to you, read on!

This chapter looks at how conversion-rate optimization can benefit your business: the importance of your website to your business and the likelihood that it may be underperforming for you; the importance of designing for effectiveness and not slavishly following "best practices"; and more. You'll see how conversion-rate optimization can increase revenue without increasing advertising spend, and finally how CRO can work together with SEO.

Your Website Is Crucial to Your Business

Do you remember what the Web looked like in 1994? Most people don't. Many were just starting to read about the coming "information superhighway." Some of the most popular websites didn't even exist. Google.com and Dell.com both launched in 1996. Facebook .com didn't show up in its original university-only version until 2004, and it was still called The Facebook. MySpace.com hadn't yet had its explosive growth or its implosive decline. Here you can see examples of how some of the most popular sites originally looked.

Yahoo in 1994 was the search engine leader, providing links to most of the known Internet.

Google in 1998 quickly overtook Yahoo as the world's most popular search engine.

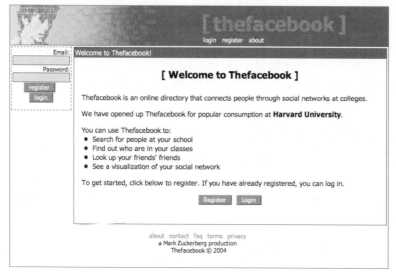

Facebook at its launch in 2004; it has since had many more redesigns than Yahoo or Google.

Back then, when I began my first web-design business, websites didn't get a lot of attention. Many of the businesses that hired me considered their sites inconsequential novelties or, at best, "brochures" that most customers would never see or interact with.

Businesses could afford to ignore the Web then. Only the geeky few of us with our plodding dial-up modems were online to see their websites, anyway!

Today, everything has changed. The Web is our daily companion. We connect with friends through social networks and get product and business information wherever we are with our mobile devices. The Web is our most important source of information and social interaction.

The average American spends between 22 and 34 hours per month online, and that number jumps much higher if you count mobile web browsing. Consider the Media Metrix research by comScore.

Average online time

Not only is the Web ubiquitous, but it's also highly influential. Up to 90 percent of purchasers are influenced by online research before making an *offline* purchase, according to a study by Experian.

We have a unique situation right now: the *importance* of the Web is still in a dramatic upswing, but the *performance* of most website experiences is still severely below potential. In other words, the experience and results of websites aren't living up to their owners' expectations and their performance potential. This translates to your online business getting fewer actions than you deserve.

The good news is that this has created a huge and growing opportunity gap. The potential to get more actions and better return on investment (ROI) is very real. Better yet, the book you're holding can give you a framework to get the extra revenue your customers *want* to give you!

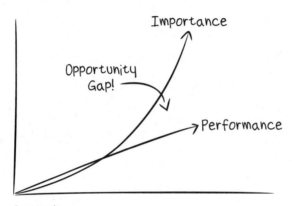

Opportunity gap

This is one reason I'm excited about the long-term prospects for careers in conversion-rate optimization. The discipline, processes, and skill set needed to *consistently* improve web experiences will be valuable for a long time to come, and the necessary skills are also highly adaptable to other media.

Your Website Is Underperforming

To tell you that your website is underperforming is a pretty bold claim because I may have never even seen your website, much less analyzed your performance metrics. Nevertheless, I can confidently tell you exactly that: your website is underperforming its potential.

All Websites Can Be Improved

I've never seen a website that couldn't be improved. In fact, the best online companies in the world are committed to continuous improvement on their websites. Some of the best-known examples include Google constantly tweaking and testing its algorithm and website design, Facebook testing, releasing, and modifying new features rapidly, and Amazon, which is well known for evolving its website through testing.

More important, let's think about you. What is your conversion rate for new visitors right now? 1 percent, 3 percent, 20 percent, 30 percent? Whatever it is, I'm willing to bet that you don't have a 100 percent conversion rate.

What Is a Conversion Rate? *Conversion rate* represents the percentage of visitors who complete your desired action, which may be to fill out a contact form, purchase a product, or call the sales phone number. It's calculated as follows: Conversion Rate (%) = Conversions (#) / Unique Visitors (#) × 100%

If your company is like most, the vast majority of visitors leave without indicating the most basic level of interest. Are you satisfied that the majority of your expensive traffic is being wasted? Should you be allocating the majority of your scarce marketing budget to driving more people to this underperforming website?

The sad fact is that your website is turning away most of your prospects and customers in disappointment. The good news is that your competitors are probably in just as bad shape. Let's hope they're not reading this book like you are. You may have a window of opportunity to gain a strong lead!

The Halo Effect of Underperformance

The *halo effect* is a psychological bias in which our perception of someone's strengths or weaknesses influences our perception of their other attributes. For example, if we have a favorite sports celebrity, our admiration of their sports talent will spill over into other areas, so we accept their product recommendations as valuable. That's why celebrity endorsements have worked so well.

Unfortunately, when your website is underperforming, it has a halo effect on your prospects' perception of your product performance.

Are You Fast?

For example, if you want to communicate that your product is fast, how quickly should your website load? Let's look at the website for BlackBerry smartphones. The home page includes complex hover effects with large background images and textures. The download requirements to fulfill the designer's vision cause a very slow load time. Here's what I saw for the first few seconds on the page:

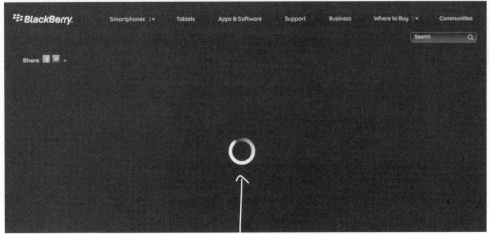

Slow page load has a halo effect on product perception.

Unfortunate irony

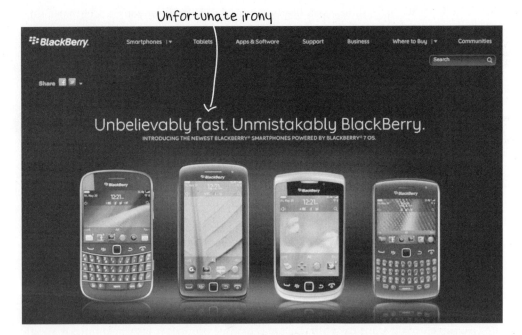

Do you see the irony of the headline that appeared once the page loaded? The website experience is negatively affecting the exact value-proposition point that this company wants to promote.

Is It Easy?

If you claim that your product or service is easy, take a look at how easy your website is to understand and use:

- How many steps are in your signup process?
- How many fields of information are required in your purchase process?

- How easy is it to find your shipping information?
- Is your product information understandable?

We'll get into more detail about how to identify these types of issues and more in Chapter 7, "Optimize for Clarity," Chapter 8, "Optimize for Anxiety," and Chapter 9, "Optimize for Distraction." The important point to understand is that the halo effect from your website's usability is influencing your prospects' perception of your product.

An Example: Rotating Offers, the Scourge of Home-Page Design

In WiderFunnel's conversion-rate optimization work, one of the most common elements we come across is the rotating home-page offer banner, or *slideshow*. It's a great example of how typical websites evolve common features that are harmful to business results. We have tested rotating offers many times and found them to be a poor way of presenting home-page content.

Our first example is the Ballard.com home-page rotating banner. Notice that each banner has small white boxes in the lower-right corner that indicate how many messages are being rotated. Each banner also has a small Learn More link, but these are white and barely visible on top of some of the images.

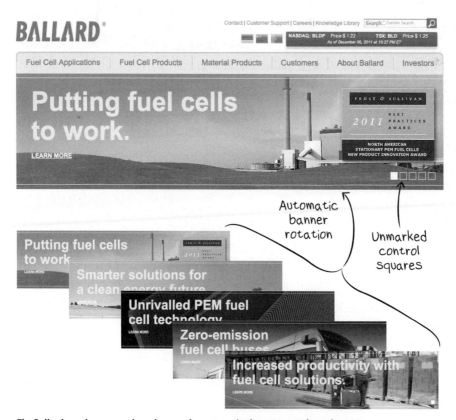

The Ballard.com home page has a banner that rotates in the sequence shown here.

The only positive these banners have going for them is that they don't have large copy blocks, which would have been unreadable. Unfortunately, most of those nice big headlines are so vague that the target audiences, products, and messages are unclear. Ballard has huge potential for improving its home page's effectiveness.

Next, consider the Forever21.com home page and its rotating banners.

The Forever21.com home page has a banner that rotates as shown here.

The Forever21 banners also show tiny boxes identifying the number of messages as they rotate.

Let's think about your visitor's experience in more detail for a moment. She arrives on your home page and needs to orient herself to your layout in order to decide which information to zero in on. A strong, page-dominant banner with a headline and bold image is where she's likely to start her focus.

Unfortunately, the message in that banner usually isn't relevant to what she's looking for. Why? The marketing department is featuring current events, offers, and news that may be important to some department within the organization, but not to the majority of visitors.

In the lucky event that your visitor sees an offer that looks interesting to her, she will want to read a little more about it. But just as she's gathered the motivation and confidence to click through and learn more, the rotator switches to the next offer.

What happens now? She's confronted with a second offer and has to decide whether to focus on reading it or getting back to the previous offer. She's feeling a little frustrated and disoriented at this point.

If she decides the first offer was really what she wanted to see, how does she return to it? She has to figure out how to control the slideshow without the benefits of an owner's manual. The web designer surely would have made it easy to navigate back and forth between offers, right?

Unfortunately, that's not the case. Your beleaguered visitor may have to locate a tiny row of dots or squares hidden among the bold, colorful photos in the offer onslaught.

You can, I'm sure, empathize with her likely reaction, which is to bounce off the site in frustration.

Web Design for Results (Rather than Aesthetics)

I sometimes give web designers and art directors a hard time about the websites they create. In reality, though, they're usually not the *only* cause of your website's conversion problems.

At some point early in the design process, the designer often asks the client for examples of websites they like. This may be a sign that things are heading in the wrong direction from the beginning.

The client inevitably selects the websites of the three competitors they think are the most "successful." Rarely do they branch out of their immediate industry environment. They certainly won't know where to look to find the Web's best-converting web experiences.

What is the basis for judging the websites the client selects? Neither the client nor the designer knows how well the chosen examples perform. Often there's no discussion of whether the example sites have similar business goals. The criterion for success in cases like this often becomes purely aesthetic.

You see, the problem with your website probably started with the criteria for judging a successful design. On one hand, the goal of the design agency is to end the project with a happy client. Of course it is. They want the client to pay the agency's invoice! Many are also motivated to win "creative" awards, which are based more on cleverness than business results. They want design samples that make their portfolio look great. The revenue attached to those designs for those awards doesn't matter.

When was the last time you saw a digital agency present the revenue improvement for each of their redesign projects on their website? If they do, they may be one of the rare breed of digital agency that cares about the end result of their designs.

On the other hand, the client usually doesn't give the design agency the proper goals to start with. They often don't tell the agency to do whatever is necessary to increase qualified leads for the sales team or lift e-commerce sales or affiliate revenue. They may just say that the current design is "tired" or "stale" or that the new CEO doesn't like it.

Often, the design is—tragically—driven more by the technical limitations of a chosen content-management system (CMS) than by lead generation and sales goals. Why is this allowed to happen? If you're paying for a new website, shouldn't it improve your business results? Clients and agencies *both* need to reevaluate the outcome of their work. If it doesn't produce measurably improved business results, it's just busy work and a waste of marketing budget. You can turn this around by ensuring that your next website update begins with the business and website goals and the criteria for measuring success in terms of specific website actions that produce more revenue.

When goals and success metrics are in place, you have a much better chance of improving those metrics. Unfortunately, even when website owners have clear goals, objectives, and metrics, they may fall into the temptation of seeking out quick-fix advice or "best practices" to follow.

Why "Best Practices" Aren't Best

It's rare to find a website where design and content have been based on research from controlled testing. Web design teams give too much credit to other sites' design teams and don't have enough time for controlled conversion-rate optimization testing.

Judging by the similarities in the layouts and design within industries, most websites are based on copying competitors. This follow-the-average approach leads to poorly performing elements becoming accepted as "best practices" just because they're common. There's a saying that "Everyone wants to be 'normal,' but no one wants to be 'average.'" Do you really want your website to be average?

To compound this copy-the-average problem, clients often feel intimidated by agency and design professionals. I've worked with some very smart and capable agency strategists, but clients often put too much trust in their agency's opinions. Agencies foster a know-it-all image, which can lead to bogus opinions that carry the weight of professional recommendations.

Clients, agencies, and designers all have to take responsibility for questioning professional opinions. Ask for the data, look for the flaws in the reasoning, and always question assumptions.

At WiderFunnel, we joke that we've chosen one of the most humbling businesses to be in. Every time we deliver a recommendation to a client, we know we'll have to test it—and not just with opinion-based user testing, but with statistically significant, scientific, controlled tests! This means our test variations may "lose," and we may be "wrong." But I wouldn't want it any other way. It's exciting to see a test we've planned deliver proven revenue lift time after time.

What is often missing in "best practice" recommendations is a consideration for your unique business environment, goals, and target audience. Your website should be a vehicle designed to uniquely communicate the value proposition of your product or service and then make it easy for visitors to take the desired action.

Whenever we find ourselves in opinionated debates about website content or design, we always have a tie-breaker argument, and I recommend you use it, too. We simply say, "Interesting idea. **You Should Test That!**"

Is There a HiPPO in the Room?

Is your organization or department run by a HiPPO? No, not the savannah, mud-rolling type of hippo. I'm talking about the *highest-paid person's opinion*. Google knows all about the dangers of this HiPPO. The Google marketing team has a very cool HiPPO mascot that they travel the conference circuit with, to make this point.

Trevor Claiborne, Google; HiPPO disguised in suit; Chris Goward

The HiPPO method is one of the ways organizations make decisions about their website design. Take a look at the decision methods that follow. Which one does your organization use?

The HiPPO Method   Imagine you're in a conference room with the stakeholders involved in your website redesign. There are representatives from Marketing, IT, Sales, Product, and Engineering. Your web designer presents the design concepts and lays them on the boardroom table. Does the majority around the table carefully hide or hedge their opinions about the design until the HiPPO has given an opinion? If so, your organization has fallen victim to the HiPPO method of decision-making. These city-dwelling, HiPPO-following organizations cause all kinds of problems.

The Black Turtleneck Method   Now imagine yourself in the same conference-room scenario. This time, a person wearing a black turtleneck and sunglasses (indoors) points at the "best" design. His opinion is backed up by a very convincing professional rationale and experience, of course! If the majority of opinions follow this seasoned expert, your company has been fooled into the Black Turtleneck method. Unfortunately, the longer these gurus are followed, the more confident they become about their opinions and the less frequently they challenge their own opinions with valid data.

The Customer Tested Method   The third method of decision-making uses the scientific method of hypothesis and testing to find optimized solutions. You formulate hypotheses about which page layouts will encourage the highest conversion rate and use controlled A/B split testing to find out with statistical confidence. In this scenario, when your designer presents design alternatives, you say, "Those look like interesting design options. **We Should Test That!**"

Of course, I recommend the third method. If you get good enough at it, you'll be so successful that you, too, can roll in the mud or wear sunglasses indoors!

The Risks and Costs of Website Redesign

You may be considering a website redesign to fix your conversion problems. Often, companies that need to improve their website results believe a redesign is necessary. In some cases, we've had clients put their redesign projects on hold once they learn about the options conversion-rate optimization presents.

Redesigning the site has the benefit of giving you a clean slate and letting you fix everything at once. It may seem like an easier task to redraw the current information architecture, wireframes, design, and content than to try to work within the constraints of testing individual components.

A website redesign is a risky endeavor, though. The investment of time and money can be enormous and difficult to accurately estimate. There is always a risk of the dreaded scope creep, which blows budgets. Most important, it may not give you the results you hope for.

Many website managers carry battle scars from redesign projects that were long overdue, over budget, and underperforming. There is also no guarantee that a carte blanche do-over will improve your results.

Your New Website Design Could Hurt Your Results

A dirty little secret of website redesigns is that the new site often reduces conversion rates and revenue. You may have heard stories similar to those I have from companies that have spent huge sums only to see a significant revenue drop-off after the new site is launched.

There are several reasons for this:

- Your most valuable repeat customers may be accustomed to the current site layout and confused by a new site. Their confusion will result in lost revenue for you.
- The new design may fix some conversion problems but unintentionally introduce worse ones, with a net effect of reduced conversion rates.
- Most important, your website design may not be a problem, and the redesign could end up being a complete waste of time and money with no improvement to show for it!

Using a start-from-scratch redesign really just guarantees that you'll use the HiPPO or Black Turtleneck method on every page of your site. That's not what you want to do, is it?

Your Improvements May Be Overshadowed by Mistakes

An equally disappointing result can occur even if you *do* see a conversion-rate improvement after launching the new site design. In the process of the redesign, you'll change many hundreds or thousands (or hundreds of thousands!) of components. The changes will range from individual design elements like buttons, logos, colors, and fonts to linking structure and page flow, to page-content selection and creation. Regardless of the overall result, how do you know which of the many factors were responsible for positive or negative conversion-rate changes?

The following hypothetical graph illustrates this problem. Even in this simplified scenario with eight website changes, you can see how potentially large improvements can be masked by the cumulative effect of all the modifications.

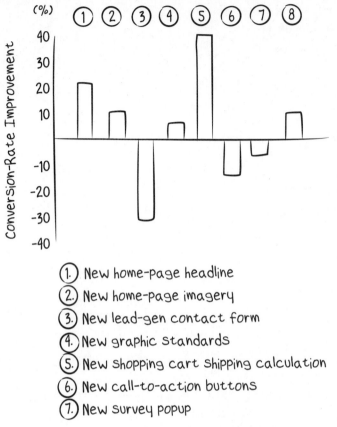

1.) New home-page headline
2.) New home-page imagery
3.) New lead-gen contact form
4.) New graphic standards
5.) New shopping cart shipping calculation
6.) New call-to-action buttons
7.) New survey popup

Website redesigns mask the effects of the many individual changes.

Imagine if you could identify the changes that yielded a positive effect and keep only those, while discarding the negative changes. Well, you can do exactly that with controlled testing. Testing the effect of one change is called an *isolated* variable, and it's an important part of experiment planning that we'll discuss in Chapter 4 ("Create Hypotheses with the LIFT Model"). By testing alternative page variations that differ by only one element, you can isolate the effect that the single element has on your revenue.

In the previous example, if you ran an isolation test on the home-page headline, you would know that it had improved your conversion rate, and you could also gain some insight into the types of messages that appeal to your home-page audience. On the other hand, if you redesigned the site without testing, you would be unaware that your new contact form is seriously hurting your results. Masking the effects of individual changes is a risky way of redesigning your website!

Use Evolutionary Site Redesign

There is a less risky approach than a complete website redesign—one that maximizes your conversion-rate improvement by isolating the impact of individual changes. This approach gives you two options: I call the traditional method a *revolutionary site redesign* (RSR), where you switch to a brand-new site all at once; alternatively, you can use *evolutionary site redesign* (ESR), where new design, layout, and content elements are tested and your website gradually evolves toward the best-performing ideal.

In an ESR redesign, you prioritize your most important pages and page templates and test new layouts, designs, and content with controlled testing. You get all the benefits of a new site design without the risks.

As you've probably guessed, ESR essentially uses conversion-rate optimization principles to redesign your site. You end up with a new site "look and feel" and conversion-rate lift at the same time.

Conversion-Rate Optimization Increases Revenue without Increasing Advertising Spend

The best thing about conversion-rate optimization is the result: You get increased revenue without the need to increase your ongoing advertising spend. You can keep spending the same amount of money, driving the same amount of traffic, and you'll get more leads, sales, and revenue from a conversion-optimized website.

Where else can you invest effort to get that kind of result?

Comparing Conversion-Rate Optimization with Paid-Search Optimization

Running tests on your paid-search ads is a great way to get more leads and sales. I highly recommend testing your ads. Consider the end result, though. Even if your testing finds a better ad that improves your click-through rate (CTR), you still have to pay for those additional clicks! And what if those extra paid-for visitors don't convert into customers?

Let's look at an example that compares the results of paid-search optimization and landing-page optimization. (By the way, the exercise we're about to look at is as complicated as the math will get in this book. In years past, you may have needed a Ph.D. in statistics to run optimization tests; but with all the great tools that take care of the calculations now, you just need a website and some good ideas. We'll spend much more time on strategy and test ideas than number-crunching.)

In the following table, we assume a $3 cost per click (CPC) using a paid-search advertising platform like Google AdWords or Microsoft adCenter and 100,000 paid search impressions.

Cost per conversion for paid-search optimization and landing-page optimization

	Paid-Search Impressions	Paid-Search CTR	Landing-Page Visits	Landing-Page Conversion Rate	Conversions	Ad Spend	Cost per Conversion
Original (Baseline)	100,000	2%	2,000	2%	40	$6,000	$150
Scenario 1: Paid-Search Optimization	100,000	2.2%	2,200	2%	44	$6,600	$150
Scenario 2: Landing-Page Optimization	100,000	2%	2,000	2.2%	44	$6,000	$136
Scenario 3: Both	100,000	2.2%	2,200	2.2%	48.4	$6,600	$136

Before beginning optimization, we discover in this example that the company is spending $6,000 to get 40 conversions, for a CPC of $150. If the company spends its effort on A/B testing its search ads and modifying its campaign structure, let's assume it can improve its CTR by 10 percent, from 2 percent to 2.2 percent. The result is 10 percent more conversions: 44 versus 40 originally. The budget has also increased by 10 percent to $6,600.

Instead of testing its ads, if the company were to spend its time A/B testing its landing page, its could increase the conversion rate by 10 percent. (Hang on for a couple more pages, and I'll tell you typical lift rates I see from conversion-rate optimization.)

The result from landing-page optimization alone is also 10 percent more conversions, shown in scenario 2, but the budget hasn't increased. The CPC has actually decreased by $14!

The best option is to do both, as in scenario 3. The company has maximized the CTR to get more visitors to the site, and it's capturing more of those prospects with an improved landing page. The result is 48 new customers (a 20 percent improvement) and much lower CPC ($136 versus $150).

For most marketers, the best return on investment and effort is to optimize the on-site conversion experience. If you have to prioritize your effort, focusing on conversion-rate optimization first will not only improve the efficiency of your PPC advertising spend. It will also multiply the effect of *all* your traffic-generating activities, such as other advertising, social media, direct marketing, and public relations.

Conversion-Rate Optimization and Your Business

Every company with an online presence can benefit from conversion optimization. But to be fair, some benefit more than others.

Your company is most likely to get the best results if it has certain characteristics. You should prioritize conversion-rate optimization if the following are true:

- You already have a high-traffic website (and the more, the merrier!).

- You have a goal of generating leads, selling products or services, or generating affiliate or ad revenue from your site.

- You want to generate more revenue (you would think this is a given assumption, but I'm regularly surprised by the non-revenue criteria some companies use for decision-making).

- You have, or are willing to foster, a culture of data-driven, scientific marketing.

If your company has these characteristics, I have great news: conversion-rate optimization can produce great results for you! As with any marketing activity, a certain amount of effort is required to run conversion-rate optimization experiments. The higher the traffic volume on your experiment pages, the greater return you'll get for your investment of effort. But even if your website is just starting to build up traffic levels, you can benefit from testing. Take care to spend time planning a test with dramatic differences, and prepare to leave it running long enough to get statistically significant results. There's no harm to be done by leaving a test running, and you never know what you may learn quickly.

Conversion-Rate Optimization Results by Industry

In our experience, there is no industry, goal, or target audience that can't get great results from conversion testing. Shown next are average conversion-rate lift results that WiderFunnel has achieved for completed experiments for our clients using the testing process and methods you'll read about in this book. The following averages are based on WiderFunnel test results for our clients from 2007 to 2012.

Category	Average Conversion-Rate Lift
Lead-generation goals	49.0%
E-commerce goals	23.1%
Business-to-business (B2B) target market	76.9%
Business-to-consumer (B2C) target market	32.3%
Overall	**39.6%**

Although these conversion lift results aren't achieved overnight and often require multiple rounds of tests, conversion-rate optimization clearly has been worth the effort for these companies, and it will be for you, too!

Calculate the Benefit of Conversion-Rate Optimization

Building a business case is more easily done for conversion-rate optimization than for other marketing projects. How often are you able to propose a program that will let you predict the benefit with statistical confidence? Not often, I'm sure.

At the most basic level, you can calculate the benefit by multiplying total revenue generated by the website by the expected conversion-rate increase. For example, suppose an e-commerce store sells $10 million annually and expects to improve its site-wide conversion rate by 10 percent. You can roughly estimate the revenue lift as follows:

$$\$10{,}000{,}000 \times 10\% = \$1{,}000{,}000$$

This is a simple top-down estimate. For greater accuracy, you can verify the revenue associated with potential experiment pages by building the numbers from the bottom up. For example, looking at the e-commerce business, you can calculate potential revenue lift as follows:

	Original	10% CR Lift	20% CR Lift	30% CR Lift
Landing-Page Visitors (Annual)	400,000	400,000	400,000	400,000
Sales Conversion Rate	1.5%	1.65%	1.8%	1.95%
Sales to Landing-Page Visitors (#)	6,000	6,600	7,200	7,800
Average Order Value	$45	$45	$45	$45
Landing-Page Revenue	$270,000	$297,000	$324,000	$351,000
Expected Revenue Lift	-	$27,000	$54,000	$81,000

Improving your conversion rate is only one possible outcome, though. We often find just as much benefit for our clients by improving *average order value* (AOV). If we assume a potential 20 percent increase in conversion rate and a 10–30 percent improvement in AOV, the calculation looks like this:

	Original	20% CR Lift and 10% AOV Lift	20% CR Lift and 20% AOV Lift	20% CR Lift and 30% AOV Lift
Landing-Page Visitors (Annual)	400,000	400,000	400,000	400,000
Sales Conversion Rate	1.5%	1.8%	1.8%	1.8%
Sales to Landing-Page Visitors (#)	6,000	7,200	7,200	7,200
Average Order Value	$45	$49.50	$54	$58.50
Landing-Page Revenue	$270,000	$356,400	$388,800	$421,200
Expected Revenue Lift	-	$86,400	$118,800	$151,200

You can see how quickly the improvement adds up!

A business that generates leads for the sales team can do a similar calculation by placing an estimated value on each lead. Each lead-generation company has to decide on a method for valuating leads as accurately as possible. A calculated lifetime value (LTV) method will give the best results.

Lifetime Value Calculating lifetime value (LTV) can be an interesting and valuable exercise for companies to go through. A customer LTV tells you the average net value of a new customer by accounting for more than just the initial purchase. If you can estimate the percentage of customers who make repeat purchases and the average order value, you can approximate the customers' total value. Determining your LTV is outside the scope of this book. For more information, you can start with the links posted at YouShouldTestThat.com/WhyYouShouldTestThat.

The visitor volumes for sites that generate leads are sometimes lower than for e-commerce sites, but the LTV often compensates for that. For example, a B2B software developer may value each lead much higher than a single consumer e-commerce transaction. Here is a typical lead-generation scenario:

	Original	20% CR Lift	30% CR Lift	40% CR Lift
Landing-Page Visitors (Annual)	120,000	120,000	120,000	120,000
Lead-Generation Conversion Rate	5%	6%	6.5%	7%
Leads Generated (#)	6,000	7,200	7,800	8,400
Lifetime Value per Lead	$45	$45	$45	$45
Landing-Page Revenue	$270,000	$324,000	$351,000	$378,000
Expected Revenue Lift	-	$54,000	$81,000	$108,000

Note: The numbers for your business will likely be different, but this should give you a framework for thinking through the upside potential. For more in-depth calculations to help you build a business case for conversion optimization, you can download free online calculators at YouShouldTestThat.com/YouShouldTestThat.

CRO Works alongside SEO

Companies are often concerned about how conversion-rate optimization will affect search engine optimization (SEO) efforts. We all know that an effectively search engine–optimized site is a beautiful thing. Traffic flows in from natural search rankings without you needing to spend fees for pay-per-click ads.

However, that site traffic is useless unless those visitors become customers, and that's where conversion-rate optimization is required. Without conversion-rate optimization, all the SEO in the world will, at best, increase your traffic levels. But your conversion rate won't improve. Or worse, unsophisticated onsite SEO techniques will actually lower your conversion rate. (You know the type of site I mean: the copy is so stuffed with repetitive keywords that it's impossible to read. That's a credibility killer.)

SEO and CRO Can Play Well Together

Fortunately, the principles of SEO and conversion-rate optimization are totally compatible. Here are some foundational principles that apply to both SEO and CRO:

- You'll achieve better search engine rankings with pages that focus on a single topic or product. This will improve your conversion rate, too.

- Testing clear and relevant headlines instead of overly clever headlines (such as your ad agency's big idea) will improve both SEO and CRO.
- Replacing complex content presentations and animation (for example, Flash-esque content) will usually improve your SEO and conversion rate.
- Using clear content hierarchy with proper heading tags will help with SEO and force you to think about your message progression, which will probably help your conversion rate too.

As a Google Authorized Consultant, I've spoken with key individuals at Google about potential impacts of CRO on SEO, and the company's stated policy is to *not* penalize pages that have been tested using split testing tools. They've told me that Google wants to reward pages that provide what visitors are searching for. In fact, Google has requested that I provide any examples of conversion-optimized pages that have decreased in search or quality score ranking due to conversion-rate optimization so the company can address it. I have yet to see an example.

Conversion-rate optimization can also help your SEO efforts in other ways:

- A page that's optimized for conversions is more usable and visitor-friendly, which makes it more likely to receive inbound links and referrals.
- Search engines rank pages more highly if they're updated frequently. Conversion-rate optimization activities will tend to keep your layout and content fresh.
- A conversion-rate optimization process will discover more relevant keywords that match what visitors are searching for.

How to Do CRO without Hurting Your SEO

As added assurance for those concerned about SEO, here are specific technical tips to help you during and after the running of a conversion-rate optimization test:

During Your Conversion-Rate Optimization Test

- Use a proper CRO tool that uses a JavaScript redirect, which will render your test invisible to search engines.
- Add your challenger variation pages (in the case of an A/B/*n* test) to your robots.txt file to block spiders, for a double layer of protection against duplicate-content penalties.
- Use the same title tags, meta tags, and heading content in your challenger pages as in your control page so you don't forget to include them when you implement the post-test champion page as the new control.
- Use standards-compliant code on your challenger pages, and implement SEO best practices, such as img alt attributes, search-friendly text, and CSS-based code.

- Move supplemental on-page content below the page fold if you feel it's important for SEO but not for conversions.
- It's possible to have content appear first in the page code but lower on the visible page presentation. This is a consideration if your important SEO content may be hurting conversions.

After Your Test

- Once a winning page is declared, it should be double-checked for SEO best practices, and any structural and coding modifications should be made based on your SEO protocols.
- When you replace your old page with the new higher-converting page, use a 301 permanent redirect from your variation page URLs in case anyone linked to, or bookmarked, one of the variation pages during the test.

If you follow the tips and tricks in this section, you'll achieve a powerful one-two punch for your website: maintaining good SEO brings you more qualified traffic, and good CRO converts more of that traffic into customers.

You Should Test That!

I hope you're convinced that you need conversion-rate optimization in your business. In the following chapters, we'll look at how to develop a conversion-rate optimization strategy and get the best results from your ongoing testing program. Chapter 2 will explain the scientific method of controlled testing on websites, dispel common misconceptions about conversion-rate optimization, talk about how to plan your target markets and set goals, and finally show how to use the seven-step conversion-rate optimization cycle.

As you embark on your journey, remember to always keep handy your conversion-rate optimization mantra. Whenever you come across an un-optimized page or a strong opinion about your marketing, you can say, **"You Should Test That!"**

Note: As you progress through this book, you'll see links to supplementary material and downloads. Each chapter has a section for additional resources and for discussing the chapter topic with others. For this chapter, go to YouShouldTestThat.com/YouShouldTestThat to contribute your ideas and join the discussion.

2

What Is Conversion Optimization?

*"Would you tell me, please, which way I ought to go
from here?" said Alice.*
*"That depends a good deal on where you want to get
to," said the Cat.*

—Alice in Wonderland

In Chapter 1: "Why You Should Test That," you saw how optimization can improve conversion rates. But there's even more to be gained from conversion optimization than just conversion-rate lift. When I say *just*, I don't mean to minimize the impact this has on the business, of course. I mean that the immediate conversion-rate lift is the starting point.

The results from conversion testing often generate learning that can impact the overall marketing strategy and even business strategy. It's like a gift that keeps on giving!

This chapter explores why controlled testing, above all other website-improvement methods, is required for conversion optimization. It also discusses target audience concepts and goal-setting methods. Finally, I introduce the seven-step testing method that you can use to get continuously improving conversion rates.

Conversion Optimization Requires Controlled Testing

Since the evolution of the modern scientific method began in the seventeenth century, the world has steadily become a better place in which to live. All advancements in modern society have been a result of this method. Scientists have made discoveries that have increased our life expectancies by decades, minimized infant mortality, developed fast and efficient global communications and travel, and increased worker productivity.

Yet many marketers still resist using the scientific method to advance our craft. Some probably enjoy the comfort in knowing that their work isn't tested so their opinions can't be disproven. Or they just trust their intuition and gut feeling to guide them in the right direction, much as the bloodletting physicians and alchemists did in prescientific eras.

Fortunately, we're no longer in the sixteenth century. The barriers to scientific marketing have largely been removed today. With more and more of our lives and transactions happening online, the difficulty and cost of quantitative testing in controlled environments has dropped dramatically. The golden age of marketing testing and learning is just beginning!

The Scientific Method of Controlled Testing

I want to make a clear distinction here between what many people consider testing and the *controlled* testing used in the scientific method. I've met many people who believe they're testing but have never run a true controlled test.

Test Against a Valid Control

Controlled testing requires structuring the experiment with a valid *control* that is run concurrently with the *challenger* variations. The control group is the segment of the experiment population that sees the original, unaltered web page that you're testing to improve.

In a controlled website test, the challenger variations are tested against the control, and all other factors are kept constant as carefully as possible to make sure the test results aren't polluted. This is often called the *champion-challenger* approach and is a cornerstone concept of direct-response marketing.

The following diagram outlines the controlled testing process. In an A/B/*n* test, sometimes called a *split test*, you assign each of your experiment visitors to see one of several challenger variations, numbered from A to *n*, where *n* represents any number of test variations.

1. Each visitor in your sample audience on your website or test page is entered into the experiment, unaware, and is randomly assigned to either the control or one of the challenger variations.

2. The visitor sees the same page variation on each subsequent visit to your site, ensuring a seamless user experience and valid test results.

3. When the visitor completes the test's goal, such as filling out an inquiry form or purchasing a product, a conversion is recorded for that visitor's assigned variation.

4. The testing tool calculates which variation delivers the highest conversion rate and when statistical significance (that is, it's unlikely the test results are due to chance) has been achieved.

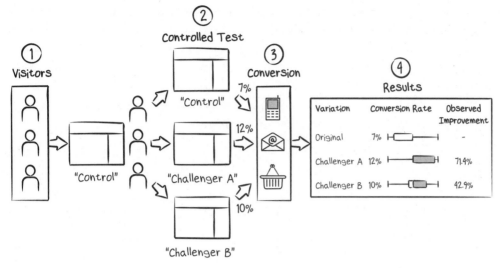

Variation	Conversion Rate		Observed Improvement
Original	7%	⊢□─┤	–
Challenger A	12%	⊢──▬─┤	71.4%
Challenger B	10%	⊢─▬─┤	42.9%

Controlled A/B/n testing

Data is collected until statistical significance is achieved and you have found a new champion, which can then replace the old page to become the new control for the next test round.

Selecting a Sample (Not a Free One, a Statistical One)

In scientific terms, an experiment *sample* is a portion of the entire *universe* that you want to test. Because you can't test every potential customer, you'll select a sample that represents the entire audience. Your experiment sample in this case is a portion of your website visitors.

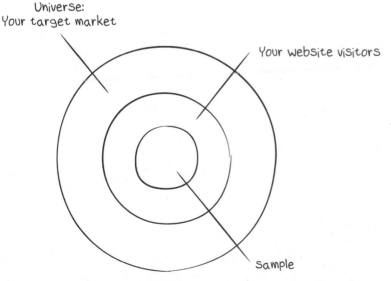

Select a representative sample of your visitors.

The visitors to each test page must be selected from the sample group to get meaningful test results. Your test audience should be homogeneous, meaning that each variation should receive the same type of visitors or mix of visitor types. If you test by choosing the visitors for each variation from different traffic sources, your results won't be useful.

Yes, We're Making a Sampling Assumption

If you're a statistician reading this, you'll notice that we've made an assumption that our website visitors are a representative sample of our target-market universe. Although this isn't 100 percent accurate, it's "close enough for jazz," as we used to say in the band scene. ;-) In other words, the cost of finding a totally accurate target audience sample would outweigh the benefits in business results.

This is a problem many web marketers encounter when they try to run a test manually without a proper controlled testing tool. I've seen many examples of marketers using different paid search ads, ad groups, or even traffic sources to drive visitors to variation pages to run a test. Google AdWords, for example, shouldn't be used to run conversion-optimization tests, because it doesn't properly track experiment participants and goal conversions to unique visitors. You'll get skewed data that is likely to mislead you.

You can get a valid sample by using a tool designed for controlled website testing and making sure to run the experiment long enough to achieve statistical significance.

Using a Tool Designed for Controlled Testing

Selecting valid samples isn't the only advantage of a conversion-optimization tool; this type of software also has all the other features built in so you can run controlled A/B/n and multivariate tests on your website. Each testing tool takes a slightly different approach to how tests are set up, managed, and run, but they all have similar characteristics. All testing tools do the following:

- Split incoming traffic randomly (and approximately evenly) between the variations.

- Set cookies or a similar control mechanism to ensure that each visitor in the experiment sees the same variation each time they return to the test page.

- Track the goal conversion rate(s) for each variation page (or combination of variables in the case of multivariate testing).

- Provide reports showing the conversion rates for each variation.

- Show the statistical significance of test results so you know if and when a test is complete and a winning page can be declared.

As shown in the flowchart, there is a typical series of server interactions for common JavaScript-based testing tools.

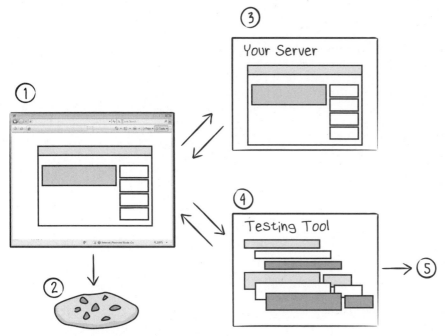

Typical testing tool dynamic content delivery flow

The process looks like this:

1. Your visitor's web browser requests your web page.
2. A cookie or similar tracking method is set to identify this visitor as part of the experiment group.
3. Your site server delivers the control page's content.
4. The testing tool server replaces variable content areas that you have defined with the variation content. In the case of a multivariate test, multiple sections are swapped independently. In the case of an A/B/*n* test, the entire page's content may be swapped, or the visitor may be redirected to a different page URL.
5. The testing tool provides results reports through a web login interface.

See the appendix "Additional Resources" for an intro to many of the common testing tools you can choose from.

"Best Practices" Are Not Conversion Optimization

As conversion optimization has become more popular, many people have confused it with best-practice consulting. Be sure you don't make the same mistake.

Web design experts at one time or another have given all of the following best practices tips:

- Green buttons work best... (they don't)
- Red buttons work best... (nope)
- No, use orange buttons... (not always)
- Minimize form fields... (depends on the situation)
- Minimize clicks to conversion... (not necessarily)
- Emphasize security icons... (bad idea)
- Security icons raise anxiety... (sometimes)
- Sex sells... (usually not, unless you're selling sex)
- Always include a smiling person... (uh uh)
- Never include people... (test this)
- Use long copy landing pages... (in some cases)
- Minimize your copy length... (in many cases)
- Lead with benefits... (not always)
- Lead with features... (sometimes)

And so on. (You get the picture, right?) Many recommendations from the experts have proven to be untested.

For example, some conversion consultants recommend making your security badges (like McAfee or HackerSafe) as prominent as possible. After all, "you're paying for them, so you might as well make them obvious," they'll tell you.

How do you know if that's good advice? Well, we've tested it. In some cases, adding security icons helps, but we've actually seen that making them too prominent or introducing them too early in the purchase flow can reduce conversion rates and sales! That's a conclusion you might not be able to guess without testing it.

The only best practice I can recommend is this: when you hear a best-practice recommendation, say, "You Should Test That!" You may be surprised.

The discipline of testing and validating hypotheses is very different than taking the opinions of "experts" as fact. Don't take experts' opinions without testing for your-self! What an expert "feels strongly about" may just be the latest thing they're paid to promote.

Another problem with expert recommendations is that they can't take into account all the complexities of any particular situation. You're facing a unique set of environmental variables. A consultant may have seen similar situations and be able to make some helpful suggestions that could lead to great test hypotheses. But without testing those suggestions in your particular situation, you shouldn't be confident about taking the consultant's word for it.

That's not to say that bringing in a consultant or conversion expert won't be helpful. It often will! But you should look for consultants who do a lot of testing and then make sure they're willing to follow through on executing the tests to take responsibility for the outcome.

The Before & After Method Is Not Conversion Optimization

At WiderFunnel, we have had marketers call us looking to improve their conversion rates who tell us that they already do conversion testing.

Too often, it turns out they're using the Before & After (or Pre & Post) method rather than controlled split testing. They make changes to their website or landing pages and then look at their web analytics data to see if their results improved from a prior time period. If the conversion rate or revenue increased, they attribute it to the change they made and consider it a success. If results drop, they revert back to the original and call it a failure.

This is a dangerous practice. It ignores so many uncontrollable, external influences and statistical uncertainties as to make the result entirely meaningless. That's right—I said meaningless!

Let's look at a typical example of how this works. You're looking at your analytics reports for an important page on your site; maybe it's a high-traffic landing page or a product category page. You notice that it has all the signs of a poorly performing page: high exit rate, high bounce rate, low conversion rate for entry visitors, and so on. It looks like a great candidate for conversion optimization. So you gather your team together and come up with ideas for improving it, or hire a consultant for a page critique and redesign it based on the consultant's input.

You launch the newly designed page and use the Pre & Post method to evaluate the results. After a few weeks of data gathering, your analytics results look like this:

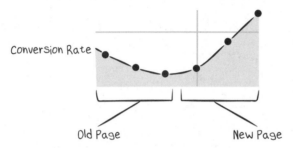

Before & After assumed success paints a pretty picture.

Clearly, your conversion rate with the old page was low and declining, and your new page has turned the conversion rate upward almost immediately. Pop the champagne corks!

Not so fast! The long-term story may be very different. Here's what the following weeks of data could look like.

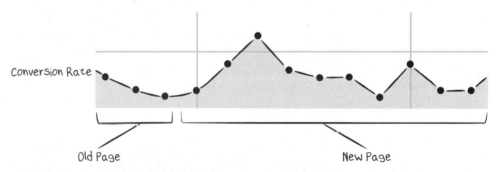

Before & After real results tell a different story!

External Factors Mess with Your Data

In WiderFunnel's experience, external factors often wreak havoc with Before & After tests. If you don't control for all other variables, it isn't a valid test. Any of the following external factors may change your conversion rate in either the positive or negative direction without your knowledge, and invalidate the results of Pre & Post tests.

Competitive Activity

Your competitors are always active. They're changing tactics and strategies, adding new products, testing offers, and running marketing campaigns.

Do you know when their email marketing blasts are released? Do you know their promotional schedule for discount offers? Of course you don't. And their activities can have a significant influence on your conversion rate.

For example, let's say you run a cruise vacation website featuring Alaskan cruises. You offer up to 60 percent savings, which you mention in all of your main traffic-generating Google AdWords ads.

Alaska Cruises 2012 Deals
Alaska Cruises & Land Tours. Up to
60% Off. Welcome Aboard & Save!
www.alaskacruiseexperts.com/Alaska

You recently changed your landing page design and are monitoring the results using the Pre & Post method. You're carefully watching your booking conversion rate in your web analytics tool to see the impact the new design makes. Little do you know, though, that a few days after you switched to the new test landing-page design, two competitors changed their ads to promise savings that are much more compelling than yours.

Your competitive environment impacts your conversion rate.

Your competitive environment has changed, and your landing-page conversion rate may be impacted one way or another *regardless* of the changes you made to your landing page.

Seasonality

Be aware of any predictable fluctuations like these:

- Does your business have any seasonality to your customers' demand level?
- Are there fluctuations in conversion rate on different days of the week?
- Is there any change during cold or warm months?
- What about during popular vacation weeks?

If you observe any seasonality in your businesses, you can be sure that the results of a Pre & Post test will be misleading. Even if you don't operate in a highly seasonal business, fluctuations in demand and perceived urgency will render a Pre & Post test worthless.

Marketing Activity

Can you keep your marketing silent for several weeks while you try to run a Pre & Post test? Most companies would find this requirement too restrictive. It would leave you unable to respond to competitive activities or limit your testing ability to only small windows in between marketing efforts.

Not only that, if you can't run tests during marketing promotions, you have no way of knowing which experiment variation performs best during promotional periods. In some cases, different layouts and content perform better during higher-urgency periods.

On the other hand, if you use proper controlled testing, you can run experiments at any time, regardless of the current marketing activity. See Chapter 10, "Optimize for Urgency," to learn more about how urgency affects experiment results.

Product and Service Availability

In a product business, stock levels can influence conversion rate. Limited supply creates a scarcity reaction that motivates people to buy due to fear of loss. As you'll see in Chapter 10, the fear of loss can be a very powerful motivator. Make sure you're using it in your favor rather than being an inadvertent victim of it. During a Pre & Post test, fluctuations in stock levels affect your conversion rates continually.

Note: Someone may be discussing your products and services right now. Research shows that we trust the word of our friends more highly than other sources. Research done by Invoke Solutions shows that 64 percent of social-media users rate blog and social-media posts by friends to be either "trusted somewhat" or "trusted completely." You can find links on this topic and the original source research at YouShouldTestThat.com/WhatIsConversionOptimization.

At any time, a positive or negative comment could be said in person, on a blog, or in social media that will influence your conversion rate. You can't always control it or factor it into your Pre & Post test because you may not even know about it!

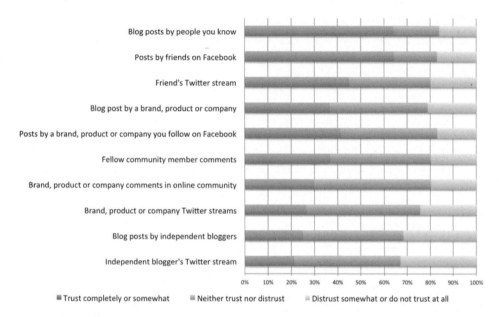

Consumers trust friends.

Have you considered how these factors are affecting your conversion rates on a weekly, daily, and even hourly basis? You may be surprised how much of an influence they can be.

The only thing worse than not testing is getting misleading results from your tests. Too many companies using Pre & Post testing have acted on this false data and are harming their business results.

Usability Testing Is Not Conversion Optimization

Nearly as bad as best-practice consulting or using the Pre & Post method is to put too much trust in individual user testing. Sometimes companies aren't testing on their live website traffic at all but still believe they're testing!

I define *user testing* as an exercise where you observe a small group or a single user attempting to accomplish a predefined task on your website. User testing can be an important method for generating hypotheses; but used alone, it isn't conversion optimization.

Don't make the mistake of following the findings from user testing without verifying using controlled A/B/*n* tests. Unfortunately, I have seen examples where research firms report findings from small groups using precise percentage results that give the advertiser false confidence in the results.

For example, if a report states that "58.3 percent of study participants value the many-options aspect of the service rather than the quality," would you be inclined to emphasize options over quality in your advertising? That 58.3 percent number looks very precise, doesn't it? But what if those findings are actually based on a survey of only 12 people? It would really mean that only 7 preferred the flexibility aspect. That result shouldn't give you confidence to change your marketing approach!

There are several reasons why using usability testing alone can lead to misleading findings:

The Hawthorne Effect

The act of observing a thing changes that thing. When people know they're being observed, they may be more motivated to complete the action. Or, knowing that you're looking for usability problems, they may be more motivated to find problems whether or not they're actually important.

Observer-Expectancy Effect

Researchers can unintentionally influence user-testing participants and change the results. This is similar to the Hawthorne effect. It's very difficult to avoid communicating with subtle verbal and nonverbal cues that direct the user.

Limited Sample Sizes

The feedback you get is only valid for the small number of people you're testing. Although you can often gain valuable insights from a small number of users, you don't know which ones are valuable. And doing usability testing with large sample sizes is generally cost-prohibitive.

Sampling Bias

The first of two selection biases, sampling or user-selection bias occurs when you have a mismatch between your actual customers and the criteria you use for selecting study participants. You may have an inaccurate view of your real customers or may skew toward the segments that are easier to attract into the study. For example, if your company develops video games, by studying hard-core gamers in the 14- to 24-year-old male category you may miss out on the growing and lucrative 25- to 44-year old females, who will clearly have very different interaction styles and needs.

Self-Selection Bias

Self-selection bias is a significant problem when users volunteer to be in a study. You'll never be able study people who don't want to participate in studies. This could be a large portion of your target audience that you'll never hear from! Look out for real customer motivations.

Preset Goals Creating an Artificial Scenario

In usability testing, the researcher sets predefined goals for the user to attempt to accomplish and then monitors their success or failure and points of difficulty.

Probably the most fundamental limitation of this type of user testing is that the scenarios are artificial. The task you choose for the user may not be the task a typical user would choose. It's also not likely to be relevant to the particular user you're testing. In other words, you're asking a person to imagine and act as if they were the type of person who wanted to accomplish the task you want them to. That's asking a lot!

Conversion Optimization Involves More Than Just Usability

Usability tests give you an indication of interface problems and clarity of navigation, but they usually don't generate ideas about the layouts, content, and value proposition that would be more persuasive. Steve Jobs was once quoted in *BusinessWeek* saying, "It's really hard to design products by focus groups. A lot of times, people don't know what they want until you show it to them." Your customers don't know how you can motivate them, and they can't tell you which landing page design will work best for them, either.

Researchers have similar problems when conducting focus groups, one-on-one interviews, or other qualitative methods. They know that data can't be reliable until it's verified with quantitative testing.

Traditional usability testing is valuable in exploring a variety of scenarios quickly, gaining immediate interactive feedback, and developing hypotheses that could not otherwise have been predicted. But when used in isolation, it isn't a good tool for website decision-making. The potential insights generated need to be validated through controlled testing.

I think Joel Spolsky said it well:

Usability is not everything.
If usability engineers designed a nightclub, it would be clean, quiet, brightly lit,
with lots of places to sit down, plenty of bartenders, menus written in 18-point
sans-serif, and easy-to-find bathrooms.
But nobody would be there. They would all be down the street at Coyote Ugly
pouring beer on each other.

Surveys Are Not Conversion Optimization

Surveys can be a useful tool for gathering feedback from your visitors, but they alone won't optimize your conversion rate. Website surveys have become very popular for marketers like IKEA and MacWorld to gather direct feedback from visitors.

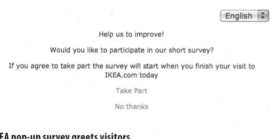

IKEA pop-up survey greets visitors.

MacWorld popup survey by ForeSee

Survey tools like these can help gather qualitative data on customer satisfaction. They're especially useful for finding customer-service lapses, because customers who are disgruntled with your product or service are most likely to express their frustration.

Surveys won't tell you how to create the best layouts and content to maximize your conversion rate, however. Only the most serious usability problems will be revealed with a survey.

Click Heatmap Tracking Is Not Conversion Optimization

Some fantastic tools allow you to monitor how visitors interact with your website. With some, you can view visual overlays on your pages, showing where people click most often.

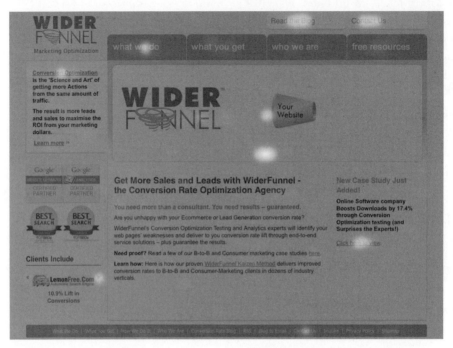

A click heatmap of the WiderFunnel.com home page, generated by CrazyEgg, shows click concentrations on the animated demo and blog links.

Some tools can also record videos of individuals' screens as they navigate through your website. It's almost as if you're looking over the visitor's shoulder. The technology is awesome!

Interaction tracking like this can give you some ideas about which areas visitors may expect to be clickable. You may find, for example, that a lot of people click an image, perhaps expecting to be able to view a larger version of it.

Tracking like this can't tell you why visitors act the way they do, however. You won't know why people are clicking an image or what they expect to see next (and each person may have different expectations). More important, it also can't tell you whether changes will lift conversions!

Surveys, user testing, click tracking, and other similar technologies are not, in themselves, conversion optimization, but they're all methods for developing hypotheses for conversion optimization.

By now you should see that conversion optimization doesn't happen without controlled testing. All the observations, analytics, and gut feelings you can gather may improve your results, but you'll never know for sure until you test them. By all means, gather the data; then You Should Test That!

What Is Conversion Optimization?

Now that you've seen many of the common misconceptions and understand what conversion optimization is *not*, let's look at what it *is*. True conversion optimization lives in the intersection of persuasion marketing, experience design, and the scientific method.

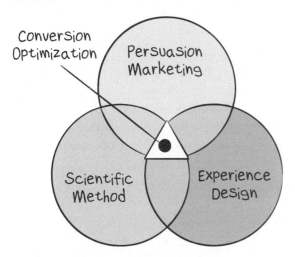

- In *persuasion marketing*, a skilled conversion strategist knows how to communicate the value proposition and build desire in the prospects. This is where you create motivation for completing the call to action. It involves communicating the right message to the right people at the right time with clarity.
- *Experience design* is where you facilitate that action. When you've created motivation, your prospects need a seamless, painless, and even enjoyable way to complete the action. Experience design is focused on the transactional elements of your marketing.
- The *scientific method* is how you test the hypotheses you create within the first two areas. This requires using a rigorous process of continuous testing, iteration, and improvement.

Who Are Your Target Audiences?

The concept of a *target audience* is a way of describing the people you would like your marketing messages to reach. Understanding your audience is critical to being able to create products and messages that they can relate to and will respond to.

Target Markets and Personas

In recent years, marketers have debated the benefits of using target markets versus the newer concept of a persona to understand their customers. Almost all marketing departments have target-market definitions, but detailed personas are still a rarity.

Whether you use target markets or have detailed personas, conversion optimization requires putting yourself in your customers' shoes. Practicing the art of empathizing with their perspective, needs, and experience will make you a better conversion optimizer.

Target Markets

Marketers use the concept of target markets (or segments or profiles) to help understand whom they're marketing to. Target markets are based on similar demographic data, such as age, household income, and life stage, as well as psychographic characteristics, including interests, perspectives, and religious or political views.

The benefit of target markets is that they're relatively easy to develop, understand, and communicate. A typical target-market description could look like this:

- Age: 35–54
- Marital status: Married
- Gender: Skews female
- Household income (HHI): $75,000+

Some companies have several distinct target markets, and each summary allows the marketer to select media and messaging to reach and persuade them.

Target-market summaries are often criticized for lacking insight into the individuals. It can be difficult for you as a marketer to really connect with your customers if you can only think of them as a faceless mass labeled with these cold data points. That impersonal feeling has led to the popularity of *personas* as a marketing tool.

Personas

Personas take a more individualistic approach to understanding your audience. Many companies go to great lengths to develop these detailed descriptions of their typical customers.

The characteristics that are included in personas vary greatly depending on who develops them. There are few common standards for persona development.

Personas are especially helpful for your copywriters to paint a clearer picture of the reader and understand their situation and needs. On the other hand, highly detailed personas can lead to copywriting that is too specific to a fictional character. The individuals represented in the persona descriptions don't represent your real customers. There is no average customer, and speaking to one predominantly can alienate your real customers.

COURTESY OF THE PUBLIC LEGAL EDUCATION AND INFORMATION NETWORK OF BRITISH COLUMBIA.

Doris - Newcomer	
Profile	Doris is a 28-year-old nanny, new to British Columbia from the Philippines, working with a family in the Dunbar area of Vancouver. She is in Canada on a temporary domestic worker visa.
Goals	To stay in Canada working as a nanny and to support her family back in the Phillipines.
Attitudes	Not sure where to turn for help for legal questions. Finds Canadian legal terms to be confusing.
Behaviours	Prefers to talk with someone when seeking advice. When she uses the Internet, she uses Google Phillipines as her starting point for searches.
Computer skills	She has access to a computer at home, uses computers at the houses of friends and at the library. Uses email and chat to keep in touch with family in the Phillipines.
Legal access and history	Unfamiliar with BC or Canadian law. Worked through the immigration process.

A persona helps guide the development of copy for a new website.

Writing for multiple imagined persona types can also make the copywriting too wordy, as you try to meet all the individual needs of these persona characters. In practice, writing for personas often sacrifices brevity and clarity in exchange for over-personalization. The result can be a cluttered message and lower conversion rates!

You should use the data you have available to get a good understanding of your visitors without becoming bogged down creating overly detailed personas. A balance can be achieved without the potential complexity the persona-development projects can provoke.

Setting Goals

Before getting started on your first conversion-optimization project, you'll save yourself grief by spending time clarifying your goals. You may think goals are the obvious part; after all, you already know you want more sales, right? There is a lot more involved in goal-setting than simply deciding to increase sales, though.

You need to track and improve the activities that deliver business results. It often helps to start at the beginning by stating why the website exists; then you can identify all the possible goals, prioritize them, and pinpoint the most important ones to optimize for.

This section will cover the strategy for goal-setting. In Chapter 11, "Test Your Hypotheses," I'll show how to implement the goals as part of your test plan.

Define Your Goals

Why does your website exist? Is it there to:

- Present information about your company and products?
- Generate leads for your sales team?
- Convince visitors to "Like" you on Facebook or follow you on Twitter?
- Create your brand image?
- Sell products to new customers? Sell products to repeat customers?
- Provide customer service and warranty claims?

Maybe it has more than one of those goals, or maybe others. One thing is for sure—until your goals are well defined, you'll have a hard time knowing when you've achieved them.

You may, like many website managers, be facing the pressures of competing priorities and demands from multiple stakeholders. Especially in larger organizations, every department wants its own content featured prominently, and every time the "next big thing" comes along, someone wants to add it to the website.

Understanding your website's *raison d'être* and the specific goals needed to achieve that overall purpose will give you the rationale and the data to make sound decisions under pressure.

The Goals Waterfall

Your goals for your conversion-optimization tests should flow from your marketing goals, which ultimately flow from the organization's goals and strategy. This top-down goal flow is what I call the *goals waterfall*.

By tying your activity and decisions up the waterfall to the business goal source, you'll focus your efforts on the most productive outcomes that benefit the organization. It's easy to lose sight of the business goals in the day-to-day debates over website decisions, but developing a habit of defining the right goals will pay off.

Not only will your focus on the business goals ensure that you optimize the right things, but it can also help you get more senior buy-in and attention for your projects, and even get you the salary increase you've been hoping for. It's a win-win-win!

Prioritize Your Goals

To control the competing demands within the organization, you need to create a clear goal prioritization. You can do this in three steps:

1. Rank your goals.
2. Assign relative goal values.
3. Estimate actual goal values.

Business Goals

Marketing Goals

Conversion Optimization Goals

The goals waterfall shows that conversion-optimization goals flow top-down from business goals.

Once you get agreement on the goal prioritization and values, you'll have very clear direction to set up your conversion-optimization goals.

Rank Your Goals

You can take a first pass at ranking your goals by simply creating an ordered list of your goals in terms of the relative value to the business. That list will give you a basic criterion for judging the emphasis for each competing piece of content. You'll clearly be able to see how prominent each piece of content should be on your pages.

This is, incidentally, a good opportunity to include management and other website stakeholders in the discussion. It could help you build consensus for your later proposal to start conversion-optimization testing on the site.

For example, your organization's social-media advocate is probably telling you that your landing pages should include badges for Twitter, Facebook, LinkedIn, Google+, and all other manner of social activity. With your prioritized goal list that is tied back to the organizational goals, you can now have a reasoned conversation about where a Facebook "Like" fits on the hierarchy of information. Is it more important than a newsletter signup, whitepaper download, quote request, or product purchase? Probably not.

Let's use an example to demonstrate how to prioritize goals. Here is a typical list of website goals that has been sorted in order of importance:

Priority	Goal
1	Product sale
2	Quote request
3	Whitepaper download
4	Blog comment
5	Social-media profile activity (Facebook, Twitter, LinkedIn, Google Plus, and so on)

You can clearly see from this list which calls to action should get the most visual emphasis on your key pages. In this case, the product sale is your main conversion, and the others are secondary goals, or what we call *micro-conversions*. The quote request in some cases is also a primary conversion if it leads to a sale for a different product or a higher-value order.

Your landing-page visitor should have no question that their primary decision is whether to purchase a product now before evaluating the secondary conversion options. The call-to-action for purchasing should be the most prominent action button on the page.

Conversions vs. Micro-Conversions   Your main conversion is the goal action that is most closely tied to revenue. Any other goal is called a *micro-conversion*. I've created names to differentiate two types of micro-conversion actions:

Micro-step conversion: A step along the way toward a full conversion, like an add-to-cart or a visit to a quote-request form

Micro-indicator conversion: An indicator of interest in a future full conversion, like a whitepaper download or social-media interaction

Assign Relative Goal Values

After ranking your goals, you should then take your prioritized list one step further by assigning relative values to each of the goals. The values don't have to be absolutely accurate revenue-producing numbers for a start. Simply having magnitude context helps greatly to clarify decision-making.

Pick a median goal on your list, and assign it an arbitrary amount, such as $10. In the following example, we'll add a $10 value to the whitepaper download. To simplify this example, I'm including e-commerce and lead-generation goals, which may or may not apply in your situation. As a starting point for valuing the relative importance of your goals, you can estimate the value of the other goals up and down from that median value, as in the next table.

Priority	Goal	Value
1	Product sale	$250
2	Quote request	$100
3	Whitepaper download	$10
4	Blog comment	$2
5	Social-media profile activity (Facebook, Twitter, LinkedIn, Google Plus, and so on)	$1

In most cases, as in this example, you'll start to see a dramatic split between goals that are closely tied to revenue and others that are more speculative. This should give you even more motivation to optimize for the high-value goals. You can now pull out this handy list in a web-design debate and ask, "Would we rather have a $1 Facebook 'Like' or a $250 product sale?" That's one question that doesn't take any testing to answer!

Estimate Real Goal-Contribution Values

The relative goal values will get you close to what you need for the purposes of optimization, but you may want to refine them further. For example, the product-purchase and quote-request amounts in this example can likely be estimated more accurately.

> **Note:** The value of a product purchase, for an e-commerce website, may simply be your average order value. Or, to make it more useful, you can split the product purchase amount into new customer product purchases and repeat purchases. As discussed in Chapter 1, you can use a lifetime value (LTV) for the new customer purchases for greater accuracy. For more information on options for calculating LTV, see YouShouldTestThat.com/WhatIsConversionOptimization.

To improve your estimated quote-request value, you can calculate it by identifying the sales that came from your web quotes. If you already have your sales quotes tagged in your sales-management system, you'll have no problem pulling the sales that originated from quote requests. The value of a quote request can be calculated as follows:

S = Your total sales from quote requests

Q = Your total quote requests

Quote-request value = S / Q

For example, if you have $180,000 sales from 1,000 quote requests, the value of a quote request is

$180,000 / 1,000 = $180

Your other goals may not have direct revenue tied to them, but they should still be recognized with some value. You can spend a lot more time refining these values through attribution modeling and LTV exercises, but don't do that first. Especially if you haven't started your conversion testing yet, your time is best spent getting a test running. You'll get better results optimizing for an 80 percent accurate goal than waiting until your goals are 100 percent accurate!

The updated goal-value list looks like this:

Priority	Goal	Value
1	Product sale	$229
2	Quote request	$180
3	Whitepaper download	$10
4	Blog comment	$2
5	Social-media profile activity (Facebook, Twitter, LinkedIn, Google Plus, and so on)	$1

If the difference in value between your main goal and your micro-indicator conversion goals is large, you should track the single goal in your tests. The KISS ("Keep It Simple, Superstar") principle applies here. Tracking many micro-conversion goals for conversion-optimization tests can overcomplicate the analysis unless they're clearly important steps toward a main conversion.

Now you have the tools to prioritize your goals. You need to decide which action or actions on your site to identify as goal conversions. There may be several steps along a purchase or lead-generation funnel that can be tracked.

Should You Optimize for Micro-Conversions?

The most common reason people optimize for micro-step conversions is to speed up their experiments. Remember that a micro-step conversion is simply a small action on the way to a full revenue-producing conversion.

Because the length of time needed to run your A/B/n or multivariate test depends, in part, on the amount of traffic and conversions you get, and because most websites get many times more micro-conversions than sales or lead conversions, their experiments may complete faster using micro-conversions as test goals.

For example, consider a typical gated form that a software company uses to generate leads for a sales team.

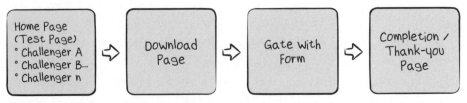

A gated software-conversion path

At each step, there is a certain drop-off rate. If the home page gets 100,000 visitors monthly, the counts for each page in this hypothetical scenario could be as follows:

a) Download page: 20,000

b) Gate with form: 15,000

c) Thank-you page: 5,000

Setting Micro-Conversions as Goals

Let's say you want to run an A/B/*n* test on the home page in the previous example. You need to decide whether your experiment goal is: a) visit to the download page, b) visit to the gate page, or c) download completion.

If you choose option a), using the download page micro-conversion as the goal, your experiment will complete faster because you'll have 20,000 goals triggered rather than 5,000.

That's good news, right? You can finish the test sooner and move on to the next test.

The False Micro-Conversion Testing Assumption

But, wait. You've made a big assumption there.

If you assume there's an equal drop-off rate through the funnel regardless of the home page variation shown, it shouldn't matter which one you choose. But will your funnel-completion rate (from download to thank-you page) really be the same regardless of the home page variation?

In our testing experience, that is a dangerous assumption. Using micro-conversions as conversion-optimization goals can show misleading test results. We have seen many examples where the first step of a funnel can dramatically change the completion of a subsequent step—even a step that is several steps removed.

Here's a typical example A/B/*n* test result through the funnel:

	Home Page	Download Page	Gate with Form	Completed Conversion	Conversion Rate Lift
Control Page	100%	51%	38%	2.4%	N/A
Variation A	100%	49%	**40**%	3.1%	29%
Variation B	100%	52%	38%	**3.5**%	46%
Variation C	100%	**54**%	35%	2.1%	-13%

Depending on the micro-conversions you were counting as your goals, here's what you would have decided:

Conversion Goal	Winning Variation
Download page	Variation C
Gate with form	Variation A
Thank-you page	Variation B

Clearly, the best-performing variation is actually B. It lifted the lead-generation conversion rate by 46 percent. But if you had run the test using download-page visits as the goal, you would have chosen variation C as the winner and could have seriously hurt your results! In short, where you set your test goal influences your results.

Optimize for Revenue-Producing Actions

For conversion optimization, you should always set your test goal to be as close to revenue as possible. Optimize for direct sales, average order value, and qualified leads generated.

Please continue to track and review micro-conversions in your web analyses, but for conversion testing, stick to revenue-producing goals.

Web Analytics Goals vs. Conversion-Optimization Goals

Many of the metrics found in your standard web analytics setup aren't appropriate goals for optimization, even though they may be relevant Key Performance Indicators (KPIs) for your website.

 Key Performance Indicators With so much data available in your web analytics tool, you need to focus attention on the most important numbers that influence business results. These KPIs are the numbers that give insight into how the business is performing over time. By focusing the numbers shared within the organization, skilled web analysts are more likely to have their reports actually read rather than being filed in the round bin.

When setting up your web analytics tool, it can be helpful to set up tracking for all manner of activities. You can set various pages and micro-conversions as goals, and even track clicks, time on page, and other interactions as events. These can all be helpful as you search for insights into how visitors are using the site, and can spark new hypotheses for testing.

However, just because something is tracked and meaningful doesn't mean it should be a conversion-optimization goal. Conversion-optimization goals should be selected very carefully to only include the most important revenue-tied action or actions.

Example: Don't Optimize for Bounce Rate

Bounce rate, for example, is a common KPI and an indicator of the relevance of a particular page to visitors entering the site. If your site-wide bounce rate is 43% and a popular entry page has a bounce rate of 56%, for example, the page may not be meeting the expectations of incoming visitors.

Bounce Rate vs. Exit Rate   *Bounce rate* is a metric used in most web analytics tools. It's generally measured as a percentage of the visitors who enter your site, view only one page, and leave without seeing any other pages on your site. Don't confuse it with *exit rate*, which is also a page-level indicator showing the percentage of visitors for whom the page was the last viewed before leaving the site. Each of these may be indicators of a conversion-optimization opportunity area.

A higher bounce rate isn't necessarily a problem, however:

Example 1—Non-Target Visitors   In one case, the page in question may have a high natural search ranking for non-revenue-producing keywords, bringing in non-target visitors. Those non-target visitors aren't hurting you by visiting the page and can be disregarded (unless you can figure out a new way of engaging them in a relevant offer). Your true bounce rate for your target visitors may be lower than you think in this case.

Example 2—Successful Communication Page   In another case, your page may actually be doing a good job of communicating your message, so some visitors who aren't ready to convert can leave rather than navigating the site to try to figure out what you sell. This isn't necessarily a bad thing and may still allow for a relatively high lead-generation or purchase-conversion rate.

But a high bounce rate can suggest a problem on a page, too. So shouldn't you try to lower a high bounce rate with testing if you can?

No. If you set bounce-rate reduction as your conversion-optimization goal, you could hurt your revenue-producing goals.

Here are instances where your bounce rate could be lowered without improving revenue:

- Changing a single landing page into a multipage microsite experience could encourage multipage views without more purchases.

- Moving some key information, like pricing, onto a second page will almost surely lower bounce rate but not improve sales.

- Simply adding links to popular news or blog content could lower bounce rate but just be a distraction from sales goals.

- Replacing productive offers with free offers may have lower revenue-producing value.

If you were to test any of these options as challenger experiment variations, you could easily lower your bounce rate and believe your test was a success. But that new challenger page may have hurt revenue production while "improving" your bounce rate. In this case, you shouldn't test that!

Case Study: How Tourism British Columbia Increased Online Marketing Engagement by 44 Percent

Tourism British Columbia is responsible for the continued growth and development of the province's $13.4 billion tourism industry. Its website, HelloBC.com, represents 130+ communities and over 6,000 tourism businesses. It's also the first touch point for hundreds of thousands of local and international travelers visiting the province each year.

The Business Need

Research conducted by Tourism BC found a direct correlation between website content and user engagement on HelloBC.com. As visitors engaged with more website content, their likelihood of planning a trip to the province increased. With content readily available, Tourism BC needed a way to engage more prospective travelers.

The Challenges

For Tourism BC, brand equity isn't a problem. British Columbia boasts one of the most livable cities in the world and a natural landscape unlike any other in North America, and hosted the 2010 Olympic and Paralympic Winter Games; the organization knew that the time to capitalize on tourism dollars was now.

With the Internet playing a major factor in a prospective tourist's decision-making process, Tourism BC wanted to ensure that these visitors were accelerated down the path of booking their vacations in the province. This started with the free travel guide, which could be downloaded by registering on HelloBC.com.

Although registrations to download the guide were fairly high, the organization realized that it was losing opportunities for further engagement with website content deeper in the site, because most visitors exited after downloading.

Tourism BC knew that reengaging those visitors with website content would increase the probability of bookings; however, it needed a strategic methodology to get visitors engaged again after the download.

The Solution

Tourism BC knew that implementing new ideas on the travel-guide landing page and hoping for the best was not the way to approach this challenge. It knew that interest in the province was at an all-time high, and leaving this opportunity to chance was not an option.

Having worked with WiderFunnel previously to optimize the site's landing pages, Tourism BC knew the company could be trusted to provide an end-to-end conversion-optimization strategy that would produce the highest possible conversion rates.

WiderFunnel began with an in-depth discovery and planning phase to develop a Kaizen Plan, which produces a strategy for conversion optimization across all web properties and landing pages. By analyzing website statistics and performing heuristic analyses, the WiderFunnel conversion strategy team identified and prioritized optimization opportunities, one of which was the testing of an often-overlooked step in the conversion funnel—the thank-you page.

Original (control) thank-you page

Using its proprietary LIFT Model, WiderFunnel analyzed the HelloBC.com thank-you page and identified a number of opportunities for improvement, specifically for information clarity and call-to-action prominence. The WiderFunnel strategists recommended a multistep approach to conversion-optimization testing, starting with one test to identify the best general page layout and then a second test to isolate individual hypotheses and continue improvement.

Continued

How Tourism British Columbia Increased Online Marketing Engagement by 44 Percent *(Continued)*

Test 1: Establishing a Baseline for Success

WiderFunnel developed several page layouts and design hypotheses using the original as a control page against which to compare each variation's results. Each variation's goal was to engage visitors on the thank-you page after visitors downloaded the travel guide, by inviting them to view more content deeper in the HelloBC.com website.

Because of the relatively low traffic of thank-you pages, WiderFunnel created dramatically different page variations to be tested against the original control page. Even though the strategists had many possible hypotheses to test, testing too many variations would have lengthened the test duration.

The strategists dug into WiderFunnel's central database of test results to identify past results with situations similar to Tourism BC's in order to find layout approaches that had a high likelihood of improving conversions.

The winning variation resulted in a 22 percent lift in visitor engagement compared to the control page.

Round 1 winner

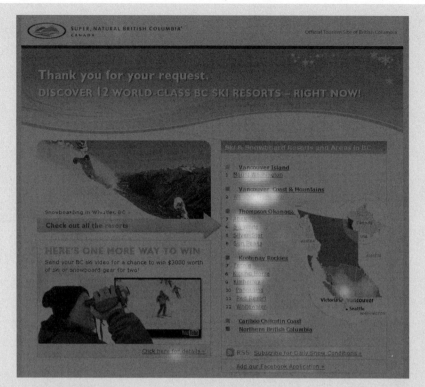

Click heatmap from round 1

Test 2: Making Refinements

Using insights gathered from the first test, including findings from a heatmap analysis, WiderFunnel generated new hypotheses and integrated them into new test variations, which were implemented in an A/B/*n* test against the winning variation of the initial test:

> **Variation A: "Interactive Map"** was developed to test the main hypothesis that a clickable map of British Columbia would entice thank-you page visitors to continue their exploration of the province by accessing more website pages.

> **Variation B: "Catalogue"** tested the main hypothesis that highly visual and informative representations of BC's key regions and cities would appeal to page visitors and draw them back into the website.

Variation B was found to increase visitor engagement by a further 18 percent on top of the 22 percent lift realized during the first test round.

Continued

How Tourism British Columbia Increased Online Marketing Engagement by 44% *(Continued)*

SUPER, NATURAL BRITISH COLUMBIA®
CANADA

Official Tourism Site of British Columbia

BRITISH COLUMBIA

THANK YOU. We have received your order for your FREE **BC Escapes®** e-Guides. You should have received your guides in your inbox already.

Discover BC's six regions and start planning your getaway now!

Cities

Vancouver

Discover the duality of Vancouver: urban sophistication and natural splendour.
• Vancouver is a cosmopolitan city with all the urban amenities - fine dining, shopping, museums, galleries, music and theatre - plus endless opportunities for outdoor activities.

Whistler

Revel in the four-season resort town of Whistler. Spring brings an array of adventures.
• Enjoy fresh air and walking trails, shopping, spas, entertainment, fine restaurants, golf, train tours and much more.

Victoria

Get to know the quaint charm and friendliness of the province's capital city, Victoria.
• Victoria boasts fabulous shops, restaurants, museums, and city parks, complementing world-class golf courses, ski hills, hiking trails, and fishing expeditions.

Regions

Vancouver Island

Vancouver, Coast and Mountains

Thompson Okanagan

Round 2 winner

The End Result: A 44 Percent Lift in Visitor Engagement

Cumulatively, the two testing rounds resulted in a 44 percent gain in visitor engagement. Furthermore, the insights provided from the tests revealed more opportunities to engage visitors on thank-you pages. This has allowed Tourism BC to dramatically reduce exit rates as well as increase downstream engagement on HelloBC.com.

The Continuous Improvement Cycle

In our personal lives, we are continually given opportunities to learn, change, and grow. Our daily interactions can be like miniature experiments where we receive feedback from the world and have opportunities to try different ways of interacting. Some choices we make are more or less effective than others, as my former girlfriends will attest, and the world gives us the appropriate feedback.

Looking at the bigger picture, the same can be said for how life on Earth evolves by experimenting with different variations of each species. Life is a continuous improvement experiment!

Our businesses have the same opportunities to evolve. Rather than meeting the fate of the dodo or dinosaur, however, we can consciously run experiments to keep ahead of the competition.

Business theories have been developed to recognize and capture these optimization opportunities, such as the Shewhart Cycle. Systematic processes like this for planning new ways of doing things, checking the results, and following the better-performing actions have improved business quality dramatically in the past half century.

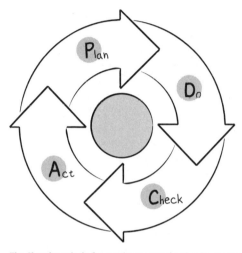

The Shewhart Cycle for continuous production improvement

As in life and business, our websites have opportunities to receive feedback and improve on a continuous basis.

Continuous Improvement Is Key to Success

There is an unfortunate misconception that conversion optimization immediately results in a perfect, "optimized" page or website. It's tempting to hope for an ideal page to quickly emerge from one or two test rounds. That perfect page doesn't appear instantly, however. Conversion optimization is best approached as an ongoing process of improvement.

Companies that view their optimization efforts as a one-time project don't get the best results. They're easily discouraged if the first test doesn't give immediate leaps in their conversion rate and miss learning opportunities that can be gained from each experiment. Each test is an exciting opportunity to learn how your real visitors respond to new experiences, and those insights can have powerful effects if you let them.

Our experience at WiderFunnel shows that the companies that plan with us for an ongoing series of experiments get the best results. The compound learning that is gained from each test leads to even more ideas for improvement and often much larger conversion-rate gains on the third and fourth test rounds on a page.

The Seven-Step Conversion-Testing Process

At WiderFunnel, we developed and use a seven-step testing cycle that aligns with the scientific method and the Shewhart Cycle.

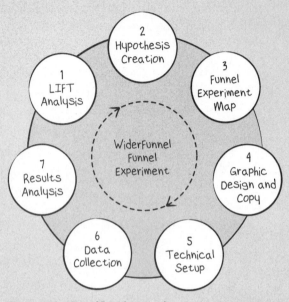

The seven-step Funnel Experiment cycle

In this process, the challenger variations we test are never arbitrary modifications to the page. They're always based on data-driven hypotheses from a conversion strategist. Although you might be tempted to take a shortcut by hiring a designer or copywriter to come up with alternatives to test, this process doesn't engage them until step 4.

The process is set up so the test variations are driven by marketing hypotheses rather than artistic aesthetics. Most important, this process works to consistently deliver results for our clients.

Step 1

The LIFT Analysis is a key component of the observation step, which also includes watching how existing visitors use the site through web analytics data, usability studies, surveys, and other observation methods. The components of the LIFT Analysis are explored in Chapters 4 through 10.

Step 2

The hypotheses you create are the questions you ask of your visitors. Creating valid, testable, and powerful hypotheses is one of the most important skills of the conversion strategist. Getting better results with your tests simply requires creating better hypotheses.

Step 3

The Funnel Experiment Map (or FunEx Map) is what we call the test design document. Proper documentation is very important to ensure the tests are set up correctly and results can be analyzed. See Chapter 11 for details about how to plan your test structure.

Step 4

Graphic design and copywriting are necessary parts of website content testing. It's important to note that this step doesn't happen before the previous steps. If there's no hypothesis behind the experiment variations, it's not a scientific test!

Step 5

Run your experiments using an A/B/*n* and multivariate testing tool that keeps a proper test control and reports on statistical significance as the experiment progresses.

Step 6

Monitor the test data as it's collected to make sure the variations are being served approximately equally and that conversions are recorded properly. Avoid jumping to conclusions by declaring a winning variation before statistical significance is achieved!

Step 7

Once your test reaches statistical significance, you can analyze the data to gather learning and infer the "why?" behind the result. These conclusions can be confirmed with follow-up tests or related new hypotheses for the next experiment. The continuous-improvement process then continues back to step 1.

One of the most important keys to testing success is having a consistent process to follow for executing tests. According to Econsultancy research:

...four variables most strongly correlated with improved overall conversion in the last year are perceived control over conversion rates, a structured approach to CRO, having someone directly responsible for conversion and incentivising staff based on conversion rates.

Econsultancy Conversion Rate Optimization Report,
October 2011, emphasis mine

 Note: For a link to this Econsultancy report and more, visit YouShouldTestThat.com/WhatIsConversionOptimization.

Progress from Macro to Micro

The great sculptor Michelangelo began by removing large chunks from a granite block. He gradually progressed to removing smaller bits with finer tools and eventually to sanding and polishing to reveal the finished sculpture, as in his *David*.

Michelangelo's *David* began as a rough granite block.

It would have been a wasted effort for him to polish the rough granite block before chiseling away the large chunks. The form needs to be defined before the detail. Similarly, your conversion optimization should begin with testing the overarching concepts and major page elements before moving in to refine the fine details.

We often begin by testing the layout, funnel flow, or value-proposition concept of a landing page. Once we've determined the best approach, the details of the containing elements can be tested, including headlines, imagery, copywriting details, and call-to-action buttons.

Note: You can access on-demand webinars for more information about the LIFT Model at YouShouldTestThat.com/WhatIsConversionOptimization. You can also add your comments about this chapter and start a conversation there.

In the next chapter, you'll learn how to prioritize your conversion-optimization opportunities using data and the three-component prioritization framework.

3

Prioritize Testing Opportunities

Data is what distinguishes the dilettante from the artist.
—George V. Higgins

You've decided that you need to use conversion-optimization testing to improve your conversion rate. But where should you start?

You may be managing a website with many dozens, hundreds, or thousands of pages. You can't test all of them at once. With limited time and resources to commit, the prioritization of those test opportunities is an important part of your optimization planning.

Even if you had unlimited resources to plan and create tests, you'd face a limiting factor in your traffic volume and seasonality. As you'll see in Chapter 12, "Analyze Your Test Results," your tests need to collect enough visitors over an appropriate time period to give you meaningful results. Even with the highest-traffic websites, prioritizing tests is necessary.

In this chapter, we'll look at how to prioritize to get the best return on your conversion-optimization effort. You'll see how to prioritize your testing opportunities by understanding the data you should look at, the three criteria you'll use for prioritization—potential, importance, and ease—and additional qualitative research you can gather to help develop your test plans.

Use Data to Prioritize Tests

You *could* simply choose a test page based on your gut intuition about which pages are most important, or throw darts at your information architecture diagram, but by now I hope you realize that I'm going to recommend looking at some data to help you decide. Even with all the data available, some intuition is involved in prioritizing your test pages. Although the data may point to a problem in one area, the real problem can sometimes be at an earlier stage in the conversion funnel.

For example, I have often seen examples of high shopping-cart abandonment in e-commerce sites. In many cases, the problem can't be fixed on the shopping-cart page, though. Visitors are moving from the product detail pages and category pages into the cart to try to find the shipping and returns information, but that information should have been available on the product detail pages. You can often reduce shopping-cart abandonment by optimizing the earlier stages of the buying decision.

You may believe that your conversion-killing culprit is obvious and you already know which page you need to test. Perhaps your website has only a handful of pages or you're working with a single landing page. If that's your situation, you can safely skip this chapter.

For most of us, though, prioritizing test pages isn't that simple—yet we do need to prioritize our test effort. Part of the answer lies in your web analytics data.

Your Web Analytics Data

Your web analytics data will be your most valuable resource to prioritize your tests. There are many options for web analytics tools, and although each has unique features and capabilities, all of them should give reports similar to the Google Analytics reports we'll look at in this chapter.

Why Google Analytics? Of the seven enterprise-quality web analytics companies Forrester identified in its Web Analytics Wave, Q4 2011 report, Google Analytics is by far the most ubiquitous tool. In fact, many companies that have paid tools like Adobe SiteCatalyst also use Google Analytics to get another perspective and validate each tool's information against the other.

Throughout this book, most examples use Google Analytics in the screenshots and reports, because they're most widely relevant. You should be able to find similar reports regardless of the tool you use.

A lot of people will be tempted to skip this chapter and start testing on their home page, thinking it's "obviously" the most important page. So, we'll start by addressing that assumption.

Your Home Page Isn't Your Front Door

Have you noticed how much attention companies pay to their home page? Yet other areas of the website are often more important for driving revenue.

In many organizations, you could add a picture of the Flying Spaghetti Monster to one of your product detail pages and no one would notice; but add a call-to-action button on the home page, and the HiPPO will call to ask if you've violated the Graphic Standards Policy. Take a look at your web analytics "top landing pages" report, and you're likely to see many pages getting entrances and page views. Some may even have more entrances than your home page!

The Graphic Standards Manual Many organizations use a document called the Graphic Standards Manual to maintain consistency in their communications. Although these tools can allow the organization to decentralize design work, they can often be too restrictive, especially when the graphic standards they maintain don't follow tested conversion principles. I look forward to the day when organizations define and evolve their graphic standards documents based on the results of controlled graphic-design tests. At WiderFunnel, we create a testing Playbook that can be used in a similar way but is based on tested results. Need graphic design best practices? You Should Test That!

View Data at the Page-Template Level

Even if your home page is the most popular single entrance page, that often isn't the case if you aggregate all the pages that use the same template. You should do this to determine where you have opportunities to test site-wide template layouts in addition to individual pages.

You may get only a fraction of your entrance visits to any one of your product detail pages compared to the home page. But if you add all the visits to *all* the product detail pages, there are probably many times as many entrances as occur on the home page.

Let's look at a typical example of an e-commerce site that sells jewelry. If your site has Google Analytics installed, you can follow along by viewing your own Landing Page Visits report: navigate to Content › Site Content › Landing Pages.

Looking at this report, you see the list of the example site's most popular landing pages. The home page (/index.html) appears at the top with 43,470 landing-page visits in the time period selected.

These use the category page template.

	Landing Page		Visits ↓	Pages / Visit	Avg. Visit Duration	% New Visits	Bounce Rate
☐	1.	/index.html	43,470	12.97	00:07:56	50.90%	18.43%
☐	2.	/category_Rings.html	10,377	12.22	00:07:18	60.67%	18.74%
☐	3.	/category_Engraved.html	4,773	7.81	00:05:16	72.49%	29.71%
☐	4.	/product_detail/203577	4,287	4.79	00:03:57	72.20%	43.83%
☐	5.	/category_Tiffany_Jewelry.html	4,198	8.08	00:04:15	81.54%	26.99%
☐	6.	/category_Bead_Bracelet.html	3,776	8.17	00:04:26	82.73%	24.66%
☐	7.	/product_detail/256368	3,674	9.11	00:06:51	83.02%	26.95%
☐	8.	/product_detail/208597	3,650	4.43	00:04:07	87.32%	42.85%
☐	9.	/product_detail/254668	3,179	10.08	00:07:22	12.46%	40.04%
☐	10.	/basket.jsp	3,150	6.13	00:03:34	76.41%	29.46%

Primary Dimension: Landing Page Other ▾

Plot Rows | Secondary dimension ▾ | Sort Type: Default ▾

These use the product detail page template.

Google Analytics landing-page visits for a jewelry e-commerce store

This clearly shows the home page as the most popular single page. But this doesn't mean the home page gets more traffic than all other page *templates*. When we combine all the same types of pages together at the page template level, we'll see a clearer picture. If your website uses a content-management system, blog platform, or e-commerce platform with page templates, your testing plan, which we'll discuss in Chapter 11, "Test Your Hypotheses," will need to consider whether to test against individual pages or the site-wide templates as your control pages.

What Is a Landing Page? The page that a visitor sees when they first arrive on your website is the *landing page* for that visit. A landing page may also serve multiple purposes—as a category or home page, for example. Or, it may be a stand-alone, single-purpose page, designed to work with an advertising campaign.

Roll up your pages to the template level in your Pages and Pageviews reports to see the templates with the highest traffic volume. Then you can decide whether to test against a site-wide template or an individual page.

By default, each page in your site shows up as a separate row of data in web analytics if it has a unique URL. Notice that the website in the earlier Google Analytics

report uses a URL-naming convention in which all the category pages include `/category_`
in the URL and the product detail pages include `/product_detail/`. Page-naming URL
conventions like this make it easy to aggregate the metrics for the same types of pages
by adding a search filter to the list.

To try an example, let's start by aggregating all the category pages. To do so,
add `/category_` in the search box at the top of the list, which looks like this:

We end up with a display that filters the report data and only shows the data
for category pages that are used as landing pages. At the top of the report are aggregate Visits, Pages per Visit, Average Visit Duration, % New Visits, and Bounce Rate
metrics.

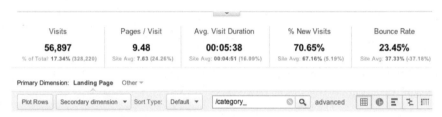

The aggregate category pages show many more visits than the home page.

In this case, you can see that the category pages have 56,897 landing-page visits
in the same period that the home page had 43,470.

Let's do the same thing for product detail pages by placing `/product_detail/` in
the report filter:

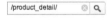

Insert graphic

Now we find that landing-page visits for product detail pages total 117,542.

Product detail page metrics show twice as many entrances as the home page.

That means more than twice as many visitors enter the site through a product detail page as enter through the home page!

Using Regular Expressions in Landing-Page Reports

Some sites have URL structures that make aggregating landing-page data more complex than the example we've used. If your site is one of them, don't despair! Google Analytics supports the use of regular expressions (RegEx) to filter the landing-page reports. To learn about RegEx, we recommend that you ask your web developer about how to use them, and also visit YouShouldTestThat.com/Prioritize.

We've only scratched the surface by looking at two site templates. When you consider the many other types of pages on your site, such as those for services, about your company, careers, brands, blog posts, PR, and social media activity, single-purpose landing pages, and more, you can see how quickly the home page can lose its position on the organizational pedestal. Fortunately for you, this means you can safely let the rest of the organization fight over home page real estate while you start on other important pages.

At WiderFunnel, when we begin a series of tests with our clients, we prefer to start optimizing any page *other than* the home page to avoid political barriers. When we're ready to approach the home page, we have already done good work under the radar and have test results showing conversion-rate lift to enhance the case for testing the HiPPO's sacred cow: the home page.

Let's look at how to prioritize the conversion-optimization opportunities beyond just the home page.

The PIE Prioritization Framework

You need to consider three criteria in prioritizing which pages to test and in which order. They are as follows:

Potential   How much improvement can be made on the pages?

Importance   How valuable is the traffic to the pages?

Ease   How complicated will the test be to implement on the page or template?

You can quantify each of your potential opportunities based on these criteria to create your test priority list. The most important consideration is the importance of the pages to the company.

Prioritize Pages with High Potential for Improvement

That is, look for the really bad pages. Although I've yet to find a page without some potential for improvement, you can't test everywhere at once and you should prioritize your worst performers.

A certain amount of the personal judgment and experience of the conversion champion comes into play at this stage. This is also where some qualitative data like surveys and user testing can help you generate test hypotheses.

Your web analytics data will point to some of the clear, problematic pages—landing pages with high bounce rates, for instance—but some problem areas won't be so obvious. If the problem is a high rate of shopping-cart abandonment, for example, your web analytics won't tell you that your visitors are struggling to find shipping and returns information in earlier stages of their decision-making process. If you work on optimizing the cart, where web analytics points to the problem appearing, you won't be able to fix the issue. You may actually need to test on your product detail pages, category pages, or the site-wide header or footer area.

None of your data sources, used in isolation, will perfectly identify your conversion opportunities. Let's look at how to combine information from various sources to paint a more complete picture of your visitors' experiences on your site.

Top Exit Pages

The last page that someone sees before leaving your website is called an *exit page*. Your exit rate, which Google Analytics labels % Exit, shows the percentage of visitors to a page who leave your website immediately after viewing that page.

> **Exit Rate vs. Bounce Rate** Exit rate is often confused with bounce rate. A bounce is similar to an exit, but with a bounce, the visitor has seen only a single page before leaving the website. Someone who's exited from your site may also have visited other pages. The exit page is simply the last page they saw before leaving.

Your top exit-rate pages can identify problem areas. Often you'll find that people are leaving because those pages aren't compelling or informative, or the content may not be relevant to the media that drove the visit.

Of course, there also may be a good reason for them to be exit pages, like a post form-fill thank-you page, for example. You need to evaluate the pages in the context of their purpose.

You can find your top exit-rate pages in Google Analytics by navigating to Content › Site Content › All Pages and then sorting by the % Exit column.

Click here to sort by exit rate.

		Page		Pageviews ↓	Unique Pageviews	Avg. Time on Page	Entrances	Bounce Rate	% Exit	Page Value
☐	1.			408,004	114,404	00:00:41	13,091	35.68%	6.33%	$0.00
☐	2.			283,525	233,300	00:00:43	202,235	16.93%	18.68%	$0.00
☐	3.			273,845	184,312	00:00:30	36,491	16.66%	6.50%	$0.00
☐	4.			142,783	105,083	00:00:32	15,514	29.60%	10.05%	$0.00
☐	5.			100,139	73,888	00:00:33	10,650	24.12%	9.32%	$0.00
☐	6.			82,668	62,283	00:00:28	7,014	23.30%	8.19%	$0.00

If you sort by exit rate, though, you'll probably end up with a useless report showing 100 percent exit rates for very obscure pages with single-digit visits. Although those may be problem pages, they're clearly not priorities for testing!

Clearly, these aren't important pages.   Click here to make this more useful.

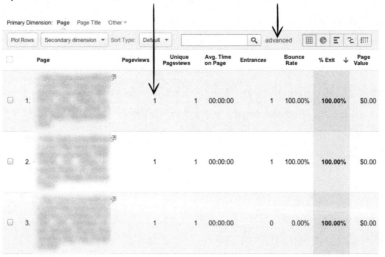

To make this report more useful, you can add a filter to show only high-traffic pages.

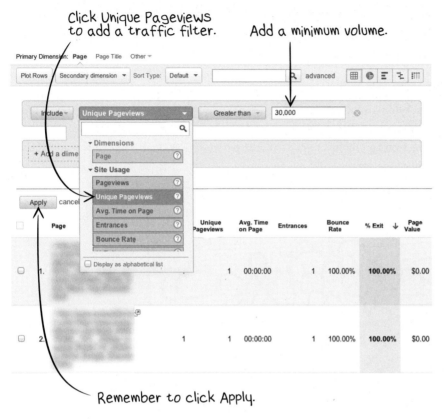

Click Unique Pageviews to add a traffic filter.

Add a minimum volume.

Remember to click Apply.

Click the Advanced link. Then, in the Page drop-down, select Site Usage › Pageviews and enter a minimum number, like 30,000. Click Apply to generate the report.

	Page	Pageviews	Unique Pageviews	Avg. Time on Page	Entrances	Bounce Rate	% Exit ↓	Page Value
☐	1.	30,785	30,460	00:00:56	28	42.86%	45.43%	$0.00
☐	2.	32,987	22,580	00:01:02	17,803	44.10%	37.89%	$0.00
☐	3.	39,345	24,199	00:01:23	18,645	43.70%	33.49%	$0.00
☐	4.	42,661	29,822	00:01:03	19,882	40.07%	31.17%	$0.00
☐	5.	34,217	31,738	00:00:28	1,027	41.87%	27.54%	$0.00
☐	6.	69,619	51,741	00:00:46	34,769	25.17%	22.64%	$0.00
☐	7.	31,526	23,039	00:00:57	13,834	27.17%	20.72%	$0.00

Filtered exit-rate report showing only high-traffic pages

Now you're starting to see a useful exit-rate list! This report will give you some good candidate pages. Many of these are problem pages that should be prioritized for conversion-optimization testing. You Should Test That!

Analyze Your Conversion Funnel

So far, I haven't discussed the conversion funnel concept. It's an important part of identifying problem pages. I'll begin with some definitions.

A conversion funnel has two parts: the persuasive end, also called the top of the funnel, and the transactional end, or bottom.

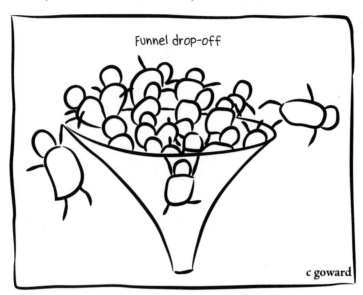

The persuasive end of the funnel includes your home page, product or service pages, landing pages, internal search results pages, and basic information content pages. These are the areas of the website where you present your value proposition and persuade your visitors that they need to act.

The bottom end of the funnel is where the transaction actions occur. These are transactional pages with forms, shopping carts, and thank-you pages.

The web analytics data we've looked at up to this point shows the persuasive end of your conversion funnel. In most cases, those top-visited, entry, exit, and bounce pages reports don't show the transaction end. But the bottom of the funnel is still important.

The visitors to those pages have been through your site, have read about your products and services, and are considering a purchase. They may be on your lead-generation contact form, newsletter signup page, or e-commerce checkout funnel. They're your hot leads and are very valuable!

Funnel Drop-Off Rates

Your analytics funnel reports focus on the bottom end of the funnel. You can find it in Google Analytics by navigating to Conversions › Goals › Funnel Visualization. If your primary website goal is a contact form for lead generation, your funnel may show a single step.

Contact

451 visitors finished | 11.46% funnel conversion rate

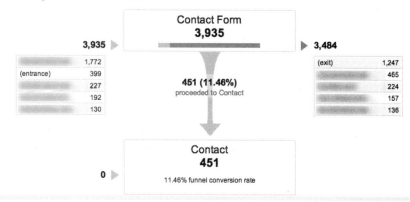

A simple lead-gen contact form funnel

In this case, you see that only about 11 percent of visitors who arrive on the contact form page successfully complete the form and become leads. If 89 percent of the visitors who decided to click a link to contact you abandoned the process, you would probably consider this a low conversion rate.

Once you've identified a drop-off step in your transactional funnel, you should ask yourself where the problem is:

- Where are visitors coming from who arrive on this transactional page?
- What could they have been expecting to see here?
- What information could they have been looking for?
- Is there anything on this page that could have stopped them from completing the call to action?
- Did they just not have enough motivation from the persuasive end of the funnel?

We'll look in more detail at how to analyze the page to create hypotheses for testing in Chapter 4, "Create Hypotheses with the LIFT Model." For now, to prioritize where to test, you need to make a judgment call about whether the transactional page is the real problem area or if the data is giving an indication of an earlier persuasive problem.

There are lots of great, low-cost ways to improve your judgment call by gathering qualitative data from visitors too.

Gather Qualitative Data

The controlled testing required for conversion optimization is a purely quantitative process. Experiment variations are tested with the goal of achieving statistically significant results. But there is also a place within the process for collecting qualitative data sources. That place is near the beginning, before you've developed your experiment hypotheses. As such, this is another important stage in identifying and prioritizing pages whose performance needs improvement.

Qualitative information is useful in three ways:

- It helps the conversion champion identify pages or areas of the website that are causing problems for your visitors.

- It provides context for how your prospects view your products and need to use your website.

- It provides ideas for the conversion champion to develop hypotheses for testing.

Quantitative vs. Qualitative Data What distinguishes qualitative data-collection methods from quantitative? Quantitative data is collected with methods that are controlled and statistically significant. Qualitative data usually involves collecting rich, deep, open-ended feedback from small numbers of people. Quantitative data, conversely, asks a defined question of a large number of people.

There are many methods for gathering qualitative data from your site visitors, such as usability testing, surveys, eye-tracking studies, click-tracking analysis, and heuristic site analysis.

Usability Testing

Usability testing is a popular method for understanding whether visitors are able to complete certain actions on your website. It's very useful for finding areas where visitors may be uncertain how to complete an action; these may be severe conversion-funnel blockages.

You can get considerable value from simply being in a room with a prospect and hearing their direct input. When it comes to knowing your customer, there's a lot to be gained from putting a face to the other sources of observation.

The typical process for usability testing is to invite individuals to an observation room where they're asked to complete a series of specific actions, such as finding a particular product on the site or completing a form. The user is encouraged to verbalize their thinking as they go through the process, which you hope will reveal the barriers and perceptions the website is causing.

The renowned usability expert Jakob Nielsen recommends running usability tests with no more than five users each. He believes this gives the majority of insights to be gained from each study without blowing your budget on large samples. You can find out more in this blog post: www.useit.com/alertbox/20000319.html. Steve Krug, in his fantastic book *Don't Make Me Think!* (New Riders, 2005), says you can get away with testing as few as three people to get the majority of benefit.

If you set up your own usability tests, make sure you have the right equipment. You can make video recordings of the user interactions through their own computer cameras with tools like Silverback for Mac and Morae for Windows. These videos are especially useful for convincing others in the organization that your website needs conversion-rate optimization. There's nothing more persuasive for upper management than watching a video of a real visitor on your site bumbling through your carefully designed experience. Watch how quickly you get support for testing!

Silverback records mouse movements and clicks.

See the test participant's facial reactions.

Quick and less expensive alternatives to usability testing are also available online at sites like www.usertesting.com, www.trymyui.com, and www.loop11.com. With these services you can submit your pages or design comps and record how online participants respond. You can get much of the same benefit from the online services as from full usability tests, without the high cost.

You can simplify your test even more using www.fivesecondtest.com, where you can upload your page layouts, design comps, and screenshots for quick feedback. Participants are shown your page for five seconds and then asked to give their impression of what your page is about. It's a great way to gauge visitors' initial understanding of your value proposition.

The fivesecondtest keyword cloud shows visitors' first impressions of what your website is about.

Usability testing has limitations, as you know from Chapter 2, "What is Conversion Optimization?" and the cost can add up quickly. Other qualitative methods can produce similar information more quickly and at lower cost.

On-Site Surveys

Surveys of your current website visitors can be conducted quickly and economically with one of the many website survey tools available today. For a list of recommended tools, visit YouShouldTestThat.com/Prioritize. By simply adding a piece of script to your pages, you can include surveys that either are user-initiated or automatically pop up when visitors arrive on your page.

The information you gather from surveys is only as good as the questions you ask. Here are three recommended by Avinash Kaushik, who also co-founded the survey company 4Q:

- What is the purpose of your visit to our website today?
- Were you able to complete your task today?
- If you weren't able to complete your task today, why not?

A pop-up survey on the IKEA.com home page interrupts my visit.

These questions are great for finding usability challenges. If your goal is to generate ideas for conversion-optimization tests, I also recommend adding questions that aim for marketing insights, like these:

- Would you recommend our products or services to others? Why or why not?
- What do you consider to be our product's or service's main benefits?
- What product information were you not able to find?

The goal of your questions is to find nuggets of information that show which parts of your value proposition are most important and least understood. These nuggets will lead to hypotheses to be tested.

You'll be able to think of many other questions, but don't go overboard. If you want to ask more than four or five, split them into separate surveys to avoid overwhelming visitors and reducing your survey completion rate.

You may find that your visitors say they can't see information that you think is clear and prominent. This reveals a possible problem with the page layout that can be improved and tested. Your visitors aren't used to your site and have to figure out where content is placed in addition to understanding the content itself. Any problem you discover is good news. The site has improvement potential!

Although on-site surveys can be helpful to get input about your website usability and product benefits, they can also reduce your conversion rates by interrupting the visitor's experience. Any distraction can reduce sales—especially something totally unrelated to the goal of the visit. Pop-up surveys can do more harm than good if they're left on the site for too long, because many visitors find them intrusive.

Customer Email Surveys

You can avoid disrupting your on-site visitors' experiences by surveying your customers by email. You'll get a different type of information, but it's still useful to help create informed experiment plans.

Email surveys are best for learning about customer demographics, needs, product satisfaction, and company perception. The majority of useful survey questions explore the most important product and service features and visit or purchase frequency. Here are some thought-starters for questions you may find useful:

- Which of these is most important when choosing where to buy? (Select all or rank in order of importance.)
- What features are important to you that we don't offer? (Open-ended.)
- What do you like about us compared to others?
- Which of the following features that we offer were you aware of? (Multiple choice.)
- What features, products, or services do you wish we offered?
- What difficulties did you find in placing your order today? (Multiple choice or open-ended.)
- How often have you purchased this service or product in the past?
- When or in what situations do you use the product or service?

At the end of the survey, don't forget to include another call to action. These are engaged, valuable customers who can always be more engaged and valuable! Consider a purchase discount as thanks for their help, or a link to download other information, or a newsletter signup.

Email surveys can be great for understanding how your customers perceive you and your products, but they're not as useful for gaining website-specific insights. A better way to do that is to observe how real visitors use your pages. These techniques include the next two methods of gathering qualitative data: eye tracking and on-page analytics (or click tracking).

Eye Tracking

Although usability testing and surveys give you verbal and written feedback about your site and product, as they say, a picture can be worth a thousand words. That's why eye tracking and on-page click tracking can help you understand how people are interacting with your website.

With eye-tracking studies, participants are asked to complete tasks on the website, just as in a usability study. An eye-tracking sensor is added to the computer screen;

this detects the direction of the participants' retinas, which is then mapped to the location on the screen. The results from multiple participants are aggregated to produce heatmaps, showing hot spots where visitors gave most of their attention.

Eye-tracking research is a very interesting area that can reveal insights into how people think and how to guide their attention. For example, a test run by the Swedish eye-tracking tool company Tobii tested 106 participants while they viewed two product ads. The only difference between the ads was the position of the baby on the left side of the page. You can find full-color versions of these ads in the Color Gallery near the end of the book.

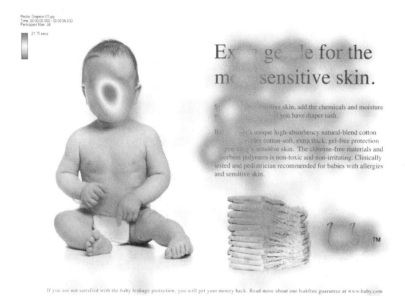

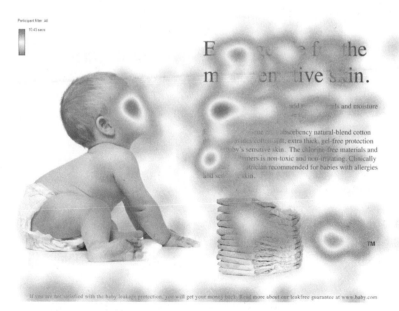

When the baby was front-facing, visitors were more likely to lock eyes with the image and less likely to focus on the page content. When the baby faced toward the text blocks, the visual hotspots followed the baby's attention and moved to the text.

This study showed that the images you choose, especially when they involve people, can impact the page's eyeflow. The implication is that images can help or hinder visitors' ability to digest the information and can impact the conversion rate.

This is exciting research, but the real impact of these images on your landing-page conversion rates can only be determined through an A/B/*n* split test. You Should Test That!

On-Page Click Tracking

On-page click tracking can give you insights into how people are interacting with your pages. Although many of the insights could be gleaned from more traditional web analytics tools, the visual presentation of click heatmaps can make it much easier for even nontechnical team members to get excited.

With click heatmaps, you can see where people click, even when they click areas that aren't links. This can lead to useful insights. For example, collecting click-tracking data on a landing page with a tool like CrazyEgg allowed us to see concentrations of clicks on an arrow that pointed to a call-to-action button.

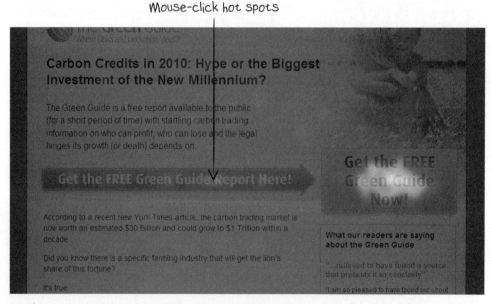

The click heatmap for this site shows click concentrations on areas other than the call-to-action button.

Without click tracking, you could have assumed that the arrow was used to guide the visitor's eye to the button. It turns out that some visitors were mistaking the arrow itself for a button. You can fix this confusion by changing the placement of the button or making the arrow clickable, too.

Another cool feature of on-page tracking tools is the scroll heatmap, or scroll-map. Its color-coded gradient shows how far down the page most people scroll.

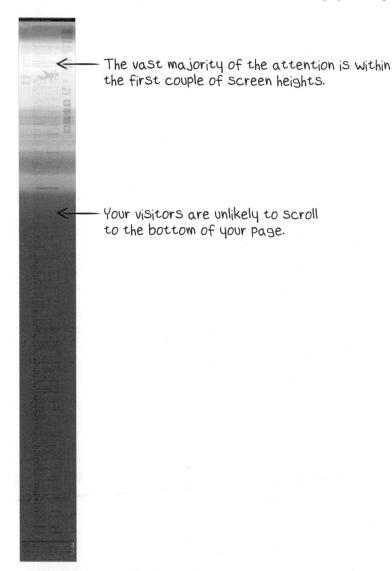

The vast majority of the attention is within the first couple of screen heights.

Your visitors are unlikely to scroll to the bottom of your page.

A scrollmap shows where visitor interest dies off.

The scrollmap shows you why the screen fold is so important. Most visitors are reluctant to scroll very far unless they're given a compelling reason to. The most important information should be at or near the top of the page. In Chapter 9, "Optimize for Distraction," you'll see how to identify distraction problems and optimize above the fold.

There are also tools, such as ClickTale, that record videos of how real visitors navigate your site. You can see what your visitor sees and clicks, page by page. This can be especially useful for analyzing forms, because you can watch people's failed attempts to complete your transactional funnel.

There's a lot of overlap in the insights gained from click tracking and eye tracking. Click tracking doesn't tell you how the content affects people's attention, but it does tell you how they act and allows you to collect data from a high quantity of visitors in real-life scenarios at low cost. You won't usually get enough additional hypotheses from doing both for the same target page.

The data from on-page click tracking can help you understand how people are interacting with the site and, when combined with surveys and real user interactions, can provide a rich source of data to generate powerful experiment hypotheses.

Ask Your Mom

Another simple technique for getting insights is the "ask your mom" method. Yes, I'm being serious.

Think of your mom as a typical consumer visiting your website. Will she understand and be able to explain in her own words what your website is trying to communicate? Marketers too often get so trapped in the bubble of their product, industry, and incomprehensible acronyms that they forget how real, live people communicate.

Now, you could literally visit your mom (and you probably should do that more often), but this can also be a mental exercise to get into your customer's mindset. As David Ogilvy said, "The consumer isn't a moron; she is your wife." By practicing empathy for your visitors and putting yourself in their shoes, your task of creating persuasive messages will become much easier.

Having an empathetic mentality is a requirement for successful heuristic evaluations.

The Heuristic Evaluation

One of the most important methods for finding conversion problems is to use a heuristic evaluation, otherwise known as "taking a walk in your customer's shoes."

A heuristic evaluation usually involves conversion-optimization experts who can identify likely conversion problems using heuristics (or rules of thumb). An experienced conversion champion can quickly identify common problems based on experience from past test results and use frameworks like the LIFT Model (see Chapter 4) to evaluate conversion pages.

A good conversion champion gathers all the data available from qualitative research sources and uses it as input for heuristic analyses.

Don't Misuse Qualitative Data

Qualitative information sources can provide raw material from which the conversion champion can develop test hypotheses, but they're often misinterpreted. There is a significant danger of overconfidence in qualitative information. I've often seen companies hold up small sample surveys and single-user testing outputs as if they were conclusive directions for website changes.

Much of the danger is the responsibility of those conducting the studies, who can be tempted to oversell the results. Watch out, for example, for user-testing results that claim something like "75 percent of respondents believe our company offers the low-cost service option" (or whatever you're interested in studying), when the study included only one or two dozen participants.

The wording in these surveys should be qualified, and you should take care to evaluate the robustness of the findings. Three practices will help avoid this misrepresentation:

- Surveys and studies should never use percentages as findings unless their results are statistically significant.
- Until quantitative testing has been done, the findings in these studies should be qualified with wording like "results imply…" or "findings point to…" or "we have directional results showing that…."
- These studies should recommend the priority findings that should be tested quantitatively rather than being immediately implemented on the website.

The information gathered from the qualitative sources we've looked at can be useful for preparing a conversion champion to develop a testing plan. They're only useful, however, as long as they aren't trusted to be definitive prescriptions for website changes.

Characteristics of Research Methods

Characteristic	Usability Studies	Surveys	Eye Tracking	Click Tracking	Heuristic Analysis	Web Analytics	Controlled Testing
Cost	High	Medium	High	Low	Medium	Low	Medium
Real-life scenarios	No	No	No	Yes	No	Yes	Yes
Predetermined tasks	Yes	No	Yes	No	Yes	No	Yes
Large sampling	No	Yes	No	Yes	No	Yes	Yes
Open-ended feedback	Yes	Yes	Yes	No	Yes	No	No
Global geography	No	Yes	No	Yes	Yes [how?]	Yes	Yes
Eliminates Hawthorne effect	No	No	No	Yes	Yes	Yes	Yes
Eliminates observer effect	No	Yes	No	Yes	Yes	Yes	Yes
Statistical significance	No	Rarely	No	No	No	Rarely	Yes

The only characteristic needed to round out controlled conversion-rate optimization testing is input from open-ended feedback to develop hypotheses. That is why combining controlled, quantitative testing with heuristic analysis and other qualitative methods is so powerful. Qualitative information helps identify areas of the site that have severe problems and provides fodder for new hypotheses to be quantitatively tested.

Prioritize Important Pages

Your most important pages are the ones with the highest volume and the costliest traffic. You may have identified pages that perform terribly, but if they don't have significant volume of costly traffic, they aren't testing priorities.

Pages with High Traffic Volume Are More Important

Your high-traffic pages are gold. You can use them to test important marketing questions, gain insights to apply to lower-traffic pages, keep your team interested in the continuous learning you're gathering, and make a big impact on the business. These pages are where you have thousands of beautiful visitors ready to give you their feedback (unbeknownst to them) about what works best.

You also need high-traffic pages to run experiments that complete in a reasonable timeframe. The words *reasonable* and *high-traffic* mean different things to different people, so I'll give you an example. If your test pages or templates have more than 20,000–30,000 monthly unique visitors, then your A/B/*n* split tests have a chance to achieve statistically significant results within a few weeks. With traffic levels lower than that, you need to prepare to run them over a longer period.

There's no harm in doing that. You just need to manage your expectations so you don't get impatient when the test doesn't complete right away. Don't plan to run many test rounds in rapid succession on those low-volume areas.

Because your tests on high-traffic pages complete more quickly, you can move on to the next tests sooner, speeding up your optimization progress. From the information you gather on high-traffic pages, you can run more experiments on lower-traffic pages.

For example, you could test five variations of the call-to-action button's color on a high-traffic landing page. If you found that orange buttons work best, followed by green, blue, gold, and aquamarine, you could decide to test only the two best performers, orange and green, on a lower-traffic page to confirm the result.

Running experiments on high-traffic pages is also more interesting and rewarding. When tests complete quickly, your team is more likely to stay engaged and supportive. In any organization, you need to manage enthusiasm and momentum to get things done. Seeing huge conversion-rate lifts from a test can be a big boost to the team. Waiting around for a test to finish over many months is a downer and can toss a bucket of cold water on your optimization momentum.

Finally, and probably most important, high-traffic pages are more likely to be important to the business. After all, more people are already visiting these pages, so they may have a greater influence than lower-traffic areas of the site. When you find a high-traffic page, You Should Test That!

Most-Visited Pages or Templates

High-traffic pages are easy to find. In Google Analytics, go to Content › Site Content › All Pages. By default, the report will sort the pages by pageviews.

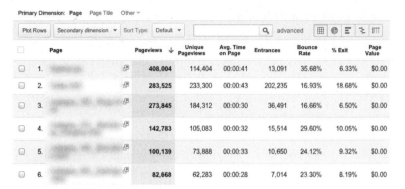

The top pages report shows your highest-traffic pages.

Your testing tool will likely report on unique visitors rather than the total number of visits. This is an important distinction to make. Web analytics reports often show pageviews as a primary metric, but pageviews include multiple views from the same people traveling around multiple pages on your site or returning for multiple sessions.

When you're running a controlled experiment, however, you're more interested in whether each unique person converted at least once. Once a person has visited your test page and converted, they should be counted as one unique visitor and one conversion. If that was the only person to visit your page, your conversion rate should be reported as 100 percent.

If you were to include multiple visits and pageviews for the same people, the conversion rate reported could be skewed too low because a person could have a single conversion with multiple visits. In that case, your single visitor could have been reported with one conversion over three visits, which would inaccurately show your conversion rate as 33.3 percent. This example underscores one of the reasons to always use a controlled testing tool to run your experiments, as discussed in Chapter 2.

Unique pageviews is therefore a more accurate measure of the traffic volume you should consider. Click the Unique Pageviews column header in your pages report to sort by unique views rather than all pageviews.

	Page		Pageviews	Unique Pageviews ↓	Avg. Time on Page	Entrances	Bounce Rate	% Exit	Page Value
☐ 1.			283,525	233,300	00:00:43	202,235	16.93%	18.68%	$0.00
☐ 2.			273,845	184,312	00:00:30	36,491	16.66%	6.50%	$0.00
☐ 3.			408,004	114,404	00:00:41	13,091	35.68%	6.33%	$0.00
☐ 4.			142,783	105,083	00:00:32	15,514	29.60%	10.05%	$0.00
☐ 5.			100,139	73,888	00:00:33	10,650	24.12%	9.32%	$0.00
☐ 6.			78,876	66,008	00:00:33	3,586	25.07%	8.82%	$0.00

Sorting by unique pageviews estimates the traffic volume for your experiments.

You can get an indication of which pages may have significant opportunities for improvement (also known as serious problems!) by looking at the Bounce Rate and Exit Rate (% Exit) columns. A page with a combination of high entrances and high bounces or exits indicates a good testing target page. I'll say more about pages with potential for improvement shortly.

Top Entry Pages

Your top-visited pages report shows the most popular pages within your site, but it's also important to look at the most important pages that people first see when they arrive at your site. These are your top landing pages, also called *entry pages*. You can find that report by navigating to Content › Site Content › Landing Pages.

Primary Dimension: **Landing Page**   Other ▾

			Visits ↓	Pages / Visit	Avg. Visit Duration	% New Visits	Bounce Rate
☐	1.		202,235	13.32	00:08:27	52.03%	16.93%
☐	2.		36,491	12.50	00:07:58	61.48%	16.66%
☐	3.		34,769	8.23	00:05:55	83.99%	25.17%
☐	4.		20,303	8.44	00:04:53	78.55%	22.87%
☐	5.		19,882	4.84	00:04:28	77.88%	40.07%
☐	6.		19,712	8.81	00:05:02	81.13%	23.86%

Top landing pages are your most popular site entrances.

Your top landing pages represent a unique opportunity because they're the first impression of your business and products for many visitors. These are opportunities for you to test and discover the layout, content, and messaging that convinces your visitors to stick around, engage with your products, and (you hope) become a lead or customer!

Pages with Expensive Visits Are More Important

The cost of bringing visitors to your landing pages is an important consideration when prioritizing testing opportunities. Given a choice between testing on two pages with similar traffic and conversion problems, one with high-cost traffic sources will provide a better return on investment from your conversion-optimization efforts.

Identify Your Visitors' Sources

How do you drive traffic to your website? Do you focus on organic search traffic by emphasizing search engine optimization (SEO), or do you use paid advertising, or a mix of both? Perhaps you emphasize social media activities or public relations to generate exposure.

You may have offline advertising driving prospects to landing pages or use rented email lists, newsletter sponsorships, or banner-ad placement campaigns to drive traffic. Any of these could represent high-cost traffic that should be prioritized. In each case, you should use a unique landing-page URL (or other tracking mechanisms) so the traffic source can be easily identified and segmented. Each offline source should drive to a specific vanity URL, like www.yourdomain.com/adcampaign, so you can track all the costs and conversions for each source. If you can identify the traffic source, you can attribute the costs and conversions.

Gather Costs for Each Source

Each of your traffic-generation sources has a cost. You're spending money either directly on sponsorship and advertising fees or indirectly for services like SEO management, social media, and PR activities.

Identifying those source media costs helps you put a value on your website's visitors. Don't forget to consider the following:

- SEO management
- Paid search management

- Social media management
- Social media advertising
- Public relations
- Email marketing
- Affiliate programs
- Partner referral activities
- Blogging
- Offline media: TV, print, radio, out of home, and so on

Tally your monthly costs attributed to each marketing activity, and associate the costs with their landing pages.

In many cases, the highest-cost traffic segment is from paid search, and usually the most popular paid search medium is Google AdWords. If you use Google AdWords to drive traffic, this can also be a very easy traffic source to identify by using your web analytics tool or the reports in the AdWords management interface.

To find your highest-traffic landing pages from paid search in Google Analytics, go to Content › Site Content › Landing Pages, click Advanced Segments near the top of the page (just below the Landing Pages headline), and select Paid Search Traffic.

Landing Pages

| Advanced Segments | Email | Export ▾ | Add to Dashboard | Shortcut BETA |

Select up to four segments by which to filter your report ⑦

Default Segments		Custom Segments	
☐ All Visits		☐ Ad Position 1	edit
☐ New Visitors		☐ Ad Position 2	edit
☐ Returning Visitors		☐ Ad Position 3	edit
☑ Paid Search Traffic		☐ Google CPC	edit
☐ Non-paid Search Traffic		☐ Keyword: conversion optimization	edit
☐ Search Traffic		☐ Yahoo CPC	edit
☐ Direct Traffic			

| Apply | cancel | | + New Custom Segment |

Don't forget to click Apply.

Select the Landing Page Dimension to find your highest-traffic paid search landing pages.

This report gives you the highest-traffic landing pages from paid search. In most cases, the first half-dozen pages represent the bulk of the traffic and also the majority of the total traffic cost.

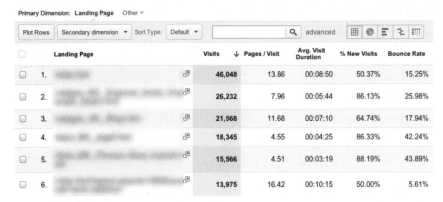

Primary Dimension: Landing Page   Other ▾

	Landing Page	Visits ↓	Pages / Visit	Avg. Visit Duration	% New Visits	Bounce Rate
☐ 1.		46,048	13.86	00:08:50	50.37%	15.25%
☐ 2.		26,232	7.96	00:05:44	86.13%	25.98%
☐ 3.		21,568	11.68	00:07:10	64.74%	17.94%
☐ 4.		18,345	4.55	00:04:25	86.33%	42.24%
☐ 5.		15,566	4.51	00:03:19	88.19%	43.89%
☐ 6.		13,975	16.42	00:10:15	50.00%	5.61%

Your top paid search landing pages are the entry points for a lot of expensive traffic.

Think about it this way: you're paying for a whole bunch of people to come to your website. For the largest chunk of those visitors, these few pages represent the first impression they have of your company. Are you giving them the best impression? Improvements you make to these pages will improve the experience and conversion rates for a significant portion of your highly qualified visitors and improve the effectiveness of your advertising budget.

Even if you don't have all your cost data available, make a best-guess estimate for each source. I'm a believer in the power of the Pareto principle: spend the 20 percent of time required to get to 80 percent accuracy. You don't need to know the costs down to the fifth decimal point to know where your biggest conversion problems are. Get the big picture as a first pass, and you can always improve your accuracy later.

Use the Pareto Principle   The Pareto principle reminds you to put your energy in the highest-productivity areas. The principle, which many know as the 80–20 rule, says that approximately 20 percent of your effort causes 80 percent of the effect. The majority of outcomes are caused by a minority of the inputs. For more on the Pareto principle, you should read Richard Koch's book *The 80/20 Principle: The Secret to Achieving More with Less* (Doubleday, 1998).

This exercise can be a startling reminder of how valuable your visitors are. Once you've gathered your costs, don't get discouraged if you see surprisingly high costs for your visitors. Rather, let it energize you to focus on improving the website experience you're sending them to!

Prioritize Easy Test Pages

The final consideration for prioritizing tests is the degree of difficulty a test will take to get running on a page, which includes technical implementation and organizational or political barriers. The less time and resources you need to invest for the same return, the better.

If you estimate that you can achieve the same conversion-rate lift from two conversion-optimization opportunities, tests A and B, and test A would require half the time and effort to implement, then your return on effort for test A will be double that for B.

Ease of testing is especially important if you're planning to run your tests without an experienced testing team and don't have a full-service conversion-optimization agency helping you with the technical implementation.

Consider Technical Implementation

Some tests take much more effort and technical expertise than others. In general, tests that include the following elements are more complicated:

- Site-wide elements like buttons, offer banners, and navigation bars
- Alternative site templates like product, category, and site search pages
- Dynamic content
- Pages controlled by a content management system or e-commerce platform
- Alternative flows where multiple pages are varied
- Complex or inflexible forms
- Pages with server-side validation or interaction
- Phone call tracking where the phone numbers need to be consistent site-wide
- Multi-goal tracking
- Experiments with multi-language support
- Pages where multiple stakeholders' opinions need to be satisfied, which isn't a technical challenge but does add significant complication

On the other hand, the more technically challenging tests can also be the most rewarding. At WiderFunnel, we have seen some of the biggest improvements from running site-wide template tests on product listing pages, category pages, product detail pages, site-wide lead-generation forms, navigation bars, and add-to-cart functions. Even though these are technically advanced test implementations, the rewards have been well worth the effort.

Site-wide tests, in particular, can be doubly rewarding because of their reach. Tests of site-wide elements and templates affect the majority of visitors to the site, so even small improvements to those pages can have a huge positive impact on business revenue. In the following case study, you'll see an example of significant revenue lift from a site-wide template test.

Case Study: 19 Percent Jump in Affiliate and Advertising Revenue for Vehicle Search Engine Website

LemonFree.com has changed the paradigm for buying and selling vehicles. Unlike other automobile marketplaces, LemonFree.com encourages greater transparency than is available on dealer-sponsored websites by offering unbiased vehicle and dealer information to shoppers.

The company's business model is supported by multiple pay-per-click and pay-per-lead revenue sources, including advertising and affiliates.

The Business Need

Over a six-month period, traffic to LemonFree.com more than doubled, reaching more than eight million pageviews per month. With no sign of traffic slowing down, company management began looking for ways to maximize the revenue from this increased traffic, including improving the conversion rate through testing.

The Challenges

In-house conversion-rate optimization tests on advertising and affiliate links had proven difficult to implement, and the results were challenging to measure, despite LemonFree.com management's fluency with testing technologies. The LemonFree.com team faced four primary challenges:

- Maintaining or improving a great user experience for LemonFree.com users
- Measuring revenue lift versus clickthroughs and form-fills
- Merging and analyzing data from the testing tool and Google Analytics (GA)
- Calculating statistical significance of Google Analytics results

LemonFree.com management's understanding of their limitations with conversion-rate optimization testing led them to seek the help of full-service outsourced conversion-optimization experts.

The Solution

LemonFree.com management chose to engage WiderFunnel to develop and execute a full-service conversion-rate optimization testing strategy for the company's website, including the site-wide listing page template. This key site-wide template contains detailed vehicle information and is accessed directly from an on-site search results page.

To ensure the accuracy of metrics, WiderFunnel kick-started the process with a planning phase called the Kaizen Plan to prioritize revenue streams and develop a reliable method for tracking revenue from each source. The Kaizen Plan identified the site-wide listing page template as a high-priority test target based on its importance as a revenue generator and potential for improvement.

Using the LIFT Model to uncover problematic areas on the web page and identify testing hypotheses, WiderFunnel recommended a hybrid test with A/B/n and multivariate characteristics.

In order to capture revenue data by source and provide actionable information, WiderFunnel customized Google Analytics to track revenue goals in addition to the conversion goal.

WiderFunnel created a total of six redesigned challenger template variations. The changes in the templates included placement and type of advertising and affiliate links and used an A/B/n test structure to isolate variables similar to a multivariate test.

The test variations included considerations such as these:

- Opening additional information pages in a lightbox versus a new browser tab
- Swapping various on-page forms
- Adding and removing links
- Placement of the advertising banner

Continues

Case Study: 19 Percent Jump in Affiliate and Advertising Revenue for Vehicle Search Engine Website *(Continued)*

The Result: 19 Percent Lift in Revenue per Visit

Of the six variations tested, all reached statistical significance and beat the original control listing page within 10 days of launch. All of the hypotheses tested had a positive impact on revenue growth, and the top-performing page template lifted total revenue per visit by 19 percent!

By making small but critical changes to remove distraction, implementing a hybrid A/B/*n*-multivariate test structure, and skillfully tracking results, WiderFunnel's new page made an immediate and significant impact on LemonFree.com's revenue.

As the case study shows, although a technically advanced site-wide test can take a little more effort to run, the resulting revenue lift often pays significant ongoing returns.

Consider Organizational Barriers

Even with the most *technically* easy test pages, you need to consider how easy it will be to get approvals for the test. If you have carte blanche authority to make changes to the website, you don't need to worry about this, and you're in a rare and wonderful situation!

In a small company, gaining consent usually isn't a challenge. In my experience, small companies can often get excellent tests running quickly and make very fast gains. This decision-making speed gives small companies the benefit of being more nimble, which allows them to often gain quickly on their slower, behemoth rivals.

In a large organization, political considerations are a big part of the conversion-optimization champion's job. You need to understand which stakeholders have a claim on each page and how much resistance you'll face in getting approvals for a test.

If you're unsure about the likely ease of approvals, start with a less visible test, such as a landing page or internal website page. After you've gotten a win, you can use the data from that successful test in your pitch to run tests on more prominent pages.

Prioritize with a Weighting Table

Once you've prioritized your test opportunity pages according to their importance, potential for improvement, and ease of implementation, you can combine these considerations into your test opportunity list. By this time, you may have spent enough time in the data that you know which page to start with. Sometimes the top-priority page sticks out clearly in the data as having high importance, potential, and easy implementation. If so, you should move on to the next chapters and start testing on that high-priority page now. Then, return here to prioritize the next test rounds.

If you have multiple test opportunities you can prioritize, use a weighting table to help with the decision. List your potential test pages in the first column, and add your rating using a scale of 1–5 in the Potential, Importance, and Ease columns. Then sum the columns in the Priority Rating column on the right.

Potential Test Page	Potential	Importance	Ease	Priority Rating
Home page	5	4	1	10
Paid search landing-page template	4	5	4	13
Product/Service category page template	4	4	3	11
Product/Service detail page template	5	4	3	12
Lead-generation form	4	5	2	11
Shopping-cart step 1	2	5	2	9
Shopping-cart step 2	3	5	2	10

You may find, for example, that your home page has a high rating for Importance in terms of the traffic it reaches and Potential for improvement, but the political barriers push it down the list. Your paid search landing pages may be just as important and potent with much easier approvals. Other pages fall within the priority spectrum, which gives you a prioritized list to focus your effort.

There are no standard rules for which pages are best to prioritize. Your website lives in a unique target market, including factors like your competition, seasonality, and internal cultural environment; all of these affect how your site is used and should be optimized. The priority rating you give each of your potential test pages will depend on this unique business environment.

Reprioritize Regularly

Finally, your prioritization should always be considered a work in progress. After each test, reevaluate the new information you gather from the test results to determine how it affects the priorities. In Chapter 12, you'll learn how to evaluate test results and assess whether to retest on a page or move on to the next priority.

> **Note:** You'll find links to all resources mentioned in this chapter at YouShouldTestThat.com/ Prioritize. You should also go there to start discussions with fellow conversion champions.

In the next chapter, you'll learn how the six conversion factors in the LIFT Model affect your conversion rates and revenue and how to create hypotheses for testing.

4

Create Hypotheses with the LIFT Model

The most serious mistakes are not being made as a result of wrong answers. The truly dangerous thing is asking the wrong question.

—Peter Drucker

The job of a conversion rate–optimization expert is to find data-driven insights that dramatically improve business results. We do this by identifying problems in a business's marketing communication and developing hypotheses about solutions to solve those problems.

The first step is admitting you have a problem.

You and your team may have created the world's best website. You should be proud of your accomplishment. But it's not perfect. It needs constant improvement to keep up with competition.

On the other hand, maybe you already know it's in rough shape. There are many examples of landing pages and websites that are really, really bad.

Don't be ashamed if you're disappointed with your marketing performance. It could be worse!

So far, you've seen why conversion optimization is important, how to approach it as a strategy, and how to prioritize your testing opportunities. Now, the focus will shift to your specific optimization opportunities.

The most important take-away from this chapter is that having a process for developing hypotheses is more important than any one-time tips or recommendations. You'll learn how to use the Landing page Influence Functions for Tests (LIFT) Model to create and categorize problems, convert them into valid and actionable hypotheses, and then use those hypotheses to create awesome tests that improve the results from your marketing.

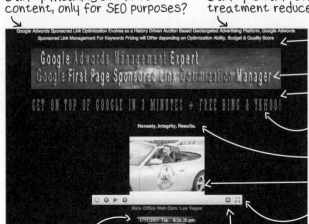

Clarity: Meaningless intro content, only for SEO purposes?

Clarity: Small, reversed type treatment reduces readability

Clarity: Copywriting above headline is likely to be skipped

Clarity: Compressed, embellished type with background imagery difficult to read

Value Proposition: Poor graphic design reduces credibility

Clarity: Red on black creates visual vibration

Anxiety: No proof points to support claims

Distract: Rotating images add to confusion

Anxiety: Auto-playing audio ad repels visitors

Distraction: Irrelevant date and weather content

Urgency: No call to action anywhere on the page

Could this be the worst landing page ever?

But never fear: this chapter will also give you a long list of tips for test ideas to help you get started.

Methodology Is More Valuable than Tips

It's not uncommon to find e-commerce or lead-generation consultants who think testing is a waste of time. After my presentation recently at a digital marketing conference, I bumped into a consultant friend of mine. Although he was impressed with the case studies I'd shown of WiderFunnel's dramatic revenue lift for clients, he asked why I do all this testing. As he put it, "Isn't it pointless to test something when you already 'know' it's going to win?"

I have to agree. If I knew, or was even 95 percent certain, that a variation would win, I wouldn't need to test it. But I don't always know which variation will win. Even after our years of testing, I learn something new from every experiment we run. There seems to be an infinite store of insights to be gathered.

Just as important, there's value in having data to prove or disprove the commonly accepted best practices. The first time we tested against a rotating-offer home page, I had a strong belief that we could beat it. But the world wouldn't have believed me without some data to back up my professional opinion.

The most interesting test results are the ones where the winner doesn't match common beliefs. We've seen many test results where a commonly held best-practices design or copy element doesn't beat a more unexpected design.

We're often asked to share tips or best practices on how to improve conversion rates on landing pages and website-conversion funnels. Although tips provide some value, their usefulness is limited outside of the appropriate context. You're always left wanting more.

I was recently asked by a Twitter follower for my top tips to improve conversion rates. Normally I wouldn't think twice about it; people ask me for conversion-optimization tips all the time. But this time it struck me.

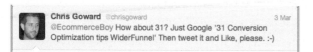

You see, I was in the midst of presenting at four different marketing conferences in two weeks about how to get better results than any "best practices" can give. The question struck me as ironic, as I try to turn conference attendees away from tips and toward a structured testing process. It seems people will always want free advice, no matter how little value it gives or how much I advise against it.

Seeking conversion-optimization tips is common—and misguided. There are no tips that you can apply to every website to improve your conversion rates. Design and content changes that work for one site can cause problems for another.

You'll get much better results by applying a process to think through your prospect's experience and develop your own test hypotheses. In the next section, you'll learn how to use a web-page analysis framework as part of your testing process.

The Gorilla in Our Brains

Our brains are like computer CPUs: we have limited processing power, and any one "application" can use it up and reduce our ability to process other applications (other streams of information). Think back to the last time you were driving a car somewhere for the first time. Maybe you were looking for street names, landmarks, or a building address. Did you turn down the music in the car?

If you did, you're not alone.

Steven Yantis, a professor in the Department of Psychological and Brain Sciences at Johns Hopkins University, has this to say about talking on cell phones while driving:

> Directing attention to listening effectively "turns down the volume" on input to the visual parts of the brain. The evidence we have right now strongly suggests that attention is strictly limited—a zero-sum game. When attention is deployed to one modality—say, in this case, talking on a cell phone—it necessarily extracts a cost on another modality—in this case, the visual task of driving.

When we focus our attention on something, we reduce our ability to think about or even perceive other things, even when those other things would otherwise have been obvious.

A research study by Christopher Chabris and Daniel Simons, authors of *The Invisible Gorilla* (Broadway, 2011), demonstrate this odd characteristic of people. In the study, Chabris and Simons instructed viewers to watch a video and count how many times the players wearing white passed a basketball.

As viewers concentrated on counting the passes, a gorilla walked through the middle of the basketball players and beat its chest. In the research, half the people who watched the video missed the gorilla, as though it was invisible. It's not that the viewers didn't recognize the gorilla—their mental processing power was simply focused on performing one task, at the expense of their other mental applications.

If you've conducted usability tests on your website or applications, you've probably wondered how people can miss the most obvious things on your page. You may have questioned how they could be so clueless.

Image provided by Daniel J. Simons (www.theinvisiblegorilla.com). All rights reserved. For links to watch these videos and download other research from this chapter, go to YouShouldTestThat.com/hypotheses.

The good news is that they're not. They're completely normal. As people, they can process only so much information at one time. Another mental process is using up their ability to see the obvious thing that you want them to.

This is an important concept to understand when conducting heuristic analyses of your communications. Even small changes to your messages, page layouts, and user interactions can have a significant impact on freeing your prospects' mental capacity so they can understand your message.

Heuristic Analysis   A heuristic analysis uses rules of thumb or expert judgment to make decisions and recommendations. When used alone, a heuristic recommendation can be misleading or harmful. But combined with controlled testing, a heuristic analysis from an experienced conversion strategist is a powerful tool for business improvement.

Understanding is the basic prerequisite to motivation. By smoothing out these mental difficulties, you'll be more successful at persuading your prospects to act.

That's where a conversion rate-optimization framework can help. By analyzing your marketing experiences from the perspective of your prospects, you can get into the mindset of minimizing barriers to cognition.

The LIFT Model

The Landing page Influence Function for Tests (LIFT) Model is the conversion rate–optimization framework I developed at WiderFunnel to improve marketers' ability to communicate, persuade, and convert prospects.

At WiderFunnel, we've used this tool as part of a structured process to lift each of our clients' conversion rates by 10 percent to more than 400 percent. For each of the experiments we run for clients, our conversion strategists conduct a brainstorming session during which we bring our individual heuristic analyses to the room and run a group LIFT analysis.

The LIFT Model shows the six conversion factors that affect your conversion rates. By testing hypotheses to improve each of these factors, you can improve the results of all your marketing activities.

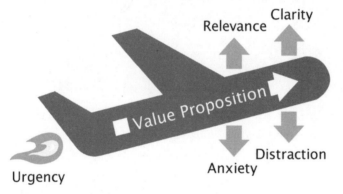

The WiderFunnel LIFT Model

The vehicle that provides the potential for the conversion rate is your Value Proposition, making it the most important of the six conversion factors.

The other five factors either drive conversion or inhibit it. Relevance, Clarity, and Urgency are the conversion drivers we can test to lift conversion rates. Anxiety and Distraction are conversion inhibitors that you need to reduce on your pages to remove barriers to conversion. We'll look at each of the factors in more detail in the following sections.

By evaluating your website, landing pages, and conversion funnel from the perspective of your prospective customer, you can identify conversion problems that can be tested and improved.

Although other fine conversion frameworks are available as well, LIFT has gained popularity, I believe, because of its ease of use and apparent simplicity that belie its powerful results. The framework is a demonstration of how maximizing Clarity and minimizing Distraction can gain acceptance!

The Value Proposition

Your *value proposition* is the full set of perceived benefits and costs, in the prospect's mind, of taking your call to action.

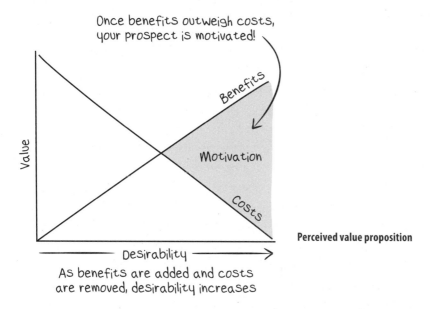

When your perceived benefits outweigh perceived costs, your prospect will have enough motivation to take action. It's important to note that I say *perceived* in the prospect's mind. Each person's perspective of your value proposition is influenced by their experiences, temperament, and past interactions with your brand and competitors.

For example, your perception of the words *value, economy, premium, quality,* and even *guarantee* may be different than mine. To some, the words *value* and *economy* imply something cheap and low-quality. To others, those same words say "smart" and "self-disciplined."

The strength of your value proposition determines your potential for conversion-rate improvement. If your value proposition is strong and the communication of it is weak, you can have large conversion-rate lift from improvements to your pages. In other words, if people want what you offer, but they can't figure out what you're saying, simply saying it more clearly will motivate more of them to buy!

On the other hand, if your value proposition is weak, or weaker than that of competitors, you'll have a difficult time improving your conversion rates, no matter how well designed your website and landing pages are.

This ability to move your conversion rate is called your *conversion-rate elasticity.* It's the amount of conversion-rate movement you observe by making changes to your communications. Pages that have more problems or are more important to your prospects' decision-making have greater conversion-rate elasticity.

When you find pages with high conversion-rate elasticity, you should rank them higher in the Potential rating that you learned about in Chapter 3, "Prioritize Testing Opportunities." These are good testing focus areas.

Testing your value proposition can produce significant conversion-rate changes. In Chapter 5, "Optimize Your Value Proposition," you'll discover how to understand your current value-proposition components and develop hypotheses to test and improve your value proposition.

Relevance

The Relevance LIFT factor asks the question, "Does the page relate to what the visitor thought they were going to see?"

When people are in a searching mindset, they switch into a faster mode of processing information. Rather than using a meaning-evaluation method to understand all the words on the page, we switch to a pattern-matching process, where we look for cues that tell us we're still on the right path.

Research as early as 2001 by Ed Chi and Peter Pirolli at the famous Xerox PARC lab showed that people look for information by following a scent trail, similar to the food-gathering techniques used by animals. As Chi put it (in *Wired*, 06/08/01, "Hot on the Scent of Information"),

> *Information scent is made of cues that people use to decide whether a path is interesting. These cues consist (of) images, hyperlinks and bibliographic citations related to the information needed. Evolutionarily, the optimization strategies that are innate in each one of us in looking for food in the natural environment occur extremely often in just about everything that we do.*

To keep your prospects interested in following the path that leads toward your call to action, you should maximize the scent trail.

The relevance of the value proposition and context of the source media are critical. Your page should use words, images, colors, and layouts that your prospect relates to and are consistent with the incoming link. If you don't, your prospect will become disoriented and leave the page. In Chapter 6, "Optimize for Relevance," you'll see examples of how to maintain your prospects' scent trail and maximize relevance.

Clarity

Does the page clearly articulate the value proposition and call to action? *Clarity* may be the most common of the six conversion factors that we find marketers struggling with. "Say what you mean" seems like such a simple directive, yet it's surprisingly difficult to accomplish.

Content and design are the two overarching aspects of clarity that should be analyzed. *Content clarity* means ensuring that the images and text combine to minimize the viewer's time needed for comprehension. When your content is clear, your imagery and copywriting complement each other. They work together to reinforce your value proposition and guide your prospect to take the call to action.

The purpose of design is to facilitate the content. Designing for clarity creates an unimpeded eyeflow, an unobscured message, and a prominent call to action. The best designers know how to use design to promote the content being communicated rather than taking attention for the design itself.

In Chapter 7, "Optimize for Clarity," you'll learn how to use content and design to make significant conversion-rate gains.

Anxiety

What potential misgivings could the visitor have about undertaking the conversion action? *Anxiety* is any uncertainty in your prospect's mind about completing the conversion. It's a function of the credibility you've built with the visitor and the trust you're asking them to have.

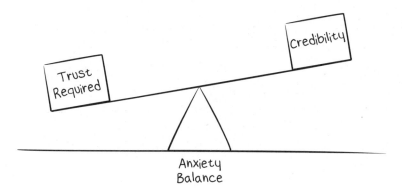

Your brand equity is an important part of your credibility. If you have a strong brand, you can get away with requiring more trust from your prospects than if you're unknown.

Think about how comfortable you feel signing up for a newsletter from a known brand like Salesforce.com, JC Penney, or eBay, for example. Contrast that with an unknown local mortgage broker's or consultant's landing page that you happen to find during a search, where a pop-up appears immediately asking for your name, email address, and zip code.

You probably expect that the known brands will respect your privacy and allow for easy unsubscribes. They have pre-established credibility. The unknown brands have to do more work to establish credibility with you before they can ask you to trust them.

Even known brands can lose their credibility quickly, though, by violating trust or usability principles. In Chapter 8, "Optimize for Anxiety," you'll see how to reduce your prospects' anxiety with design, usability, and performance enhancements.

Distraction

Are there items on the page that could divert the visitor away from the goal? *Distraction* includes anything on the page that redirects attention from the primary message and call to action. Traditionally, marketers have believed they can sell more by offering more product options. Witness the rise of endless line extensions. Coca-Cola, for example, now has over 100 drink options. But apparently the company has decided that isn't enough: it has released a beverage dispenser called *Freestyle* that lets you mix and mash up to make your own.

When I was a kid, we called this *swamp water.* I don't remember it tasting as good as the original drinks.

Research in the field of behavioral economics by Dan Ariely, author of *Predictably Irrational* (HarperCollins, 2009), shows that more choice often overwhelms people and reduces sales conversion rates. His study of jam flavors in a store in California gave a good example of the effect of choice.

In Ariely's research, he set out a display table with jams for sale, sometimes with 6 flavors and other times with 24. When there were 24 jams, 60 percent of passers-by stopped to look and try a sample. Only 40 percent stopped to look when there were 6 flavors on the table. Clearly, the 24 options created more visual interest to grab shoppers' attention and pull them in.

The interesting part, though, was the sales-conversion rate. With 6 jam options, 30 percent of shoppers purchased—but when there were 24 jams displayed, only 3 percent made a purchase! With too many options, people became overwhelmed and didn't purchase, even given this simple decision.

The more visual inputs and action options your visitors have to process, the less likely they are to make a conversion decision. Minimizing distractions such as unnecessary product options, links, and extraneous information will increase the conversion rate. In Chapter 9, "Optimize for Distraction," you'll see how to identify and reduce sources of distraction.

Urgency

Is there an indication on the page that action needs to be taken *now*?

Urgency has two components: internal and external. *Internal urgency* is based on how the visitor is feeling upon arrival at the page. Think of a marketing assistant who has been tasked to create a list of top marketing-automation tools, with prices, by tomorrow. He's on a laser-focused search for all the Contact Us forms on marketing-automation websites. There's high internal urgency to complete that task.

Contrast that scenario with a business owner who's heard about marketing automation at a marketing conference. She's in an exploratory phase to find out if it's a good fit for her business. She has low internal urgency to complete the task; and you, as a marketing-automation company, have more chance of losing her to competitors before she completes a lead form.

You don't have control over internal urgency, but you can see its effect on conversions. When internal urgency is low, your conversion-rate elasticity is high; that is, you have a lot of potential to make conversion-rate improvements through design and content changes. High internal urgency in an audience segment means they will crawl over broken glass to complete a conversion, and conversion-rate elasticity is low. Your job is simply to facilitate the conversion quickly.

External urgency, on the other hand, can be influenced by the marketer. Variables like limited time offers, seasonal reminders, and even the tone of the copywriting can affect external urgency. In Chapter 10, "Optimize for Urgency," you'll see how to test with these variables to capture more leads and sales, especially in seasons when internal urgency is low.

Problems Are Opportunities!

At this point, after evaluating some of your pages using the LIFT Model, you may be feeling discouraged about the state of your website and the challenges ahead. Look at all those conversion problems! If you've been able to identify many problems, you're in a good situation. You would be in a worse position if you didn't know about them.

The other piece of good news is that, thankfully, you don't have to fix all the problems. There is no perfect web page, and you don't have to get everything right to have a world-class conversion rate. You just have to get enough things right for your prospects to convert into leads and customers.

Fill the Marble Jar

Each person has a *conversion tipping point*, and the six conversion factors are both independent and cumulative. By that I mean, if you improve one or more of the LIFT factors enough, you can get a conversion even if some of the other factors are weak. You can compensate for a weakness with a strength.

Think of your visitor's conversion tipping point as a jar of marbles. Once that jar is filled to a certain level with motivational marbles representing the Clarity, Relevance, and Urgency conversion factors, your visitor will convert into a lead or customer. There also may be Distraction and Anxiety holes in the jar that allow the motivational marbles to slip out.

Imagine the following scenario. You manage an e-commerce gift store, and a guest (a *unique visitor* in web analytics terms) arrives with a need to purchase a gift. Let's say there is still plenty of time to make a purchase, so her internal urgency factor is low. In other words, she's only got a few shiny blue Urgency marbles in the jar. That jar needs to be full for her to make a purchase.

She arrives on your landing page, and the headline perfectly matches what she had in mind. In drop some beautiful green Relevance marbles, but the jar is still only partly filled.

Unfortunately, your copy is poorly written, and the product image is small and unclear. The call-to-action button is below the fold, and no pricing is visible on the page. There's a huge missed opportunity and, unfortunately, no transparent Clarity marbles are dropped in. You've still got a long way to go.

The good news is that you don't have significant Distraction or Anxiety on the page, so only a few marbles leak out the bottom. But how are you going to fill the rest of the jar?

"Aha!" you say. You'll create a limited-time discount offer for 15 percent off. That's a sure way to add some blue External Urgency marbles.

If that isn't enough urgency to fill the jar, the conversion still won't happen, although the visitor will go away torn because she believes the product could have been perfect for her. Her experience was just a little too frustrating.

Now, imagine the same scenario on December 15 when your guest is looking to cross off the last three names on her holiday shopping list. It's nearly dinnertime, and the kids are getting hungry. In this scenario, her internal urgency is very high. In fact, it's so high that it fills the rest of the jar with Urgency marbles, and she completes the purchase.

Your job is to fill your guest's jar with big Value Proposition, Clarity, Relevance, and Urgency marbles and plug the Anxiety and Distraction holes in the jar where marbles might escape.

We could push the analogy further by saying that different people have different-sized marbles for each color, but I'm sure you get the point. Your job is to become an avid marble collector.

Create Valid Hypotheses

Once you've identified problems on your conversion pages using the LIFT Model, you can create hypotheses from them. This is a process of changing your weaknesses into strengths that you can test.

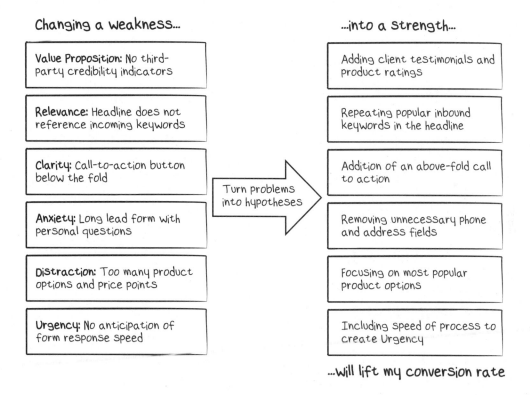

Changing a weakness...

| Value Proposition: No third-party credibility indicators |
| Relevance: Headline does not reference incoming keywords |
| Clarity: Call-to-action button below the fold |
| Anxiety: Long lead form with personal questions |
| Distraction: Too many product options and price points |
| Urgency: No anticipation of form response speed |

Turn problems into hypotheses

...into a strength...

| Adding client testimonials and product ratings |
| Repeating popular inbound keywords in the headline |
| Addition of an above-fold call to action |
| Removing unnecessary phone and address fields |
| Focusing on most popular product options |
| Including speed of process to create Urgency |

...will lift my conversion rate

Creating a strong hypothesis is an important part of any scientific experiment. The strength of your hypotheses determines the outcome of your testing. Even if millions of testable people visit your pages each month, you'll have difficulty making substantial conversion-rate gains without strong hypotheses. I'm sure it's clear by now that time spent on creating your hypotheses is time well spent.

At its core, a *hypothesis* is simply a question you can ask of your target audience or test sample. Although there is a structure for how to state a hypothesis, there is no formula for how to come up with a powerful question to ask.

The best scientists have characteristics similar to those of the best conversion champions: we're curious. Mediocre marketers aren't inquisitive. They take the test findings at face value and are satisfied in getting a conversion-rate lift. And why not? They've got the result they want, after all. I'll tell you why not: because they're missing a lot of improvement that their competitors are probably gaining.

A good conversion strategist is never satisfied with the result and is always asking questions, even after getting a great test result:

- Why does the orange button work better than a green button in this situation?
- Why does this target audience respond better to that headline than the other?
- Why does the call to action work better on the left side of the page for this website?
- How can we build on these findings?

The questions drive the development of an unending series of hypotheses to test. Some will lead to great conversion-rate lift and others won't, but in all cases you'll learn something—even if what you learn is that it was the wrong question to ask!

The Hypothesis Structure

A hypothesis has the following structure:

Changing [the thing you want to change] into [what you would change it into] will lift the conversion rate for [your conversion goal].

For example, you may believe your headline doesn't adequately communicate that your company is the leading seller in your field. Your hypothesis may be as follows:

Changing our current headline . . .

Anti-Spam underwear for less
_____

. . . into . . .

Join over 30 thousand superheroes who
wear vortex Anti-spam underwear
_____

. . . will lift our conversion rate for . . .

e-commerce sales
_____

Now that's a hypothesis you can test!

Good to Great Hypotheses

A great conversion rate–optimization hypothesis does more than just follow a scientific structure. To get powerful results, it should be testable, seek to solve conversion problems, and aim to gain marketing insights:

- **Be testable:** A *testable* hypothesis is one that can be isolated so that it can be confirmed or contradicted. If the test completes and you don't know whether it was true or false, it wasn't really a hypothesis.

  For example, this isn't a testable hypothesis:

  Our visitors prefer red headlines.

  To make it testable, it must be specific, like this:

  Changing our headline from black to red will lift the conversion rate for our lead-generation signup form.

  Over a series of tests, you can glean the "why" behind the test results by looking for patterns. After testing several elements throughout your marketing touch points, you may be able to develop a theory that your target audience responds to red elements, or value messaging, or tangible offers, or whatever. But a single test hypothesis won't prove or disprove an overarching theory.

- **Seek to solve conversion problems:** Your hypotheses should flow out of an identified conversion problem rather than just arbitrary ideas for design or content variations.

  Sometimes, testing random tips and tactics will achieve a conversion-rate lift, but if you use that method, you're relying purely on luck. That's not a reliable way to make continuous business improvement, and your conversion-optimization program is likely to end in frustration at some point.

  By creating a process where potential conversion problems are identified first, you'll learn more from each test and have a reliable source of ongoing new test ideas. This is also why WiderFunnel's seven-step testing process (see Chapter 2, "What is Conversion Optimization") places page analysis, hypothesis generation, and the test plan before graphic design and copywriting. The test planning should be strategy-led rather than based on the aesthetic whims of design or copy tactics.

- **Aim at gaining marketing insights:** The most powerful hypotheses ask questions that could impact the overall website design, marketing tactics, or business strategy.

  There's nothing wrong with tactical hypotheses that aim to improve the conversion rate on a particular page. But you can also include hypotheses that have a chance to impact the marketing strategy and even the overall business.

What if you could learn, from a series of conversion-optimization tests, that your visitors are more likely to respond to a specific and limited choice of tangible premium offers than to cash value to redeem for an unlimited choice of offers? This is an insight that can affect your marketing decision-making.

This happens to be exactly the type of insight that we were able to gain in our work with Electronic Arts for its The Sims 3 team (see the case study "The Sims 3 Doubles Game Registrations by Identifying the Most Compelling Offer" in Chapter 5). The company ended up gaining much more than just a conversion-rate lift by using that insight to restructure its team to develop assets that it could use for greater marketing effectiveness.

Starting with hypotheses that follow the proper structure is good. Creating hypotheses that solve conversion problems is better. When you find hypotheses that lead to marketing insights, you've achieved hypothesis greatness!

Tips to Get Your Testing Started

The constant requests for quick tips led us to write a blog post that lists 31 conversion rate–optimization tips, at www.widerfunnel.com/?p=1843. Even though we brainstormed those tips in under an hour, it became one of the most popular articles on the WiderFunnel blog over the next three years. Throughout the next six chapters, I'll give you those tips and many more, which you'll be able to use in planning tests on your pages.

But what do you do when you've tested those 31 tips?

Many of our clients come to us after running out of ideas about what to test. In each case, the structured methodology we use to evaluate pages and develop test hypotheses has played an important role in the conversion-rate lift we deliver for them. To get the best results, you should follow a system that generates an ongoing stream of test hypotheses.

For more discussion about creating hypotheses and to download a free printable LIFT Model poster, go to YouShouldTestThat.com/Hypotheses.

Here's one caveat as you work through the following chapters: Please don't make the mistake of taking these points as recommended changes you should immediately make on your site. Without testing them, you could be hurting your conversion rates. **You Should Test That!**

5 Optimize Your Value Proposition

Don't bunt. Aim out of the ball park. Aim for the company of immortals.

—David Ogilvy

Your Value Proposition is the first, and most important, of the six conversion factors in the LIFT Model.

- It's the driver of your conversion-rate potential.
- It's the reason your customers buy from you.

The value proposition is often approached as a logical exercise to determine your most important costs and benefits, but it also must include the emotional attributes of your company and product. The intangibles are just as important as your tangible appeals and detractions. Your brand essence plays just as much of a role as the features of your product or service.

Consider for a moment the effect of trust and credibility in the unfortunate case of Steve's Detailing in Manhattan, New York. It's a detailing shop, so you may assume that attention to detail is an important part of their value proposition. Do you think they instill confidence in their attention to detail when their sign is misspelled *Detaling*?

For you, as for Steve, what you say can be less important than how you say it.

The medium is the message, as Marshall McLuhan said. Just as your choice of advertising medium can communicate and reinforce your message, the choices in your communication design and content give cues to your value proposition.

Everything counts. Your prospects are looking for clues in every area of your business to either make a decision whether to buy or reinforce their decision post-purchase.

In this chapter, you'll learn about the components that make up your value proposition, how your prospects perceive your offering, and how to identify opportunities to strengthen and test your value proposition.

The Value-Proposition Equation

In Chapter 4, "Create Hypotheses with the LIFT Model," you saw that your value proposition is a balance between your product's or service's perceived benefits and costs. It can also be thought of as an equation in your prospects' minds.

$$\text{Motivation} = \frac{\text{Perceived}}{\text{Benefits}} - \frac{\text{Perceived}}{\text{Costs}}$$

This value proposition equation says that if the perceived benefits of your call to action outweigh perceived costs in taking action, your prospect will be motivated to act.

> **Value Proposition** The full set of perceived benefits and costs, in the prospect's mind, of taking your call to action. Your value proposition is the vehicle that provides the potential for your conversion rate, making it the most important of the six conversion factors in the LIFT Model. The other five factors are either conversion drivers or inhibitors.
>
> Ask yourself: "What are all of the elements of my offer and call to action that could be perceived as benefits and costs?"

To maximize the call-to-action conversion rates from your communications, you must clearly communicate your benefits so they will be understood, and you need to counteract or minimize the prospect's perception of the costs of converting to a lead or customer. This would be much easier if everyone saw things the same way.

Your Visitor's Perception Filters

Each person looks at the world through different eyes. Your visitors have unique frames of reference that are colored by their perceptual filters. It's as if they each wear different glasses that change what they're looking at before it reaches them.

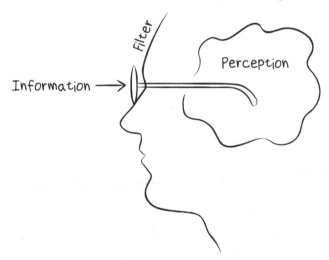

In reality, the perceptual filters are in your prospects' minds. Their perception of the information you present to them is influenced by their

- Interpretation of colors on your page
- Connotations of the words you use
- Cultural biases

- Expectations of what they will see on your page
- Current mood and feelings, which may be unrelated to your communication
- Current environment
- Previous interactions with your company
- Experiences with similar products or services
- Beliefs about quality, money, and value

In the words of George Harrison, "It's all in the mind."

These mental filters can dramatically alter how your prospects understand your messages. For example, consider an image of a smiling person.

You may think a smiling person communicates a welcoming impression, warmth, and friendliness. Or maybe you've heard the "sex sells" mantra that promotes beauty as a key to advertising success. But do your prospects have different filters that skew their impression of your image selection? Other peoples' impressions of the image may be very different. Your prospect may be thinking:

- "Marketing alert! They're trying to sell to me."
- "That's obviously a stock photo being presented as a happy customer. Can I trust the rest of their message?"
- "Why is there no cultural diversity on this page?"
- "She's beautiful. I wonder if they have any other photos of her…. What was I here for?"
- "Oh, great…another bleached blonde."

Out of curiosity, and to get a sample of some thoughts people might have, I presented that image to the `fivesecondtest.com` audience and asked this question: "I'm looking for impressions from the following image. What words come to mind?"

Here are the first 15 responses:

- "Happy, dentist, smile, close-up"
- "Blond"
- "Teeth"
- "Dental service"
- "Happy, toothpaste commercial, blonde, too happy, smile, staged"
- "Young, happy, teeth"
- "Pretty, teeth, eyes, blonde"
- "Teenager, model, high school, glamour shot, dentistry"
- "Dentistry"
- "Sweet, innocent, happy"
- "Fresh, clean, sharp"
- "Pretty, happy, smiling, a bit fake"
- "Dentist"
- "Pretty, fake, blond"
- "Bright, young, cheerful…but also sort of fake"

We can pull some interesting findings even from this small sample of responses. Not surprisingly, there were some unexpected impressions. There always are.

Quite a few responses mentioned "happy": 6 out of 15, which is good for your brand if that's the impression you want to give.

I have to admit that I didn't expect the number of people who thought of dentistry or teeth: 9 out of 15. If you're selling software or accounting services, that's probably not the first thing you want your prospects to think, right?

Notice that four of the responses said the image gave them the impression that it was "fake" or "staged." For those four responders, the feelings this image triggers are different than for the others who said "sweet, innocent" or "fresh, clean, sharp." Their perceptual filters gave them a different impression.

Although this exercise isn't a statistically valid study, it should demonstrate that there can be a wide variety of reactions to an element on your page. Different people will interpret the same images and words in entirely different ways.

The perceptual filters your prospects carry are outside of your control, and they're important to understand. By acknowledging that they exist, you can look for insights into how your target audience interprets your messages differently than you do. These filters will determine how your prospects perceive the features and benefits of your product or service. Keep the filters in mind as you evaluate how to communicate your features.

Tangible Features

A *tangible feature* is something that can satisfy a prospect's stated need. Tangible features are the facts your prospects logically use to justify their emotional decisions. They include the descriptive characteristics of your product or service and the elements of your offer, including incentives.

Product or Service Features

The *features* of your product or service are the characteristics you use to describe it. They're the attributes that can be compared to competitors.

You know you're looking at a tangible feature if it can be listed on an ad, a spec sheet, or a comparison chart, like these examples:

- "Unlimited survey questions and responses" (SurveyMonkey)
- "Build interactive dashboards with charts, graphs, and what-if scenarios to visualize your data" (Crystal Reports by SAP)
- "This collar hardware is made from solid brass, with a plated finish" (leather dog collar with name plate by GunDogSupply.com)
- "Money Back Guarantee – no questions asked" (AllPopArt.com)
- "Scalability for any size business, support for Windows and Linux OSs and complex storage needs, centralized multi-server management, live virtual machine migration, and much more" (Citrix XenServer)
- "Free Delivery & Returns" (BenSherman.com)

These are all features that you can list and that visitors can compare and check off.

The question you can answer about your features by using testing is, "Which ones should I emphasize?" If you list all your features in your ads and landing pages, you'll usually overwhelm visitors and hurt your conversion rate. You need to understand your prospects' needs and offer only the information that helps them move to the next step.

The next question you may ask is, "How many features should I include on a page?" There's no simple answer. In our testing, we've found different optimum content amounts for different situations. In some situations, a minimalist page works best. In others, the highest-converting page is very comprehensive. You should test that spectrum of content comprehensiveness.

Testing your tangible feature lists, headlines, and benefit statements will show you which are the most important to emphasize. You'll get a double benefit of lifting your conversion rates *and* producing marketing insights to build on.

Your tangible offering can also be enhanced with incentives.

Incentives and Offers

The *offer* is one of the three direct-marketing variables you can use to improve your conversion rates (the other two are *list*, or *targeting*, and *creative*). The offer is the entire package of features plus purchase incentives.

The many types of incentives include the following:

- Premiums
- Discounts
- Credits
- Buy one, get one (BOGO)
- Bundling
- Free trial
- Free upgrade
- Sampling
- Loyalty programs
- And more...

Do you know which incentives will generate the highest revenue and profit? Testing can tell you. When testing incentives, you should calculate the conversion rate for each incentive offer and then determine the profit generated by each to determine which produces the most profit. Even within the same offer, you can vary its position and test how that affects conversion.

Consider the following incentive options:

- Half off!
- 50% off!
- Buy one, get one free!

Essentially, they're all the same offer, but one will perform better than the others.

Incentive testing can provide potent insights into the offers that induce your prospects to act and maximize your revenue and profit. The case of WiderFunnel's testing with Electronic Arts' *The Sims 3* is a good example.

Case Study: *The Sims 3* Doubles Game Registrations by Identifying the Most Compelling Offer

The Sims by Electronic Arts is one of the best-selling computer game franchises in history. Since its initial release in 2000, these strategic life-simulation games have sold more than 125 million copies worldwide, won countless awards, and redefined the open-ended gameplay style. *The Sims 3*, the next generation of this global cultural phenomenon and best-selling PC franchise of all time, launched in June 2009 to 60 countries in over 22 languages.

In *The Sims 3*, players create lifelike Sims characters with unique personalities and take them anywhere in the neighborhood. The Create a Sim tool allows players to create Sims that are more realistic than ever. Players select from dozens of personality traits such as *brave*, *artistic*, *kleptomaniac*, *clumsy*, *paranoid*, and *romantic*. With Create a Sim, players can create a limitless number of truly unique Sims.

The Sims 3 allows for infinite possibilities to design the interior and exterior of the Sims' surroundings using the Create a Style feature. An extension of the game, the *Sims 3* Store, lets players customize their Sims worlds even more by offering a wide selection of exclusive *in-game content*, or virtual goods (such as hairstyles, furniture and room accessories, and clothing). Game content purchases are made by redeeming SimPoints, which are sold in bundles of $5, $10, $20, or $40.

The Sims 3 is played by a broad audience, with 55 percent of players being female. The majority of players are between 16 and 34 years of age.

The Business Need

Sales of in-game content play a major part in the business success of the *Sims 3* Store. The marketing team has crafted a conversion funnel made up of a series of micro-conversions: from anonymous player to registered player to first-time purchaser to repeat purchaser. Until a player registers their game, they're much more difficult and costly to convert to a purchaser.

The *game launcher* is a key tool used by the *Sims 3* team to pull players to the website TheSims3.com and encourage game registrations. After the game is installed on a player's computer, the player clicks the *Sims 3* desktop icon. The game launcher loads every time a player wants to start the game. This launcher is a multipurpose portal for managing new game content from the community Exchange or from the *Sims 3* Store, managing game software updates, and starting the game, and also contains promos and links to the *Sims 3* Store and Community site.

Game-registration conversions from the launcher were unsatisfactory, and the *Sims 3* team knew that even a small conversion-rate improvement could have a big impact on revenue.

The Challenges

The multiple functions of the game launcher portal were both a strength and a weakness. Although the portal provided a flexible platform for alternating offers, competing messages made finding and understanding the benefits of registration and joining the community difficult for players.

Further, *The Sims 3* has shipped millions of copies, yet a sizeable percentage of players only used the game launcher to manage their game content and start the game. Players only revisited the launcher when they were about to play the game, and they rarely clicked the various offers. Finally, customers interested in registering their game were unsure of benefits received or whether additional fees were required.

As with all websites that require users to share personal information, the *Sims 3* team wanted customers to receive the free benefits they offered in a convenient manner.

The Solution

The *Sims 3* team hired WiderFunnel Marketing Optimization to help them improve the effectiveness of their conversion funnels, and chose the game launcher as a first target for improvement.

WiderFunnel handled the project in its entirety, developing a complete test plan—including hypotheses, wireframes, graphic design, and copy—and executing the test to live players in the launcher window.

WiderFunnel developed and tested many challenger variations of the game launcher to test against the original control version. The goal of WiderFunnel's test was twofold:

1. Dramatically lift game-registration conversion rates.
2. Produce marketing insights that the *Sims 3* team could build on throughout their marketing programs.

Continues

The Sims 3 Doubles Game Registrations by Identifying the Most Compelling Offer *(Continued)*

The Result: 128 Percent Increase in Game Registrations!

All challengers created by WiderFunnel improved game registrations by at least 43 percent. The top-performing challenger, Free Town, delivered a 128 percent conversion-rate lift over the original, "control" game launcher page! The second runner-up, Free Points, also showed a fantastic 79 percent uplift, indicating that players respond best to specific offers.

Sims 3 control page   Sims 3 winning page

By using a scientifically valid method to test various offers, the *Sims 3* marketing team now knows with certainty that the winning challenger variation outperforms all others.

Bonus Result: A Marketing Insight

This test not only resulted in an improved conversion rate but also provided valuable insights into the type of offers that are most compelling for *Sims 3* players. These test results indicated that by emphasizing the offer of a free town, the *Sims 3* team could compel players to act much more effectively than by giving them the choice to spend SimPoints on any type of game add-on.

The *Sims 3* team is continuing to work with WiderFunnel to do more testing throughout the conversion funnels on their website.

In the case of *The Sims 3*, emphasizing different types of offers dramatically changed the game's marketing effectiveness. The *Sims 3* team now has insights about which tangible features to emphasize and, even more exciting, which types of features to build more of! Such insights can lead to more than just marketing changes; they can also have far-reaching organizational effects.

Tangible features aren't the only places to test your value proposition. The intangible appeals can be just as important, and sometimes more so.

Intangible Benefits

Early in my career I spent several years in sales and put a lot of effort into studying how to be a good salesperson. I spent hours on the road each day between sales calls listening to audio training and traveling to other cities to take in-person sales training seminars.

One sales trainer in particular, Tom Hopkins, made an impression on me. I can still hear him in my head saying over and over and over again, "Remember, people make a purchase emotionally and defend the purchase rationally. You must create the emotions necessary to close the sale backed up with the logic of the decision to defend it."

That is good sales advice, and it works for more than just salespeople. It applies to all of your marketing communications as well. You should provide intangible, emotional benefits that convince your prospects to buy, and give them tangible, logical features they can use to justify their decision.

Comfort. Acceptance. Power. Freedom. Control. Love. We're all longing to find satisfaction for our intangible desires. If you can provide a payoff for your prospects' unspoken needs, you'll find yourself handsomely rewarded.

Your prospects feel intangible benefits at an emotional level. These intangibles include many aspects of your company, products, and services beyond your tangible features. They include the feelings your service evokes and personal characteristics attributed to your brand.

Often, intangibles are more important than tangibles to your customers. Remember, people make a purchase emotionally and defend the purchase rationally. Think about how intangible benefits play into your own purchasing decisions.

Remember when Starbucks became popular in the mid 1990s? Before that, most people were happy to start their morning with drip coffee made in their kitchens. Starbucks changed that by creating a perceived need to drink espresso-based drinks.

But what's the real difference in features between espresso and drip coffee? Nothing! They both give you a shot of caffeine, and they taste similar. Starbucks created a set of strong intangible benefits. Espresso drinks became positioned as the choice of discerning people. And who doesn't want to be discerning?

A brilliant thing Starbucks did was to layer a tangible feature of choice on top of the intangibles. You can customize from a nearly infinite set of combinations to create your perfect coffee. That's one of the few tangible benefits people use to justify to themselves why they're spending 10 times their previous amount on their morning joe.

You can use several conversion tactics to enhance the feeling of intangible benefits for your prospects.

Credibility

Why do you trust what your friends and colleagues say? Because they have credibility with you. You believe what they say and that they will do what they say they will do.

Similarly, the credibility you build with your prospects counterbalances the trust you're asking them to have in you. The more credibility you build, the more they will be willing to share with you and believe your messages.

Credibility is difficult to gain and easy to lose. Your prospects' BS radar is on high alert, especially when they know they're reading a marketing page. Any clues that they can pick up to undermine your credibility will quickly erode whatever gains you've made.

You can test ways to enhance your credibility through the sources discussed in the following sections.

Professional Reviews

You can leverage the credibility of trusted expert sources to enhance your value proposition using professional reviews. Grasshopper shows reviews on its home page to reinforce some of its value-proposition points and add credibility to its phone call–forwarding service.

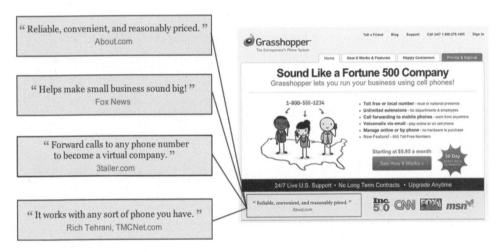

Media Mentions

Similar to displaying reviews, highlighting media mentions allows some of the media's brand credibility to rub off on your company. AllPopArt.com, for example, has been featured in many prominent TV shows and publications and promotes that fact effectively.

The credibility value depends on the media publication's brand. Be careful, because if you can only reference obscure media, the effect could be the opposite of what you want. Prospects may wonder why you've only been noticed by insignificant news sources.

Awards

Awards can add a lot of credibility, especially if the award emphasizes an important part of your value proposition. If your company promotes itself as having a high service experience, look for customer service awards. Or, try to obtain awards from frugal-shopping publications if you're a low-cost option.

Even if your company has won awards that aren't directly related to the product, general business awards can lend credibility to your company as being a leader in your field. Iron Mountain is a highly respected company and has the awards to show for it.

Professionalism

The quality of your design and copywriting can enhance or detract from your credibility. But the best design for conversion isn't always the most aesthetically pleasing or artistically creative. Professionalism comes from having design that is consistent and error-free.

Copywriting quality is also important for credibility. Your prospects have little patience for grammar and spelling errors. We'll discuss design and copy tips more in Chapter 7, "Optimize for Clarity."

Thought Leadership

Articles, white papers, books, seminars, blogs, and other popular content-marketing pieces add to your brand's impression as an innovator and leader. This is often a position taken by service companies like consultancies and agencies. Even product marketers can take this approach, as shown by 37 Signals with its home-page promotion of its popular book, *Rework* (Crown Business, 2010; and if you haven't read it, you should!).

37signals

Making collaboration productive and enjoyable for people every day.

Frustration-free web-based apps for collaboration, sharing information, and making decisions.

Basecamp®
Manage Projects
Used by millions for project management.

Highrise®
Manage Contacts
Know the people you do business with.

Backpack®
Share Internally
Simplify internal communications.

Campfire™
Work in Real-Time
Group chat rooms for your business.

Scroll down... ↓

Our book REWORK is a fresh approach to running a business. It's a *New York Times* and *Wall Street Journal* bestseller.

"If given a choice between investing in someone who has read REWORK or has an MBA, I'm investing in REWORK every time. A must read for every entrepreneur."

— Mark Cuban, co-founder HDNet, owner of the Dallas Mavericks

"The wisdom in these pages is edgy yet simple, straightforward, and proven. Read this book multiple times to help give you the courage you need to get out there and make something great."

— Tony Hsieh, CEO of Zappos.com

Case Studies

There are few more powerful tactics for establishing credibility than case studies of how your product or service has solved problems for your customers. Case studies demonstrate in detail that your solution has worked for others and allow the prospect to envision how it could work for them too.

Case studies can take many different formats that you can test. Although most companies use written documents or slide presentations, others, like Salesforce.com, use video case studies.

Salesforce + NBC Universal = [Like]

Watch how NBCUniversal has become a Social Enterprise by connecting sales teams and cross-selling for 20+ media properties.

Read more about NBCUniversal ›

Eric Johnson
VP, Sales Force Effectiveness, NBCUniversal   2:00

 NBCUniversal GROUPON Kimberly-Clark DELL   KAISER PERMANENTE.

See more customer success stories ›

Some companies use case studies as a gated lead-generation tool as well as for building credibility. That can generate leads for your sales team, but it can also discourage otherwise qualified prospects from learning more about your offering. The more information you gate, the less it spreads, and the less qualified your leads could become.

Admit it…how often have you filled in a form on a website with bogus information just to get past the gate? I've spoken to some aggressive sales companies that gate all their information. Often their most common lead name is Mickey Mouse, and the common zip code is 90210.

So, there's a balance between generating more leads and generating higher-quality leads. Before committing to an information-gating strategy, You Should Test That!

If you have any of these credibility indicators available, you should also test how and where to add them to your marketing communications. Although credibility indicators can be important in your prospect's decision-making, they're usually not the primary component of your value-proposition message. At WiderFunnel, we've often tested placement of credibility indicators and found them to be effective in a reference position outside of the main content for pages.

The placement changes completely for landing-page design, however, where credibility indicators can sometimes be very effective in the main content eye path.

Social Proof

Some social media zealots seem to think *social proof* is a new invention. On the contrary, it's been affecting people's decisions since the age of the caveman. Marketers, online and offline, have been using social proof techniques for decades. Social media technology has made it easier to use, as you'll see.

Remember when McDonald's had on its restaurant signs a tally of the number of billions of people served? That's a social proof tactic.

All those customers can't be wrong, right?

Why do dance clubs have waiting lines down the street when they're only at half capacity? Clearly, it's not providing a better purchase experience for those in line. Longer lineups tell passers-by that this is an in-demand spot.

You too can add social proof to your marketing communications through the effective tactics presented next.

Testimonials

In 1837, Hans Christian Andersen published the short story "The Emperor's New Clothes," which went on to be published in over 100 languages. One of the interesting observations about the story is how the throngs of people were happy to go along with the belief that the emperor's invisible clothing was a beautiful robe. This is the power of social influence.

Many social psychology studies in the twentieth century—notably those by Solomon Asch in the 1950s—have confirmed that people are influenced by the consensus opinions of people around them. These experiments show that people can be convinced to do and say very unusual things when a false belief is reinforced by a few peers. People will often change their opinion for no other reason than to match the opinions of others.

Social influence like this can be used to reinforce true beliefs, too! You can use this psychological flaw to your benefit by emphasizing all the people who agree with your message and support your products and services.

Shutterfly's testimonials, for example, are combined with realistic-looking photos of customers interacting with the product to provide strong social proof.

OUR CUSTOMERS LOVE SHUTTERFLY.
Don't take our word for it. See what they have to say.

" My family laughs and then cries when they open a photo book I've made for them. They love getting such amazing gifts. And, I love how easy they are to make. I can't go back to giving sweaters. "
- Dione, photo book maker since 2006

" They're not just pictures in a photo book - they're my most precious memories. This is who we are. "
- Susie, photo book maker since 2003

Testimonials have become a standard, trusted technique in the direct marketer's arsenal. But this doesn't mean you should blindly follow this "best practices" advice and plaster your page with testimonials. In some cases, testimonials have hurt conversion rates, especially where they may be perceived as artificial or contrived.

Client Logos

Even without written client testimonials, you may be able to use client logos to communicate endorsement as social proof. Using logos is generally more effective than listing clients' names. Rackspace combines client logos with links to testimonials, which adds even more verification to the social proof.

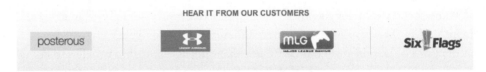

Social Media

Traditional testimonials are quickly being reinvented via social media. Using LinkedIn, Twitter, Facebook, and blog comments, you can collect followers, "Likes," and recommendations that provide social proof for your prospects.

Recommendations from social media overcome the most important problem with traditional testimonials: verification. With LinkedIn's company and product pages, your company's followers can now add recommendations, which are linked to their verified personal accounts. Microsoft's Windows Phone, for example, has 105 recommendations.

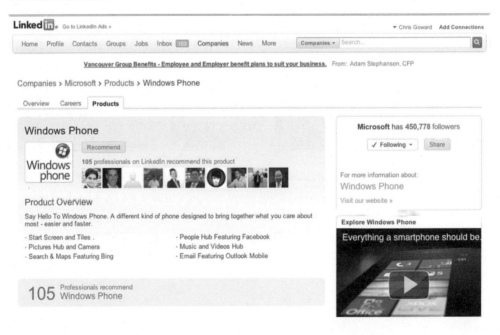

Herman B., Senior Account Manager at CRM Partners
Utrecht Area, Netherlands

Good, intuitive, plenty of apps, and CWR Mobility for Microsoft Dynamics CRM works great!

February 23, 2011 · Flag

Ram G., Project Leader at The Birchman Group
Madrid Area, Spain

Just the perfect mix for a personal & business device.

March 30, 2011 · Flag

If you don't have recommendations yet, try asking your repeat customers to add one to your company page. Make sure you thank them after they do, with a personal thanks or discount code for their next purchase.

The ubiquitous buttons for Facebook, Google+, Twitter, LinkedIn, Pinterest, and more are common social proof indicators you can use, too.

The many different forms of social media buttons are becoming a problem for businesses, though. Which ones should you include on your product pages? How many are too many? Do they clutter the page and distract from the main messages? These are all questions that can be answered through testing. Try testing the placement and number of social buttons, and see how they affect your sales.

Customer Ratings and Reviews

Much research has been done to prove the influence that ratings and reviews can have on purchase decisions. Amazon.com has been leading innovation in the field of customer reviews for many years.

Amazon was the first company to implement ratings of its reviews, then *meta reviews* or reviews of the reviews, and now ratings of the reviews of the reviews.

Comments

Track comments by e-mail

Showing 1-4 of 4 posts in this discussion   Sort: **Oldest first** | Newest first

Initial post: Jun 27, 2007 5:58:30 PM PDT

☑ Throckmorton Scribblemonger says:

What you're describing sounds remarkably like the state which Buddhists monks seek and attain - a feeling of oneness with all, purpose, and focus. Very interesting...

Reply to this post   Permalink | Report abuse | Ignore this customer
2 of 2 people think this post adds to the discussion. Do you? Yes No

In reply to an earlier post on Jul 4, 2007 4:34:17 AM PDT

☑ Erika Borsos says:

Yes, it does sound just like that. Vipassana meditation is also similar. Thank you for your comment. Erika

Reply to this post   Permalink | Report abuse | Ignore this customer
Do you think this post adds to the discussion? Yes No

In reply to an earlier post on Jul 4, 2007 4:34:23 AM PDT

[Deleted by the author on Jul 4, 2007 4:34:47 AM PDT]

Posted on Mar 23, 2010 4:00:15 PM PDT

☑ Jewels says:

Very good review. Koszonom szepen.;-)

Reply to this post   Permalink | Report abuse | Ignore this customer
Do you think this post adds to the discussion? Yes No

‹ Previous 1 Next ›

Phew…where does it stop?! And, how are other e-commerce retailers to keep up with this?

You may not have to.

Amazon has built its review system into one of its most important value-proposition benefits. I often go to Amazon to check the reviews of a book before taking it out of the library, for example, because I can be pretty sure Amazon will have more reviews than most sites.

But that may not be an important position for your company to own. There's a danger in copying what has worked for other companies without considering whether it reinforces your value proposition.

If you do need to add robust ratings and reviews, check out PowerReviews as an option. Many retailers, including Staples.com, use PowerReviews' e-commerce add-on to add rich review information to their product detail pages.

You should also test including ratings on your product-listing grid, as JC Penney has. This allows shoppers to quickly scan the product list and compare items using a social proof indicator.

Number of Customers

If you have a large customer base, you can test whether it's most effectively used as a primary or secondary value-proposition point. Rocket Lawyer, for example, uses the social proof of its 15 million customers in a landing-page headline as a primary value-proposition point.

LivePerson, on the other hand, adds its 17 million live chat engagements as a site-wide social proof indicator in its navigation bar.

Customer volume social proof

Celebrity Endorsements

Many companies today use celebrities to promote their brands. Depending on the target audience, celebrities can add credibility and social proof. Lots of people in certain target audiences trust celebrities' recommendations. MoneyMutual has built a thriving business with Montel Williams as its spokesperson since 2009.

Social proof indicators can be powerful credibility boosters. KISSmetrics, for example, places heavy emphasis on social proof indicators with industry-specific celebrity endorsements. Avinash Kaushik and Joanna Lord are both well-known celebrities with digital marketers.

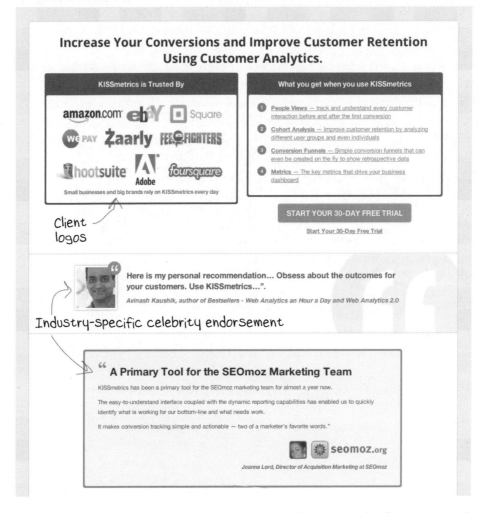

You should test using these elements on your home page, landing pages, and other marketing communications.

Personal Benefits vs. Business Benefits

If you're selling B2B solutions, you may be tempted to focus only on the benefits to the business. The logical reason that a person buys for a business is to solve the business's needs, right?

Don't make that mistake.

People are egocentric; they're looking for how a decision benefits them, even if the logical justification is how it benefits the business. Remember, people make a purchase emotionally and defend the purchase rationally.

This is different from egotism or narcissism. You don't need to have an overinflated opinion of yourself to be egocentric. It's normal for a person to think of how their decisions affect them before others. In fact, it's probably an evolutionary requirement.

Think about the emotional benefits you can offer to your customer as an individual within the business. Maybe it's peace of mind, reduced workload, time savings, stress reduction, respect from colleagues, an innovative image, recognition from upper management, or whatever.

One of the findings WiderFunnel has uncovered from our testing across industries is that people respond similarly, whether you're selling to B2B, B2C, C2C (consumer-to-consumer) or B2G (business-to-government) purchasers. We all have the same needs, wants, and aspirations, whether we're sitting in our office buying a network server or in our living room buying a summer vacation. People are people.

Costs

What would keep your prospect from buying from you?

The answer to that question tells you about your *perceived costs*. They're the reasons that keep your prospects from completing your desired action, whether that's becoming a lead or a customer.

Just like perceived features and benefits, costs can comprise tangibles and intangibles. *Tangible costs* are the monetary costs that your prospects consider to be part of the purchase, including direct and delivery pricing plus other associated costs.

Intangible costs are the flip side of intangible benefits. Examples include low credibility, inconsistent experience, missing social proof, uncertainty, and slightly less-than-professional copywriting. They can add real drag to your effectiveness.

Are intangibles real? It doesn't really matter. Your prospects may not be able to define the costs that keep them from buying, and the distinction is irrelevant if intangible costs are stopping them from buying. Whatever the blockage is, you need to uncover and clear it.

The Price

The direct cost of the product or service is the most straightforward for prospects to tally, but it can be the most complex for your business to set. In addition to the standard pricing strategy and methods your business uses to set your prices, there's also a powerful price psychology to consider. Pricing is a complex science, and discovering pricing insights can be a lot of fun!

Number-Sound Psychology

Research has shown that peoples' perception of the relative size of a number is influenced by the number's sounds. Vowel sounds produced nearer to the front of your mouth can seem smaller than sounds from the back of your throat. And fricatives like *f*, *s*, and *z* seem smaller than stops like *t* and *b*.

A study by researchers Keith Coulter and Robin Coulter published in the *Journal of Consumer Research* ("Small Sounds, Big Deals: Phonetic Symbolism Effects in Pricing," Vol 37, August 2010) demonstrated that these perceptions can cause people to make mistakes in their estimation of price discounts. Participants in the study were shown ads for ice cream, originally priced at $10. In one group, the ice cream was marked down to $7.66, which includes front-vowel and fricative-laced sixes. The other group was shown ice cream discounted to $7.22. Those in the $7.66 group perceived the price discount to be greater than the $7.22 group. In other words, a 23 percent discount seemed greater than a 28 percent discount because of the sound of the numbers.

It turns out that, in English, the numbers 3, 6, 7, and 8 create the impression of smallness compared to 1 and 2. You should test changing your prices ending in 1 or 2 to 3, 6, 7, or 8.

Price Font Size

Studies by the same researchers also showed that type size influences the perceived price magnitude. They found that a sale price is judged to be lower when it's shown in a smaller type size compared to the regular price. In fact, their results show that "the manner in which comparative price information is displayed can potentially be even more important than the magnitude of the price reduction itself." You should test reducing the type size of your sale-priced products.

The $.99 Price

We have been culturally conditioned to associate prices ending in 9 with discounts and better deals. Many retailers use round-number pricing to represent regular prices and .99, .97, or .95 for sales prices. To communicate low prices for your products, you should test price endings.

Chinese Number Perception

Vancouver, Canada, where the WiderFunnel head office is located, has a large Chinese population, and we're well attuned to the cultural implications of numbers and symbols. In Chinese culture, numbers can have strong meaning. Whereas 5, 6, and 7 are all considered somewhat unlucky, 4 is the number to avoid, because it sounds like the word for "death." Many of the newer apartment towers in Vancouver don't have floor numbers that include the number 4 (4, 14, and so on). They also skip 13, traditionally considered unlucky in Western culture, which means a tower numbered up to 50 floors may actually have only 35!

In a study in a New Zealand area with a high Chinese population, Steven Bourassa and Vincent Peng of the University of Louisville, Kentucky, showed that house numbers with unlucky Chinese numbers had relatively lower prices than those with lucky numbers ("Hedonic Prices and House Numbers: The Influence of Feng Shui," International Real Estate Review, 1999, Vol. 2, No. 1: 79–93).

Anchoring

The order in which you display prices influences your prospects' perception of their value. People can be primed to perceive prices as higher or lower by being exposed to other numbers, even if those priming numbers are unrelated and irrelevant.

In another study by Dan Ariely, he demonstrated this effect in a mock auction with his students. Before beginning the auction for items like bottles of wine and chocolate, he had the students write down the last two digits of their Social Security numbers. He discovered that students with higher-ending SSN numbers bid 60 to 120 percent higher during the auction.

Simply priming them with arbitrary higher numbers dramatically increased their willingness to pay. You can use this finding in your marketing by positioning your highest-priced packages before the economy packages, as CrazyEgg has done.

PRO	PLUS	STANDARD	BASIC
$99 /month*	$49 /month*	$19 /month*	$9 /month*
*Billed annually	*Billed annually	*Billed annually	*Billed annually
250,000 visits / month	100,000 visits / month	25,000 visits / month	10,000 visits / month
100 active pages	50 active pages	20 active pages	10 active pages
Hourly reporting	Hourly reporting	Daily reporting	Daily reporting
✓ Heatmap Report	✓ Heatmap Report	✓ Heatmap Report	✓ Heatmap Report
✓ Scrollmap Report	✓ Scrollmap Report	✓ Scrollmap Report	✓ Scrollmap Report
✓ Confetti Report	✓ Confetti Report	✓ Confetti Report	✓ Confetti Report
✓ Overlay Report	✓ Overlay Report	✓ Overlay Report	✓ Overlay Report
✓ List Report	✓ List Report	✓ List Report	✓ List Report
✓ Multiple Domains tracking	✓ Multiple Domains tracking	✓ Multiple Domains tracking	✓ Multiple Domains tracking
Sign Up Free	Sign Up Free	Sign Up Free	Sign Up Free
30-day Trial for $0	30-day Trial for $0	30-day Trial for $0	30-day Trial for $0

In countries that read from left to right, more people will view the larger pricing first with this layout. Once that highest price is anchored in their minds, the other packages seem relatively low.

Basecamp takes a different approach to anchoring by using a stacked pricing layout. This is even more likely to cause anchoring in all countries, but it reduces clarity by making feature comparisons between packages difficult.

If you have subscription packages with different prices, You Should Test That!

Consider these five new aspects for price points when adjusting and testing your pricing. There is a lot to test around pricing.

Exclusive Pricing

Traditional economic models that assume demand decreases reliably as price increases are flawed. In some cases, demand can actually be increased with higher pricing.

Social psychologist Robert Cialdini, author of the bestselling book *Influence: The Psychology of Persuasion* (Collins, 1998), says that this happens when price is used as a stand-in for quality. If your product is consulting, rare artwork, or other goods and services that are hard to compare with competition, raising prices can allow you to take the premium quality positioning in the market.

Higher prices can be a benefit in themselves, even if they don't imply higher quality. Luxury and premium priced items are often known to be of similar quality to lower priced options. Their owners want to be seen as being able to afford them.

A study of environmentally friendly shopping behavior published in the *Journal of Personality and Social Psychology* showed that consumers are more likely to buy green products when they're more expensive than other options. The "green premium" price is part of the appeal. These consumers want to be seen as making a sacrifice for the sake of the environment rather than just having the intrinsic motivation to "do the right thing." As the study's co-author, Vladas Griskevicius, a social psychologist at the University of Minnesota, says, "The modern alternative to being luxurious is spending extra money to broadcast that you are a pro-social, pro-environmental individual."

Delivery Cost

Why do so many websites hide their shipping costs?

Every shopper needs to know the total price including shipping, but on many websites, determining the shipping cost seems to require a Ph.D. in Investigative Economics. Perhaps the sites think that by hiding the shipping cost, people won't notice that they have to pay for shipping. Unfortunately for them and their shoppers, they're only causing frustration.

For shoppers, the only thing better than easy shipping costing is getting shipping for free! The most successful companies understand the power of free shipping. Look how prominent Zappos, Amazon, and Banana Republic make their free shipping offers.

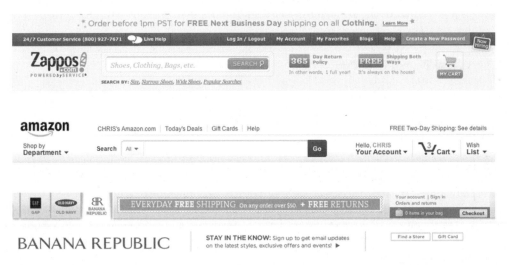

If you can remove the nagging question of shipping from your prospects' minds, you'll *free your customers* to buy. (Yes, pun intended.)

The Incredible Power of *Free*

The power of *free* goes beyond shipping costs. *Free* is the most powerful word in the conversion strategist's verbal arsenal.

In his excellent book *Predictably Irrational* (Harper Perennial, 2010), Dan Ariely shares the results of his experiments into peoples' irrational exuberance for free things. In one experiment, he and colleagues set up a stand offering two kinds of chocolates: gourmet Lindt truffles and ordinary Hershey's Kisses. They first priced the truffles at 15 cents each and the kisses at 1 cent each.

You might expect people to load up on both kinds of chocolates at those great prices! But the researchers added a twist: a sign above the table said, "One chocolate per customer." The customer had to make a choice.

Not surprisingly, more people chose to enjoy the Lindt truffle at such a bargain price. About 73 percent selected the truffle over the kiss.

Then, Ariely's team changed the prices to test the effect of *free*. When they reduced the price of each candy by one penny, customer behavior changed radically. With Lindt truffles priced at 14 cents and kisses for free, the percentage of customers choosing a kiss changed to 69 percent, up from 27 percent when priced at 1 penny. The relative value of each chocolate had remained the same, but that single penny price change for both options had more than doubled demand for the kiss!

Josh Kopelman of First Round Capital proposed the idea of the *penny gap* to illustrate this. His interest is in why business models with free services are more successful than those with even a tiny fee. The concept isn't limited to startups, though.

Traditional economic models assume that the demand curve is a straight line starting at $0 and declining steadily to the maximum price anyone would pay for a product.

Traditional economic model

This model assumes that the marginal difference in demand for the first penny of the price is the same as every other. In other words, each penny of price change has the same impact as the next on demand.

This isn't the case when you look at actual price-demand behavior. It turns out that the first penny has a many times greater effect than any other. The difference between charging $0 and $0.01 has a dramatic influence on demand.

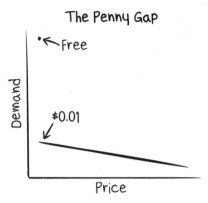

The penny gap

Look in your business model and offering for ways you can offer something free, and test the impact it can have on your demand.

I would refine the penny gap theory even more to include the other price inconsistencies you've already seen: number sounds, the $0.99 effect, and Chinese number perception.

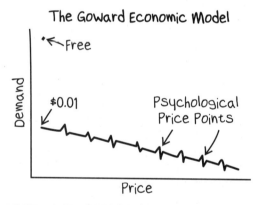

The Goward economic model

People's relationships with prices are much more complicated and interesting than economists have traditionally believed. Companies that test with their pricing and offers are gaining a competitive advantage by understanding these complex pricing relationships. You Should Test That!

Associated Costs

Gillette was the trailblazer of the *freemium* business model. The company found that a free razor-blade handle was an offer people couldn't refuse. By giving away the handle and charging for the blade, Gillette essentially started individuals on a subscription plan for ongoing blade replacement.

The model that began with Gillette many years ago hasn't changed much since, and it's still powerful, but people are more skeptical and discriminating than ever. Does your product or service require maintenance fees or ongoing purchases? Inkjet cartridges, disposable razor blades, batteries, software-support services, and broken shoelaces—your prospects have caught on to the total cost of ownership (TCO) concept and are considering it in their evaluation. If you can develop a TCO advantage, it can be a strong component of your value proposition to tip the purchase decision in your favor.

By saving your customers money over the long term, you can also support the value-proposition positioning that you have your prospects' interests in mind. You're the honest one who educates them and fully discloses your business strategy. This is a win-win opportunity to gain credibility and sales.

Okay, now that you've learned about all these value-proposition considerations that your prospects are bearing in mind, you need to apply them to your marketing.

What Is *Your* Value Proposition?

Your value proposition includes many features, benefits, and attributes. You couldn't possibly explain everything in every advertisement or landing page. Doing so would be overwhelming and unnecessary.

You need to focus and prioritize your message. Your most important features and benefits are those that are most important to your prospects and customers. That may seem obvious. But many companies instead emphasize the features that they added most recently or that were most difficult to add.

To find the important attributes of your products and services, you should look at your points of parity and points of difference from your prospect's perspective.

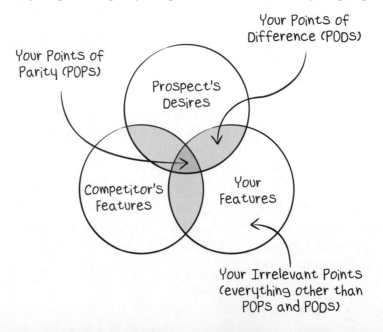

Your *points of parity* (POPs) are the features you offer that are important to your prospects but that you also share with your competitors. Think of them as the basic entry requirements to the game. Your prospects need to know that you offer the POPs, but emphasizing them won't impress anyone.

Your points of difference (PODs) are where you can win the game. They're the features that are important to your prospects and not available with your competitors. These are the features you can emphasize that will move your prospects to action. They're your differentiators.

But PODs aren't created equal. Some will be more important than others and some will only be important to certain customer segments.

Test Your Value Proposition

No matter how much effort and research you've put into your value-proposition points, You Should Test That! At WiderFunnel, we often run experiments on landing pages and home pages in which we create and test value-proposition alternatives. When combined with data from surveys of customer and market perceptions, these tests add quantitative validity to the qualitative insights. The learning from these value-proposition tests often generates powerful marketing insights that impact the overall marketing strategy.

For example, one client of ours is a large organization in higher education. In one of our ongoing series of tests, we worked with the client's team to define four different overall positioning statements for one of their schools.

We created four landing pages with the same layout and design for each and just varied the headline and copywriting in each.

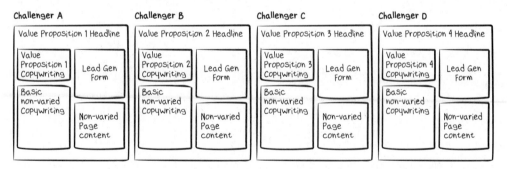

Don't underestimate the power of a few important words. In this case, the winning value-proposition positioning statement improved the new-applicant conversion rate by 40 percent!

Not only does the marketing team have a better-performing landing page, but they now have a positioning statement that has been shown to persuade more of their prospects to act. They came away with a greater understanding of the motivational triggers to use throughout their marketing communications.

Each of the value-proposition components in this chapter can be tested. To start testing your value proposition, select your most important entry page to test strategic variations of your tangible features, intangible benefits, and costs.

 Note: For more discussion about value proposition, start a conversation at `YouShouldTestThat` `.com/Value-Proposition`. In the next chapter, you'll see how to make your value proposition relevant to your target audience. You'll learn how to test your landing pages and conversion funnel with messages that give your visitors exactly what they're looking for. This includes tactics for maximizing the relevance to the source media, your prospects' needs, seasonality, and competitive actions.

6   Optimize for Relevance

A squirrel dying in front of your house may be more relevant to your interests right now than people dying in Africa.

—Mark Zuckerberg

Your prospects are animals. They hunt, forage, and consume just like their wild counterparts. Only today, they're no longer roaming the savannah searching for wild deer or prairie shrews. They're on their laptops, tablets, and phones hunting for information, entertainment, and consumables to buy.

Animals have evolved refined biological algorithms that constantly evaluate feedback from their environment to adjust their hunting paths. If the scent of their prey weakens on the path they're following, they return to a previous location to find a stronger scent path. This algorithm has been refined to locate paths where the scent of their prey gradually increases. This is what we think of as the *scent trail* foraging behavior.

Your prospective customers use a similar mental algorithm when searching for the online information they need. They may be engaged in a focused search with a particular need in mind. Or they may have been interrupted by a message that triggered a desire response and began a hunt down a foraging path. Either way, once they're on a hunt, they use primal foraging behavior to identify the information and products they need.

You can enable this hunting behavior in your marketing by providing the scent trail prospects are looking for. Your effectiveness at capturing and maintaining your prospects' attention from interest through to purchase is, to a great extent, determined by your skill at creating a strong and encouraging information scent trail.

In this chapter, you'll learn how to create that scent trail, called *relevance*, to gain more conversions, customers, and revenue. You'll see, with examples, how to maximize these five areas:

- Relevance throughout the marketing funnel
- Relevance to the source media
- Relevance to the target audience
- Relevance for the competitive environment
- Relevance to the visitor's navigation preferences

We begin by looking at how your website fits into your marketing funnel.

Marketing Funnel Relevance

Your marketing funnel begins long before your prospect arrives on your website, and your messages should maintain relevance throughout.

 Relevance The relevance of your page is a function of how closely it matches your prospects' expectations and perceived needs. Ask yourself, "Does your page relate to what the prospects thought they were going to see?"

If you look from the perspective of your website, your landing page is the first point of contact with a prospect; but to your visitor, it's just one step along a foraging path. The scent trail needs to maintain its strength to carry them to your desired action of becoming a lead or customer.

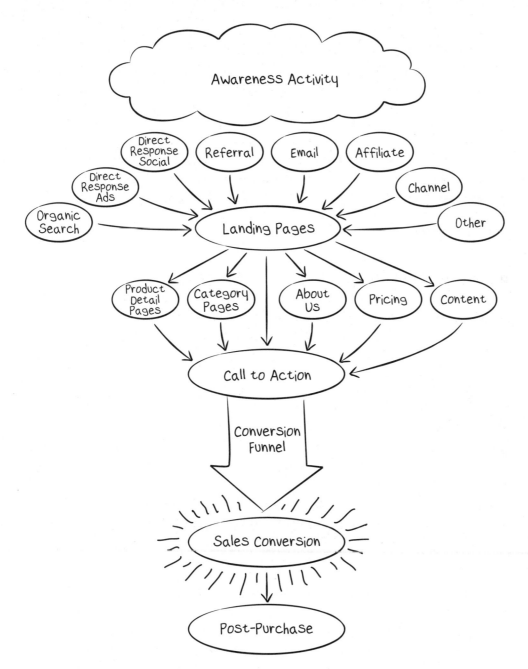

Your prospect's funnel includes all of the touch points:

- Their original awareness of your brand and solution
- The action-promoting interception via an ad, email, social interaction, or other referral source

- Your landing page
- The exploration of your company, products, and services
- Your conversion transaction via email, online forms, phone calls, bricks and mortar, channel partners, or other response channel
- Your salespeople (for lead generation)
- The post-purchase experience

A consistent scent trail through all of these touch points can become a positive experience that creates brand equity. An inconsistent experience with reduced relevance creates dissonance, which can harm the brand and reduce conversions.

Source Relevance

The martial art of jiu-jitsu teaches fighters to use an opponent's momentum rather than fight against their movements. It's much easier and requires less strength to pull someone in the direction they're moving rather than push them in a new direction. It's the martial art of efficiency. Use minimal force for maximum effect.

Although clearly it's counterproductive to view your prospects as opponents, you can still use jiu-jitsu's principles of "unifying with the other" to create more effective marketing campaigns. By acknowledging and unifying with your prospects' momentum, you can guide them to your conversion.

Visitors to your ad or website arrive from somewhere, and you can take that source medium into account to understand their intentions. They may have been searching for a product or service like yours or been interrupted while doing something unrelated. In either case, they were motivated by the ad's message and responded to your call to action.

Once they've arrived and are viewing your message, you need to keep your visitors engaged and motivate them to move to the next step in your conversion funnel. What is the first thing you should say to them?

Some believe you should state all your benefits in your headline: "Save Time! Save Money! Satisfaction Guaranteed!" it would yell.

But that's often ineffective. The first problem with such headlines is that their generic benefits are overused. So many products claim to save people time and money that those claims have lost their effect. You're better off using your specific advantages.

The second problem is that the scent trail is lost. You need to satisfy the hunter's scent trail before selling your benefits. Your prospect's primal urge to follow the search scent is strong, and you should satisfy it first.

Relevance to Ad Messages

Ads that interrupt people are much less effective than ads with high relevance. This is why ads for relevant keywords on search engines get vastly higher click-throughs and conversions than ads on social media sites. When people are on a search engine, they're in a frame of mind that looks for a solution. They're looking to sniff out a scent trail to find their goal.

When they're on Facebook, they're looking for photos of their friends. They're seeking entertainment and connection, not your product. In that mind frame, your ad is a nuisance!

Recently, I came across a video-review website in a search for a video-editing tool for an employee. What I found is a good example of both good and not-so-good relevance.

The ad, for a tool called PowerDirector 10, was highly relevant to the site and a typical visitor's intention for being there. Most visitors to that site are looking for video-editing software to make movies. The ad's message, "Make the Perfect Movie," implied that the marketer had a clear understanding of the target audience's needs.

The ad's bold design and clear value proposition caught my attention. I clicked the ad, interested to see how the site would pay off that promise. Unfortunately, the landing page was a disappointing disruption in the scent trail.

Headline loses scent trail

Nothing about how to "Make the Perfect Movie"

This landing page could have improved relevance with this headline:

"Make the Perfect Movie with PowerDirector 10 Deluxe"

I'd advise this advertiser: You Should Test That!

Then they should improve relevance even more by testing how the copywriting could fulfill that "Make the Perfect Movie" promise.

Once your prospects have shown enough interest to click your ad, your most prominent message in the following steps should match the ad message. Any message mismatch tells the visitor that they may have a weakened or lost scent trail and should return to the previous page or search engine.

Relevance to Search Keywords

Visitors who come to your website from search engines are in a better mindset for action than those from most other advertising media. Search-engine visitors are actively looking for a solution or information to solve their needs.

Your challenge is to give searchers the strong scent trail they need to continue through to your website and conversion funnel. The relevance of your ads and landing page to the keyword phrases is an important part of that relevance.

Synonyms Are Invisible

Your visitors may use different words to describe your product than you would, and you'll create a more effective scent trail by using their language. If you offer "Legal Will & Testament Services," your prospects may not use those words to find you. They'll probably search for something like "create a will" or "make a will" or "download will template."

It's important to understand that even if what you say means the same thing as their search term, synonyms or similar phrases don't maintain a scent trail. They can be as good as invisible to the searcher. The reason: the searcher isn't processing all the words for understanding.

An example search for "create a will" shows that most ads have lost the scent trail before the prospect even clicks them.

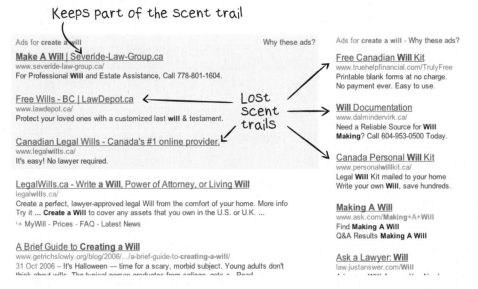

The most closely matched ad says "Make a Will," which is at least 50 percent similar to "create a will," so it's doing better than the competition. You should carefully target your ads to match as closely as possible the search terms your prospects are using.

Unfortunately, the closest-matching ad's landing page loses the plot.

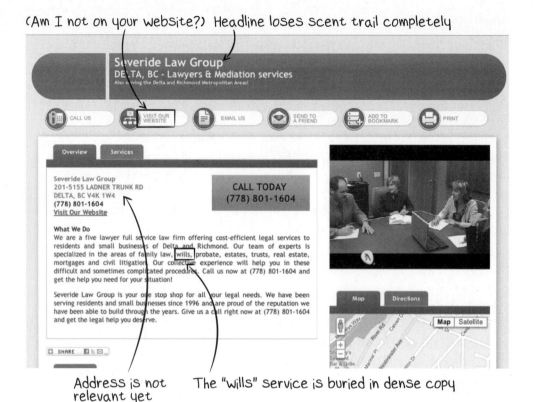

(Am I not on your website?) Headline loses scent trail completely

Address is not relevant yet

The "wills" service is buried in dense copy

This company may employ excellent lawyers and probably provides a will-creation service that some prospects are looking for, but the scent trail is lost. Among other problems, this page has very low relevance to the words the prospect used for searching and the ad they clicked to get to the page.

This company seems to be using a generic overview page as a landing page. It wouldn't take much effort to create a more relevant experience by at least directing ads to specific service pages.

This problem is common. At WiderFunnel, we see companies of all sizes that send much of their expensive traffic to their home page rather than relevant product pages or, even better, customized campaign landing pages. Creating relevant landing-page experiences doesn't have to be burdensome, but it does take some planning.

If I were to help this firm improve its campaign conversion rate, at least one of the challenger test variations would focus on improving the relevance of the landing page.

Subhead introduces their (assumed) value proposition

Headline has high relevance to the ad and search term

Relevant next step in the call to action

This new layout test includes several important changes that focus the content on the most relevant value-proposition statements. I'd recommend that the firm have a landing page like this for all the common services potential clients might search for, such as trusts, probate, and so on.

I would recommend testing more than just this one challenger against the control page, too. Testing only two pages at a time gives you some potential for learning and improvement, but it's limited. This company could test plenty of other hypotheses to increase relevance. For example:

- Adding an image of a sample will document
- Adding an image of a typical customer
- Copy focused on the will-creation process
- A headline that speaks to the risks of not having a will
- Replacing the video with a will-specific message
- Adding social proof with testimonials of people who have had wills created
- And lots more!

A conversion champion who thinks from the perspective of the visitor will find many ways to test elements that increase relevance to the source media.

Pattern Matching

When people are in search mode, they switch from a processing mind frame to a pattern-matching mind frame. A processing mind frame takes significantly more time, energy, and mental bandwidth than pattern matching. A person on a search doesn't have time for all that processing. They just need to find their goal as quickly as possible so they can move on to the next task.

To illustrate how this pattern-matching system works, imagine that you're searching for a solution but you can't understand the text because the site is written in a language you're not familiar with. For example, let's replace a set of search ads with words written in an Inuit dialect called Inuktitut, which is only used in the far Canadian north. (If you do understand Inuktitut, please bear with me for this analogy.)

Imagine that you're looking for a solution to this phrase (translation: "Where's the toilet?"):

ᓇᐅᕝ ᐊᓇᖅᓯ

You enter the search term into your Inuktitut search engine and see a set of ads that looks like this:

ᑐᑭᓯᐊᕈᑎᑦᑕᐅᑦ
www.ask.com

ᓇᐅᕝ ᐁᑯ ᐳᑦ
www.allexperts.com

ᐳᑭᖅᑕ ᓴᕐᓯᐊ
www.question.com

ᓇᐅᕝ ᐊᓇᖅᓯ
www.diaroogle.com

ᓂᖅ ᐊᒻᒪ ᓴᖅ
www.wolframalpha.com

I'll bet you found the most relevant ad to click pretty easily. You didn't even need to understand the words to find the best result. You just used the pattern-matching mental process.

People's brains are extraordinarily good at pattern matching, but it can become a liability in their search results. If a prospect searches for "create a will" they could miss a great solution just because it's worded differently. An ad that says "Create a Will" has much higher relevance and is more likely to be clicked than another that says "Personalized Legal Contracts," even though both ads could lead to the same type of service.

Dynamic Keyword Insertion

Search engines provide a feature called *dynamic keyword insertion (DKI)* to help automate the inclusion of keywords in ad text. You can use this feature to have a searcher's search terms automatically inserted into your ads. A search for "leather wallets," for example, shows the contrast in relevance between ads with keywords inserted and those without. Which do you think appear most relevant to a pattern-matching searcher?

Dynamic keyword insertion can increase relevance!

Ads for **leather wallets**   Why these ads?

Leather Wallets | AspinalOfLondon.com
www.aspinaloflondon.com/**Leather-Wallets**
Classic **Leather Wallets** By Aspinal. Free Express Shipping to USA!

Full Grain **Leather** Bags | Saddleback**Leather**.com
www.saddleback**leather**.com/
Handmade Men's **Leather** Bags Built To Outlast You. 100 Year Guarantee!
120 people +1'd this page
↳ Briefcases - Gadget Sleeves - Laptop Bags - Wallets

Leather Wallets | ebay.ca
www.ebay.ca/
Fantastic Prices On **Leather Wallets**. Buy & Sell Today.

This automated keyword insertion can be useful for large search campaigns where manual customization is too time-consuming, but you also have to set up your campaign carefully to avoid inserting keywords that you can't deliver on.

Armpit Sweat Pads
Find **Armpit Sweat Pads**
save up to 50% by visiting us now!
www.Sport-Outdoor.best-price.com

Or worse:

DKI Fail!

Ad for **used ladies**   Why this ad?

Used Ladies - Fantastic Prices On **Used Ladies** | ebay.ca
www.ebay.ca/
Deal With Canadians And Save.

> **Note:** You can find more examples of funny dynamic keyword insertion fails and more resources at http://YouShouldTestThat.com/Relevance.

Whether you choose to use DKI or to manually set up relevant ads, you should make sure the relevant messages carry through to your landing pages.

Relevance to Emails

If relevance to ads and search is important, providing a relevant experience in your email campaigns is even more so. You know a lot more about members of your email database than about new website visitors; and with a little forethought, you can provide an awesomely customized experience.

For example, an email campaign from Banana Republic in mid-April created seasonal relevance by including a reference to tax season (although I would debate whether that creates a desirable brand connection).

It could have been even made more relevant by customizing it to the recipient's gender. The web page has the user's purchase history and, assuming it has seen a pattern of women's clothes purchases, could use that information to show more relevant imagery and emphasize the link to women's clothes.

The 40 percent discount offer is compelling, though. The call to action isn't prominent, but if the reader is in the market for new office wear, she may be motivated enough to put effort into finding the link.

She probably has questions that the email didn't answer, such as which items are included and what the "Up To" part of the email headline means. Will this offer apply to the cute dress she's had her eye on? Will she get the full 40 percent discount?

Unfortunately, once she clicks the link, relevance is lost.

The landing page has no mention of the offer, the products the discount applies to, or the prospect's unique discount code.

Even after clicking through to the product category page, she sees no sign of which products are included in the sale and what the discount rate is. The shopper may have some interest, but the effort of figuring out the offer and the confusion over the missing relevance has added an unnecessary barrier for her to overcome.

When creating offers, you should plan the entire experience for visitors. Don't make them figure out how your offer works. Answer their questions when they're thinking of them, and create a strong scent trail—they will reward you.

Three Ways to Create Landing-Page Source Relevance

To maximize landing-page relevance to your search advertising, you need to consider the keywords and ad copy. You can take three approaches—targeting, customization, and standardization:

Targeting   You can direct each of your ads to the most relevant landing page that matches the search keywords and ad copy. If your site already uses relevant landing pages, this can be the easiest way to improve relevance, compared to sending all ads to a generic landing page or your home page.

If you don't have matching landing pages already created for targeting, there will be initial setup work involved in building the relevant pages. You should consider the maintenance cost of updating the pages and build them using templates to minimize that maintenance effort.

Dynamic Customization If the majority of your landing-page content is relevant to all of your incoming ads and keywords, you can increase relevance by including dynamic headlines or other text snippets to strengthen the scent trail. This can be done very easily with a few lines of code that detect the source of the incoming visitors.

Dynamic customization can be an easy way to boost relevance, but it can become unwieldy if more than a few small pieces of customization are needed. If the overall product or service needs to be customized, targeting could be easier.

Standardization If you have many minor variations in your target keywords and ads, you may find that aggregating them into larger, similar target groups can be more profitable than creating many landing pages. Targeting and customization may not provide enough of a conversion-rate boost to justify the added complexity and cost.

Standardization is also useful for testing overall value-proposition and positioning approaches for your entire audience. If your incoming traffic is split into too many smaller groups with targeting or customization, each group may become too small and divergent to test your main messages meaningfully.

If you have to choose between testing your overall value-proposition position and targeting, you should begin with overall message testing with the largest traffic group you can aggregate. Then, once you have refined your main messages, test the added benefit of message customization and targeting.

Target Audience Relevance

Great copywriters seek to understand the target audience before they write a single word. Great conversion champions do the same. Understanding your audience will help you answer important questions about your pages, like these:

- Do your messages meet your prospects' needs?
- Does the page content match what they expect to see?
- Is your value proposition appealing to them?
- Are your calls to action appropriate for their buying behavior?

Without understanding your audience, you won't be able to evaluate aspects like these, and your hypotheses will be less likely to make a positive impact.

Customer Segmentation

Your target audience isn't all alike. Your customer base may consist of distinct groups who have unique needs. Segmenting your audience can be a way to tailor your message more closely to your prospects' needs.

Here are a few ways to do that:

- **Database Segmentation** If you know the average order value for a customer, you can test bundle offers within their range, or slightly higher, to find out if you can move them up. Or, if you know that visitors have previously attended one of your webinars, you can relate an upcoming webinar or white paper to their interest.

- **Ad Source Segmentation** By detecting the paid search keywords and ads that brought your visitors to your site, you can make inferences about their interests and stage in the purchase-decision cycle and customize your landing page with an appropriate offer.

- **Media Source Segmentation** Visitors from social media are in a different mindset than those from search or email campaigns. Social media visitors usually need a more entertainment-oriented or early-stage call to action, whereas search landing pages can be more directive and email landing pages can be very focused.

- **Landing-Page Segmentation** Once visitors have reached your website, you can provide links to segment-specific content and offers.

The more you know about your reader, the more relevant your messages can be.

There are drawbacks to segmentation, though. It adds message maintenance costs, can reduce relevance by labeling your prospects, and can overcomplicate your pages with unnecessary decision-making.

Maintenance Costs

Segmentation adds time and complication to your message management. Don't just segment your messages because you've heard it's a good idea. The value of segmentation depends on the audience. The key question to ask yourself is, "Are there distinct segments that have unique needs and need unique messaging?"

Consider the cost: if you have six products, you have a minimum of six pages to maintain and update. No problem, right? But if you have six products that each have three customer segments with unique messaging, you have at least 18 unique pages to manage. You can test whether offering uniquely segmented messages for each audience improves conversions and justifies the added maintenance cost.

Labeling Risk

If you've decided to test segmenting your messages on your pages, think about the labels you use to segment. Just because you refer to a segment as "IT Professional" doesn't mean your visitors identify with that label. An individual in that segment may think of herself as a network administrator or a systems analyst or a web developer!

An affiliate network, for example, could segment its audience as two groups: Affiliates and Vendors.

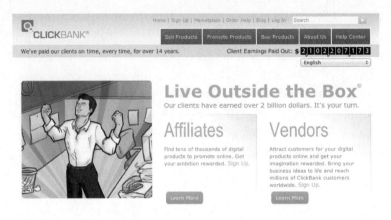

But what does someone in the Vendor audience think of himself as? Maybe he thinks he's an advertiser or marketer or something else. What about the Affiliate group? Maybe an affiliate thinks of herself as a publisher or a blogger. Even with the best intention for using segmentation, you can inadvertently reduce relevance by using your internal labels for people.

You should test the labels you use for your audience segments and consider carefully whether segmentation enhances or reduces your messages' relevance. Targeting your segments at the source whenever possible will also minimize labeling risk.

Decision Complication

Your landing pages should minimize decision-making for your prospects. By adding a segmentation decision, you risk confusing and complicating their decision before they have enough motivation. Your prospects may also wonder why they're being forced to choose a different path than others and will often open both paths to find out whether the other segments receive better offers.

If the messages for each audience aren't significantly different or justifiable, you'll get better results by creating a more compelling landing page that applies to all segments.

Call-to-Action Relevance

Are your prospects ready to buy immediately, or do they need to gather more information first? Are they looking for a quote, or do they prefer to collect more data?

Your prospects have expectations for the type of action they want to take next. By testing the types of calls to action to emphasize, you can make dramatic improvements in your results.

Think back to the PowerDirector 10 landing-page experience earlier in this chapter. In addition to losing the scent trail from the banner ad, the landing page assumes too much about the visitor's motivation level.

Clicking a banner ad indicates a low level of interest—perhaps only curiosity. By confronting the visitor with an immediate "Sell! Sell! Sell!" message, the landing page disconnects from the visitor's need.

The PowerDirector 10 landing-page experience would have more success if it paid off what the visitor was looking for. For example, it could provide helpful tips for how to use their software to make the perfect movie or emphasize features to support that promise.

At the very least, the landing-page headline should match the ad, even if the rest of the page is an unchangeable template for many products. But it would be well worth the effort to rethink this landing-page experience to create a more relevant solution payoff.

There's a balance to be struck that provides enough helpful information to keep your prospect engaged, while positioning your product as the solution to your prospect's needs and giving a strong reason to convert into a lead or customer.

With your ads and landing pages, you should test the spectrum between relevant, helpful content and hard-hitting calls to action to find the balance that maximizes conversions and revenue.

Tone Relevance

Thirteen-year-old girls respond to very different words, images, and design than 45-year-old corporate buyers. Different target audiences tolerate and respond to varying degrees of marketing messages.

In WiderFunnel's testing, we've seen distinct target audience groups, like software developers and data analysts, who have very sensitive marketing detectors and are turned off quickly. A classic example is a test we ran on a trial software-download page for Safe Software. The target audience of GIS professionals rejected one design we created that included some elements that have worked well in other scenarios, such as testimonials, a hero shot, and a curved arrow.

The underperforming page

That marketing "best practices" challenger even underperformed the original page. In this case, a minimalist design without elements that set off marketing alarm bells increased trial software downloads by 15.5 percent!

> " I don't know how you people did it, but you have created a nearly flawless spatial data conversion product that is **flexible and not intimidating to use.** Now this work is no longer rocket surgery! "
>
> Richard Clement,
> State of Alaska, Department of Natural Resources

Note: For Linux or Unix, please contact eval@safe.com or 604-501-9985 x261

The winning trial software-download page

Ralph Waldo Emerson said, "Who you are speaks so loudly, I can't hear what you're saying." Fortunately, with your marketing, you can test how the tone of your message affects your audience. The following case study shows an example of how testing the design tone to appeal to a particular target audience can lead to dramatic improvements in relevance and results.

Case Study: Multivariate Testing Increases Conversions by 162 Percent for W3i.com, an Application Network

W3i is a leader in monetization and user-acquisition solutions for free-mium apps. The company has an experienced app marketing team and the technology to optimize revenue and user retention.

W3i gets traffic from various sources, including its owned and operated sites Freeze.com, Screensaver.com, Wallpapers.com, and Profile-Pimp.net. It has distributed over 700 million applications since inception and averages 7 million app installs each second.

The Business Need

W3i wanted to increase the conversion rate on Profile Pimp, a site that features a free desktop application for customizing social media profiles. The application generates cut-and-paste HTML code for MySpace profiles and comes preloaded with backgrounds, layouts, graphics, music, and more.

Using a combination of paid, organic, and affiliate traffic-generation strategies, Profile-Pimp.net receives a significant number of visitors and a conversion rate well above industry standards. In an effort to increase the conversion rate, W3i's own optimization efforts had produced conversion lifts of up to 16 percent.

The Challenges

Like many organizations that create, design, and launch A/B/*n* split testing in-house, W3i eventually hit a conversion rate plateau. Despite some initial conversion-rate lift, the web marketing team at W3i saw subsequent rounds of testing result in the conversion rate leveling out.

W3i recognized that it needed to use the expertise of an external conversion-optimization specialist services firm to create more meaningful hypotheses and design test-page variations that would convert more visitors into users.

The Solution

W3i engaged WiderFunnel to develop a testing strategy guaranteed to increase the conversions on Profile Pimp.

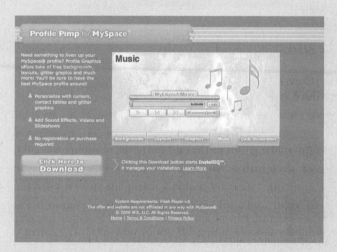

The Profile Pimp control landing page

Continues

Case Study: Multivariate Testing Increases Conversions by 162 Percent for W3i.com, an Application Network *(Continued)*

WiderFunnel evaluated the free application's landing page, previous test results, web analytics, and pay-per-click data to identify conversion-optimization opportunities. Based on their findings, the team at WiderFunnel concluded that multivariate testing provided the best opportunity to increase conversions. WiderFunnel developed a test plan including hypotheses, wireframes, graphic design, and copy, and implemented a multivariate test.

The team understood that the target audience of teenage girls responded to different motivators than other audiences. WiderFunnel's conversion strategists, designers, and copywriters crafted challenger variations that matched the expectations of what it took to be "cool" to these girls.

By dividing the test page into three variable-content boxes, WiderFunnel produced 44 page combinations to determine the optimal design and content that would generate the highest installation conversion rate.

The Result: Conversion Rate Lift of 162 Percent

Out of the 44 test page variations, 43 beat W3i's original control page. Not only that, but 36 of variations generated a conversion-rate lift of more than 95 percent. The top-performing variation achieved a 162 percent lift over the original control!

The winning test-page variation

As this case study showed, by understanding your audience, you can create more relevant landing-page experiences that will produce significant lift in results. You can also test different types of experiences to get quantitative knowledge about your visitors' needs, wants, and interests.

The relevance of your ads and landing pages is just the beginning of the conversion funnel for your prospects. You need to maintain relevance throughout the entire conversion funnel.

Navigation Relevance

Can your prospects intuitively see and find your products and services that meet their needs? Can they locate your products using navigation methods they're accustomed to? Some of your prospects like to find products using search on websites. Others like to browse through categories. Some look for product names or descriptions in text links. Others click images. Some are deal hunters. Others are spec seekers. Does your website navigation facilitate all styles, or is it oriented toward one preference?

You increase navigation relevance by displaying product and navigation options that get your prospects to their desired products easily and accurately. As an example, Walmart's mobile site forces visitors to use search alone to find their products. The default navigation includes only the following:

- A daily special (which is out of stock today, at 8:04 a.m.!)
- Sale items (which they call *rollbacks*)
- Local advertised specials
- Pharmacy refills
- Photo printing
- Order tracking

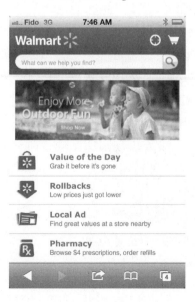

There's no department list to choose from. This ignores the types of visitors who prefer to browse within departments or product categories rather than using search.

What if I'm looking to browse a product category—say, for summer clothing? First I need to think about a particular type of item I might want: for example, "summer shorts." The resulting search results page shows one of the limitations of relying on search.

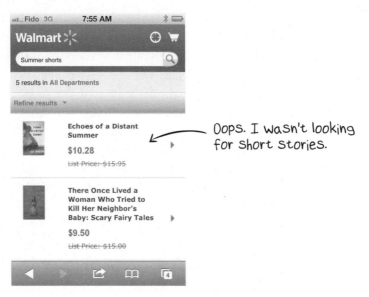

That search term has other meanings that clearly aren't relevant to my need for beachwear!

Incidentally, Walmart's desktop site does an excellent job of including departmental navigation and search options.

If I navigate to the mobile rollbacks page, it shows a good example of a departmental browsing navigation option.

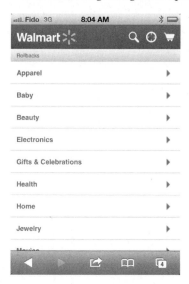

If I were Walmart, I would hire WiderFunnel to test the current mobile home page against new challenger pages. One challenger we could test would facilitate browsing by department as well as search.

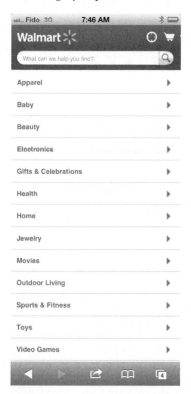

We could also test a hybrid that included specials and offers plus a link to browse by department.

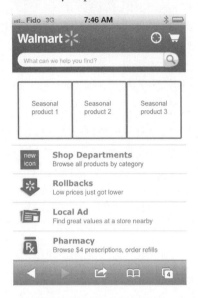

I can think of many more challenger permutations we could test as well! Once you identify a conversion problem, you can imagine an unlimited variety of ways to solve it. By testing many variations and iterations, you can find the optimized page that provides the most relevant navigation experience for your prospects.

The following case study details a test in which WiderFunnel created dramatically different variations of navigation and product-merchandising options, with significant lift in e-commerce sales as a result.

Case Study: GPS Central's Home Page Conversion Optimization Increases Retail Sales by 15 Percent

Based in Calgary, Canada, GPS Central has risen to be a major player in the highly competitive GPS retail market space. The company has established strong relationships with top-tier suppliers, carrying an extensive range of leading recreational, automotive, and marine GPS products for consumer and business markets.

GPS Central operates the `http://gpscentral.ca` online store and an offline retail location. It's also aggressively expanding its online presence in the United States and internationally.

The Business Need

Widespread adoption of GPS products, the proliferation of GPS technology providers, and the ever-growing presence of online retail channels have put severe pressure on end-user prices. Faced with thinning margins and increasingly fickle consumers, GPS Central recognized that delivering an impeccable online visitor experience had become a necessity.

The GPS Central management team had hired a creative agency to redesign the company's website and was about to launch the new design when they were introduced to WiderFunnel. Although the GPS Central team loved the look of the newly designed website, they were concerned about hurting sales by implementing it without testing. The team was particularly nervous about the new home page and didn't know how it would affect sales conversions. They believed that a conversion-optimization testing strategy would minimize the risk of hurting revenue and also provide a reliable method for ongoing improvement.

The Challenges

The GPS Central management team knew they needed expert guidance to tackle their unique challenges:

Impact on search engine optimization (SEO) efforts. The company had invested heavily in SEO for its website and needed to ensure that its efforts wouldn't be negatively impacted by conversion-optimization testing.

Dual role of the home page. The home page also served as a landing page for the company's PPC campaigns. The test structure needed to take this dual role into account.

Integration with third-party e-commerce technology. As a NetSuite user, GPS Central anticipated technical challenges tracking purchases during an A/B/n or multivariate test.

Faced with these unique challenges, the GPS Central team acknowledged the need for outsourced conversion-optimization expertise.

The Solution

On the advice of their SEO agency, the GPS Central team chose to work with WiderFunnel to develop and execute a conversion-optimization strategy for the company's home page. WiderFunnel handled the project from end to end, beginning by analyzing website metrics and ad campaigns, and then developing test hypotheses, designing, copywriting, coding, assisting with NetSuite technical integration, and launching the test—all while ensuring compatibility with SEO efforts.

Continues

Case Study: GPS Central's Home Page Conversion Optimization Increases Retail Sales by 15 Percent *(Continued)*

WiderFunnel planned the test to include the original page in a controlled A/B/*n* test. A total of three home-page layouts were created and tested against the original (control) design.

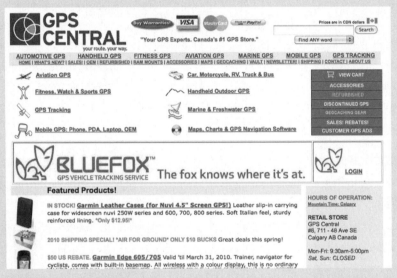

The GPS Central control home page

An A/B/*n* test structure was selected in order to test dramatically different layout approaches and establish a strong baseline.

To ensure a consistent visitor experience, WiderFunnel's variation pages maintained the tone of the existing graphic-design treatment. The team focused on layout and copy modifications that improved the effectiveness of merchandising attractiveness, value proposition communication, and content relevance to the incoming advertising copy.

Variation A: "Category Rows"

This design organized product categories into rows of subcategory thumbnails, thereby creating a comparatively long page.

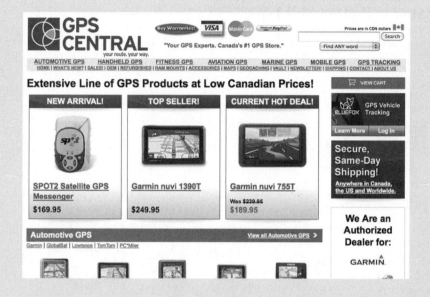

Variation B: "Images and Tabs"

This variation made category navigation highly visual with a 4×2 grid of large images using up most of the above-the-fold real estate.

Continues

Case Study: GPS Central's Home Page Conversion Optimization Increases Retail Sales by 15 Percent *(Continued)*

Variation C: "Left Column"

In this variation, category navigation was added to the left, and the most popular products were featured as a grid of thumbnails.

The Result: 15 Percent Increase in Sales

All three variations outperformed the original home page in sales conversion rate. The winner, Variation B: "Images & Tabs," lifted sales by 15 percent.

By making conversion-rate optimization an integral part of its website redesign process, GPS Central was able to reduce risk and even capture revenue that it might not have realized by simply implementing its new design. The winning variation is now the new home page, and ongoing testing can continue the improvement.

As you can see, by testing to improve the relevance of your marketing for your audience, you can make a huge difference in conversion rates.

The final factor this chapter considers is relevance to your competitive environment.

Competitive Relevance

How does your value proposition stack up against competitors? If you're like most companies, you create your ads and landing pages by comparing several options beside each other. You may lay them out on a boardroom table to choose the creative option that is most appealing.

But do you lay out your creative beside your competitors' ads too? Do you modify your messages based on competitive activity?

Your competitors' value proposition and messages impact your conversion rates directly and should be considered in your planning process. Take a look at a search for "trademark lawyer" as an example. These two ads show significantly different pricing.

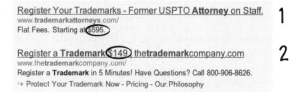

The first landing page, for TrademarkAttorneys.com, needs to work hard to justify its 4× price difference over The Trademark Company. It needs to add a lot more value proposition to give a compelling reason why its service is worth the price. The company's landing page falls short, though.

The second landing page, for The Trademark Company, is far from perfect, but at least it maintains the scent trail with the price in the headline. And with a price that's 25 percent of the competition's, the company has a strong head start on building its value proposition.

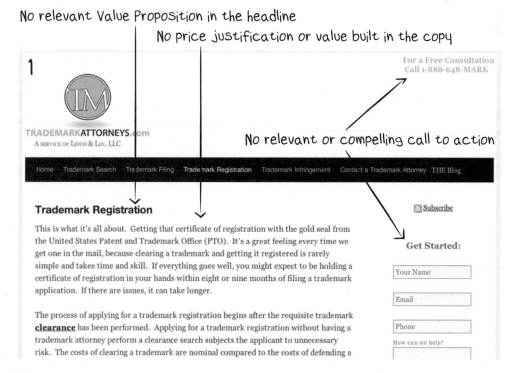

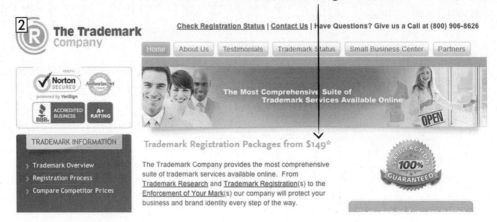

At least the headline has high relevance to their ad!

As important as price is, it's not the only aspect of your competition to consider. As part of a competitive review, you should consider all aspects of your competitive environment and look for opportunities to test new positioning for your offering against your competitive set.

Note: You can get printable PDFs of the case studies in this chapter and start a discussion about optimizing relevance at YouShouldTestThat.com/Relevance.

In Chapter 7, "Optimize for Clarity," you'll see how to move beyond relevance to test and maximize the clarity of your value proposition, including clarity of your page's design, call to action, and copywriting.

7   Optimize for Clarity

Everything should be made as simple as possible,
but no simpler.

                                 —Albert Einstein

The Dalai Lama walks into a pizza joint.

The server asks, "What can I get for you?"

The Dalai Lama considers carefully for a few moments and then says, "Can you make me one with everything?"

(Pause for effect.)

Don't underestimate your prospects' ability to misunderstand you.

There are some who believe conversion-rate optimization involves sophisticated persuasion techniques to motivate prospects to convert into customers. And they're correct. You can use many advanced tactics to enhance motivation, some of which you saw in Chapter 5 ("Optimize Your Value Proposition") regarding pricing. The field of knowledge is growing rapidly with the research WiderFunnel and others are conducting in the areas of marketing, psychology, and behavioral economics.

Although persuasion is important, clarity is even more so. In many of the website tests we've run, improving clarity alone has led to dramatic improvements in conversion rate and revenue.

Your visitors want to understand your value proposition, but they have a limit on the mental processing they will invest in doing that. By optimizing for clarity, you minimize the cognitive load for prospects, which frees up their mental bandwidth to make the conversion decision. The goal of clarity is to minimize cognitive load. Once you've optimized for clarity, you can layer on other persuasion techniques to make even greater improvement.

Clarity includes the communication of your value proposition and calls to action through your visual design and copywriting. In this chapter, you'll learn to test changes in your information architecture; graphic design, including eyeflow, images, and colors; call-to-action offers and buttons; and copywriting, including 15 tips for copywriting with clarity.

Clarity Communications with high clarity are understandable, cohesive, and accurate. They communicate the value proposition and call to action quickly.

Ask yourself: "Does the page effectively communicate the value proposition and call to action?"

Information Hierarchy Clarity

The *information hierarchy* is the organization system you use to show how information is related. At the website level, this means how the site's pages are organized; and at the page level, it means how content within each page is organized.

Website-Level Information Hierarchy

You should consider the website-level information hierarchy when testing pages or templates within a larger website. The practice of information architecture (IA) deals with how website pages are organized and linked. An IA *site diagram* is a type of document commonly used to define where each page sits within the site structure.

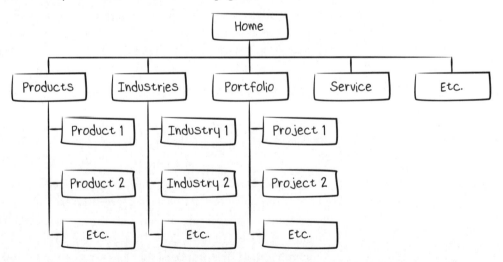

You can test your information hierarchy with hypotheses about how to organize your website's content on the page or through navigation. Should your top-level pages provide links to category pages, subcategories, individual products, or to calls to action? Should product pages sit within subcategories or be shown as larger product groups with more filters instead?

In the case of Colonial Candle, changes on the individual pages modified the site architecture by changing the depth of the links shown. It affected more than just the on-page layout.

Case Study: Colonial Candle Gets 20 Percent E-Commerce Conversion-Rate Lift

For Colonial Candle, a 100-year-old retailer, WiderFunnel tested the main store page to determine how an improved product architecture would affect sales. Challenger variations included a shorter page with overall category tiles and a longer page with individual products and category subheads.

Original page

Continues

Case Study: Colonial Candle Gets 20 Percent E-Commerce Conversion-Rate Lift *(Continued)*

Challenger A

Challenger B—winner

Conventional wisdom says "less is more," and most people involved in the project predicted that the shorter design would win. On the contrary, the redesigned longer page with clearer images and category rows worked best. That variation modified the site architecture, reducing the number of clicks needed to get from the main page to the individual products. The result was a 20 percent sales lift, producing a $20,000 increase in revenue in the first month.

Visitors on the winning page were able to view all product categories on a single page and click directly through to individual product types. On the original page, arriving at those products could have taken several clicks, and the visitor on the top-level page might not have known those products were offered at all.

Page-Level Information Hierarchy

You can also affect the information hierarchy at the level of the individual page. At the page level, a *wireframe* is a useful tool for planning. It tells you where the content boundaries are and defines the hierarchy of information. A wireframe is a diagram with a simplified view of the content blocks that shows how the main pieces are arranged. It helps focus attention on the eyeflow and content placement without the graphic design or specific copywriting in place.

Wireframes should be in black and white to avoid preoccupation with design elements and are intentionally not pixel-precise. At the wireframing stage, you should be thinking about eyeflow, the content hierarchy, and the visitor decision-making process.

When WiderFunnel ran a landing-page experiment for the CanaDream travel company, for example, we created a wireframe for each variation, as we do with every A/B/n test.

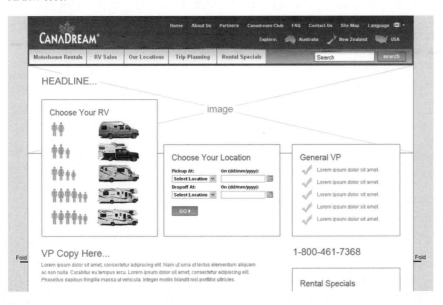

Notice the Fold markings on either side of the wireframe. This tells you (very roughly) the end point of what most page viewers will see when viewing the page. The fold is important to understand when planning your page layout, because it helps define that first impression your page creates. The location of the fold is different on every device, screen size, and web-browser configuration, and you should consider the most common screen resolutions for your visitors.

By planning your information hierarchy and structuring your content, you allow your readers to use less mental energy orienting themselves and deciding where to look first. The organization of your information relates closely to design clarity.

Design Clarity

Conversion optimization requires design that's on the far end of the "form follows function" spectrum. At the opposite end of the spectrum is design for the sake of aesthetics alone. Design like that is best enjoyed in an art gallery—not on your website.

The purpose of web design is to facilitate communication. Design for conversion doesn't draw attention to itself, but promotes the content alone. The best design disappears behind your content.

Your design should reinforce your value proposition and positioning. Should it be minimalist or embellished? Bold or subdued? Warm or cool? Your design approach communicates as much about your brand as the words you use. Your understanding of your audience, value proposition, and positioning help inform your design choices.

Design includes more than just colors and graphics. The wireframe you create for your pages, which determines placement of content sections, plays a leading role in how easily your reader's eye can move through your content.

We'll get to tactics for enhancing eyeflow clarity in a moment. First you should understand the difference between readability and legibility:

- *Legibility* tells you whether words can be deciphered. Are they too small, fuzzy, or faint to be read?
- *Readability* is a less binary, yes-or-no question. It's the degree to which the text treatment promotes easy reading. Something can be legible without being very readable. Do the color, size, font, and placement of your text entice the reader to want to keep reading, or is reading a struggle? The answer to that question is your readability.

Eyeflow Clarity

The placement of images, graphics, and copy either guide your reader's eye or block its flow. An ideal content structure minimizes the strain on your reader and allows fast comprehension.

Columns

An experiment that WiderFunnel developed for an online catalog retailer provided a clear example of the importance of eyeflow. In the test, we created several challenger variations to test against the site-wide e-commerce product page template.

Without changing the product descriptions or images, we were able to increase the sales conversion rate by more than 20 percent. The improved content placement and design in the new layouts allowed shoppers to find and understand product information more easily. The website became easier to use, and more visitors to the site made purchases.

Two of the variations we tested are particularly interesting and illustrate the influence of eyeflow. The wireframes were identical three-column layouts with just one change: the left and right columns were swapped. In Variation A, the product image was on the left with the pricing and add-to-cart button on the right. In Variation B, the product image column was on the right, with the price and add-to-cart on the left.

Variation A

Variation B

Variation B, with this single change, produced 16 percent greater sales than Variation A. That's a dramatic impact for any change, especially one that you might consider relatively insignificant.

Why was the column location that important? It changed the eyeflow and content emphasis.

Looking at the context, we understand that many of this retailer's products have discounted prices. Moving the price to the left column increased the emphasis on the price and reinforced the discount value proposition.

This layout doesn't work for all retailers and shouldn't be taken as a general rule. Further testing is likely to find even better layouts for this retailer. This test does demonstrate, however, how important your layout's eyeflow is when it clarifies your value proposition.

As a general guideline, our tests have found that reducing the number of columns improves conversion rates. This is especially true for forms. I've never seen a two-column form out-perform a single column form in a head-to-head test.

2-column form

1-column form

Guides

Shapes, lines, and patterns can also block or guide eyeflow. Using horizontal rules and boxes around content tells your readers that they should stop reading or that the content is related to different subjects. These elements should be used carefully to encourage reading.

In the *Sims 3* case study in Chapter 5, you saw the result of testing in the game-launcher window. During the development of that test plan, one of the important LIFT

Analysis points that WiderFunnel's strategists identified was that the boxed content inhibited eyeflow.

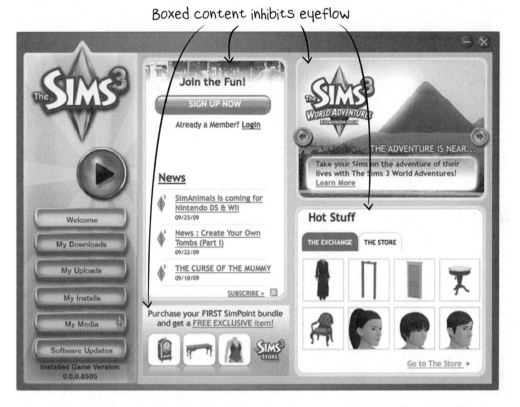

Boxes and lines between content like this create visual barriers for the reader. These barriers create a disjointed eyeflow and increase the reader's cognitive load.

You can also use visual elements to direct eyeflow patterns toward where you want people to look. Remember the eye-tracking study showing the baby's visual gaze from Chapter 3, "Prioritize Testing Opportunities"? You can use graphical motion with similar effect, as in this example of a test we ran on a webinar ad, which nearly tripled webinar signups. See Chapter 10, "Optimize for Urgency," for the full case study of that test.

You can even use graphic elements in your tweets. Check out the arrow call to action!

Chris Goward @chrisgoward 23 Apr
Do you use the 7 Critical Steps for Winning Conversion Tests? The webinar to find out is in 2 days. j.mp/HXxPtu <-- Sign up here!
Expand

You should test using visual elements to guide your readers toward important content.

Your images can also act as visual guides to bring the reader's eye to your call to action. If you add captions to your images, they will be some of the most highly read text on the page. I call captions that include an offer statement *action captions*. You Should Test That!

Image Clarity

The images you use should communicate and support your value proposition. Images that are added just for decoration risk confusing your prospects and reducing clarity.

Particularly for online retailers selling physical goods, the quality of images can affect your sales success. Enlarging images and adding zoom-in functions will help shoppers compensate for their inability to touch the items.

You can also improve clarity and reduce visual processing effort for your visitors with consistent alignment of your images. One of the problems we identified during the LIFT Analysis for Colonial Candle was misalignment of images.

Misaligned, small images reduce clarity

Shop for Candles

Taper Candles
- Handipt® Taper Candles
- Classic Taper Candles
- Grande Classic Taper Candles
- Taper Candle Holders
- Taper of the Month Club

Fragranced Jar Candles
- Oval 2-Wick Jar Candles
- Round Madison Gift Candles
- Seasonal Jar Candles
- Candle of the Month Club

Diffusers
- Reed Diffusers
- Electric Diffusers
- Electric Diffuser Refills
- Botanical Potpourri

Pillar Candles
- Smooth Pillar Candles
- Textured Pillar Candles
- Colonnade Pillar Candles
- Pillar Candle Holders

Tealight Candles
- Tealight Candles
- Tealight Candle Holders
- Large Tealights & Holder Sets

Votive Candles
- Votive Candles
- Votive Candle Holders

SimmerSnaps® Wax Melts
- SimmerSnaps® Wax Melts
- SimmerSnaps® and Candle Warmers

Candle Accessories
- Votive Holders
- Tealight Holders
- Taper Holders
- Pillar Holders
- Candle Snuffers
- Wax Buttons
- Other Accessories

Larger, symmetrical images

In the winning variations that WiderFunnel created, we enlarged the category images with consistent sizes and visually aligned them horizontally and vertically. Enlarging the images made the detail easier to see, and the consistent alignment removed flaws that attracted the viewer's eye, which left them free to focus on the image subject.

Images are also important for companies with intangible products or services. The challenge for intangibles is how to make the product or service seem more tangible.

Software vendors have traditionally done this by showing product boxes, even for software that can only be purchased via download. Others use screenshots of the product interface so prospects can imagine themselves using it.

Some image concepts can be too clever and cause confusion. For example, Singular Software has developed a popular video-editing support tool called PluralEyes. It synchronizes audio and video clips automatically, dramatically reducing the time and effort needed to edit multi-camera, multi-take, and dual-system audio productions.

When WiderFunnel's strategists analyzed the PluralEyes landing page, we discovered that their feature image was using an analogy.

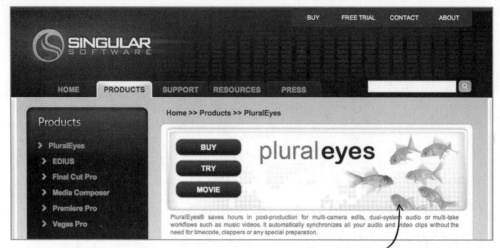

"Too clever" image reduces clarity

The analogy of the goldfish could be interpreted as the multiple elements (video or audio sources) "streaming" toward a single one. It's a clever concept. But visitors won't spend enough time to figure out a clever analogy like that. The first thing that might jump into their minds is, "Is this site selling software or fish food?" The full case study reveals other interesting findings from the test.

Case Study: Conversion-Optimization Testing for PluralEyes Software Boosts Downloads by 17.4 Percent (and Surprises the Experts)

Singular Software used conversion-optimization testing to increase free trial downloads of its PluralEyes audio and video synchronization software by 17.4 percent. The new landing-page design is a scientifically proven performer and will pave the way to future hypotheses, tests, and incremental improvements. And perhaps best of all, the results stumped the client and the experts!

The Client: Singular Software

Established in 2008, Singular Software is a pioneer in the development of workflow-automation applications for audio- and video-editing professionals. Singular Software's flagship product, PluralEyes, significantly cuts the time and effort needed to edit multi-camera, multi-take, and dual-system audio productions. By analyzing audio information, PluralEyes synchronizes audio and video clips automatically, without the need for timecode, clappers, or any special preparation.

The Business Need

From experience, Singular Software management knew that once editors realize how much time and effort they save by using PluralEyes along with their favorite video-editing software, they buy the product. The company's online marketing strategy of driving prospects to download free trial versions of PluralEyes software reflected that insight.

However, management also knew that in order to have more buyers, they needed plenty of tryers. First and foremost, Singular Software management needed to lift the initial conversion rate for the free 30-day trial versions and get editors to put the software through its paces.

The Challenges

Management wanted to redesign the landing page for the PluralEyes software to increase the free trial uptake rate, but the company lacked the internal resources and/or expertise to develop a sustainable experimentation strategy and clear hypotheses that would measurably improve the conversion rate. As a result, Singular Software turned to WiderFunnel to improve the conversion rate on its PluralEyes landing page.

The Solution

WiderFunnel used its Kaizen Method to plan and execute the PluralEyes conversion-optimization strategy. This included an in-depth analysis of the PluralEyes landing page using the LIFT Model.

The LIFT Analysis revealed several areas that were contributing to a poor conversion rate:

Competing Calls to Action The PluralEyes product control page had three competing calls to action that were vying for visitors' attention. On the landing page, web visitors could do all of the following:

- Watch a video
- Buy the software
- Download the free trial

No Clear Value Proposition The landing page was also lacking a clear, benefit-driven headline and copy to explain the value proposition, how easy the software was to use, and the pain points it addressed. Plus, for a tool that works seamlessly with so many industry-leading editing programs, such as Apple's Final Cut Pro and Adobe's Premiere Pro, the tie-in to these products was grossly understated.

No Compelling Visuals The existing web page relied on creative imagery that didn't communicate anything about the value of the product or the problems it solved. For example, there were no screenshots of the product in use.

Continues

Case Study: Conversion-Optimization Testing for PluralEyes Software Boosts Downloads by 17.4 Percent (and Surprises the Experts) *(Continued)*

After identifying the main challenges of the web page, WiderFunnel developed solutions to these three key challenges that could be used across all test variations. These included the following:

Focus on a Single Call to Action Because the primary goal of the page was to increase trial downloads, WiderFunnel took the emphasis off two of the competing calls to action and put the main focus on the download option—all while improving the copy of the primary call to action from "Try" to the more direct "Download Now." The call to action was kept consistent across the test variations.

Bring the Value Proposition to the Fore WiderFunnel wrote a new headline that used *loss aversion* to convey the hardship of life without PluralEyes ("Skip Endless Hours of Tedious Manual Syncing") and a subheadline that clearly communicated the value proposition ("Synchronize Video & Audio Clips Quickly & Affordably"). The headlines were kept constant across the test variations.

Test a Static Screen Shot against Video Because the control page lacked communicative imagery, WiderFunnel recommended testing different visuals to convey the value of downloading a free trial. By isolating a screenshot and an overview video as variables, we were able to compare these two different content approaches, and Singular Software's target audience got to pick the winner.

WiderFunnel's conversion strategist assumed that video would be the clear winner: "My gut said that video would win because it's interactive and can convey so much more than a static screenshot." Others close to the experiment, including the client, agreed. After all, video seemed like the perfect tool to communicate the benefits of a software product—especially for end users who work in video every day!

With these three elements in place, WiderFunnel proposed three design variations to test against the control (original) page:

> Variation A: "Minimalist." This design variation took a stripped-down approach by clearing a lot of clutter from the original design. The focus was on the new, stronger headline, focused value proposition in the introductory copy, a strong and visually appealing call-to-action button, and thumbnail logos of the compatible editing software brands.

Variation B: "Screenshot Isolation." This variation used the same headline and intro copy but added new, three-step, illustrated "How PluralEyes Works" copy and client testimonials under the main section. Variation B also introduced a prominent screenshot of the product in use above the fold and beside the call-to-action button.

Variation C: "Video Player Isolation." This variation was a duplicate of Variation B except that, in place of the static screenshot, WiderFunnel embedded an overview video.

The Results: Conversion-Rate Lift of 17.4 Percent

Once the test reached statistical confidence, all three variations showed significant improvement over the control, with the winning version showing a 17.4 percent boost in conversion rate for downloads of the PluralEyes software.

All three variations (two radically different layouts) beat the control, reaffirming the importance of clear and compelling headlines, copy that communicates the product's value proposition, and focusing attention on a single call to action. Deploying any of the three test pages would have solved the major problems found in the LIFT Analysis.

Variations B and C beat the minimalist approach of Variation A, driving home the power of showing the product in action. However, what really caught everyone's attention was that Variation B—featuring the static screenshot—came out ahead of Variation C's embedded video! In other words, the static screenshot beat the embedded video, showing a 35.9 percent relative improvement!

There could be several reasons for this result. Although video is a compelling medium, prospects are often in a tremendous hurry, and they may not need video to be persuaded in certain contexts. Most embedded videos load showing a still frame from the clip, and the still frame in this experiment might need to be optimized. Or the content of the video itself may not resonate with the target audience.

Whatever the underlying reason, this experiment opened the minds of all involved to new and exciting hypotheses. A new design and layout is a great way to kick off an optimization process. So is a 17.4 percent lift in conversion rate. The client agrees that this experiment is likely the beginning of a long (and profitable) learning process about what really works when it comes to conversion.

Color Clarity

Color is important for emphasizing significant page elements and enhancing readability. If you have an established brand, most of your color choices are predetermined. In this case, you probably have a graphic standards manual that dictates your color and design choices. If you don't have graphic standards set, you have more flexibility in choosing colors for graphic elements.

Regardless of whether your business has graphic standards set, you can use color selectively to emphasize important elements over supporting content.

Color Contrast

Three main components of colors are important to understand: hue, lightness (or brightness), and saturation. The *hue* is what most people think of as the color's name: blue, red, green, aquamarine, and so on. It can be visualized as the color's position on a color wheel or spectrum. The farther apart two hues are on a color wheel, the higher the contrast between them. But hue alone doesn't tell you whether two colors will work well together or even be legible. Hue is less important for readability than lightness.

Contrasting *lightness* is the most important of the three color components for readability. Lightness refers to how bright the color is. Think of holding a colored piece of paper and walking from a dark room into a lighter room and then out into a bright, sunny day. The lightness of the paper's color is different in each of those environments.

Lightness can be affected by the hue as well as the degree of shading added to the hue. Yellow is naturally a lighter hue than blue, for example, but you can increase the lightness of blue by adding white or darken the yellow by adding shade. For maximum readability, you should have high lightness contrast between the text and background colors.

A color's *saturation* level is the degree to which the hue is fully expressed, at one extreme, or closer to gray, at the other. Saturation is important for design aesthetics, but it's the least important of the three color components when considering readability.

The combination of black and white is the highest-contrast color choice. The worst combinations use colored text of medium lightness on backgrounds with similar lightness. You can often increase the clarity of your pages by testing dark text on a white background for high contrast. Remember, the purpose of this testing is to increase readability and decrease the readers' cognitive load.

In a landing-page optimization test we developed for MerchantWarehouse.com, for example, we identified low-contrast text as one of the clarity LIFT Analysis points.

Low contrast made this hard to read

By redesigning the page with greater readability (among many other changes), we increased the lead-generation conversion rate on that page by 15 percent.

Do you have large blocks of white copy on a dark background? Try black text on white. Reversed type (light text on a dark background) can work if the type size is large enough and copy blocks aren't too long. Reversed type stands out more than standard dark-on-light type, but large blocks of it create eye fatigue.

Color Meaning

Various colors have connotations, and those vary according to cultural expectations. Green can communicate a positive feeling, a "go" from a traffic signal, environmental friendliness, or the color of money in America. On the other hand, it can also imply envy or remind us of Montezuma's revenge.

Some say that red is best for calls to action because it commands attention. We can't help but look at a red object in front of us. The color red is actually built into our physiological makeup to grab our attention. Red is also considered to be an auspicious color in traditional Chinese culture, symbolizing good luck and happiness. But it can communicate "stop" or a warning. As the saying goes, when you're angry, you "see red." It's true. When your body senses anger or increased adrenaline, a surge of blood goes to your eyes and tints your vision red. You literally are seeing red!

For conversion optimization, the clarity of the color and design of the elements are usually more important than perceived connotations.

Consistency

Visual consistency is even more important than visual prominence. Although you can use color to highlight important information or draw attention to calls to action, those colors should be consistent throughout the conversion funnel.

Many sites have customized their link colors; for example, the most common standard is to use blue for links. That was originally the only color possible for links, and many people (other than the very young) are accustomed to looking for blue links.

Messing with web standards is done at your own risk. If you're inclined to use different colors than your visitors expect, You Should Test That!

Call-to-Action Clarity

The sole purpose of your page is to persuade your prospects to respond to your call to action (CTA). I'm often surprised at the effort some websites seem to take to hide their CTAs. It's as if they're embarrassed to ask for the sale.

There's a successful sales principle you should apply to your landing pages. It says, "Close early, and close often." Whatever form your CTA takes—text link, button, phone number, or embedded form—it should be prominent.

Your CTA will work best if it's accessible as soon as your prospect has read enough and decided to act. In most cases, calls to action work best when they're above the fold and at the bottom of your content. You Should Test That!

Buttons are the most popular type of CTA, and many people gravitate toward testing buttons when they first begin testing. Bigger buttons can help on a lot of landing pages that have never been optimized. If your call-to-action buttons aren't clearly visible on the page, they probably need to be larger.

But where do you stop? At some point, your button will be too large—eventually it may even stop looking like a button. Clearly, the advice to "make your buttons bigger" doesn't apply to all pages.

There's also been much (useless) debate about the best button color and design. The best button treatment depends on the rest of your site design, color scheme, brand identity, and target audience. Take a look at the variety of buttons we've tested on winning pages. You'll find the color versions of the buttons in the Color Gallery at the back of the book.

During one string of tests, we tested Big Orange Buttons, and it became an acronym around the WiderFunnel office. We call him BOB. He works hard ;-)

Hi, My Name is BOB.
(Click Here)

The wording of your CTAs can be even more important than the design and color. At WiderFunnel, we've often seen double-digit conversion-rate lift by testing copywriting alone.

Copywriting Clarity

"People don't want to buy a quarter-inch drill. They want a quarter-inch hole!" So said Harvard Business School marketing professor Theodore Levitt. You may be selling features, but your customers don't just buy features. They buy solutions. Your prospect may be solving a purely emotional want or a rational need. It may be definable and specific or intangible and general. Your copywriting tone and the value proposition you emphasize will depend on their needs.

If your prospects understand your product and are comparison shopping, emphasize the features they're looking for. Tell them about the carbide tip and high tensile steel in the drill bit first, and then give them the benefit of those features.

If they're less informed, they need to understand the benefits up front. Lead with how long-lasting your drill bit is or how fast and cleanly it makes holes compared to alternatives. Then use features as supporting points.

As your industry and the needs of your target audience evolve, so should your copy approach. By continuously testing your copy, you'll make sure your communications evolve along with the market. Whatever the needs of your prospects may be, a confused prospect won't buy.

"I'm sorry I wrote you such a long letter; I didn't have time to write a short one." This comment, attributed to Blaise Pascal, underscores the challenge of writing with clarity. Concise writing is hard to achieve, yet is just as important for web copywriting as it was for Pascal's letters.

Here are 15 tips you can use for high-clarity copywriting:

Test Headlines Your headline should encapsulate your value proposition and CTA. Testing headlines is one of the easiest ways to find your most powerful motivational trigger message.

State the Offer Up Front The CTA is the conclusion to your story. Unlike the story in a novel, you shouldn't wait to get to the conclusion. Test using a *Johnson Box*: a highlighted section at the top of the page that states the offer. It's worked in direct marketing for decades.

Use Proof Points Support your claims with evidence to build credibility. If you promise money savings, tell prospects the average savings or add a testimonial from someone who saved. If you're promoting a product as high quality, point out features that demonstrate quality against competitors. Look for opportunities to use visuals as proof points.

Break Up Your Copy with Subheads and Bullets People don't read sequentially. They skim, skip, and scatter. They skim over sections when they get bored, skip through subheads to find interesting parts, and scatter their attention all over the page, jumping from column to column, side to side, and top to bottom. Give them a format that allows skimming.

Keep Your Columns Narrow Narrower columns are better for readability. Consider how narrow newspaper columns are. They're designed for readability. This is especially true when your readers are on mobile devices.

Write Short Paragraphs Attention spans are at an all-time low.

Write Short Sentences Long sentences lose readers.

Use a Large Type Size Large type reduces reading strain and encourages your prospect to continue.

Test Long Copy vs. Short Copy In most cases, you should put yourself on a word diet. As Steve Krug says, "Cut your copy in half; then cut it in half again." But the long-copy approach works in many scenarios, too. It works best for consumer products or services where you need to build an emotional need and close with a sale. The challenge for long copy is to craft a story that keeps readers engaged.

Be Real Your customers are people, just like you. They're just as fed up with the corporate BS we're all exposed to. If you can communicate with an empathetic voice, you can gain their trust and respect. I avoid using the word *authentic* here, because social media gurus have overused it. Be real. Your customers will appreciate it.

Avoid Acronyms Your prospects don't understand your business like you do. They probably know less than you think they do. They don't understand your acronyms and business jargon. They also won't complain about your over-complicated copy, because they don't want to look stupid.

Use the Mom Test Think about a real person who is unfamiliar with your topic when you're writing. For example, think about whether your mom would understand your marketing copy. If she would (and assuming she doesn't work in your industry), you may be communicating with more clarity.

Use Active Voice When you write about something being done by someone, you're writing in passive voice. When someone is doing something, it's in active voice. Active sentences are just that—action oriented. And that's what you want on your website. Action.

Reduce Adjectives Fantastic, fabulous, flawless, fresh. Adjectives are overused. They set off marketing alarms in your reader. Choose the right nouns and verbs, and you won't need as many adjectives. Except when they work. Research by Brian Wansink, director of the Food and Brand Lab at Cornell University and the author of *Mindless Eating: Why We Eat More Than We Think*, shows that nostalgic, sensory, and branded adjectives can increase sales on restaurant menus. You Should Test That!

Manage Expectations What should your visitors expect once they complete the CTA? How fast can they expect product delivery, or how soon will they get a lead-generation response? Clarifying expectations reduces anxiety and can dramatically improve conversion rates.

In a landing-page test for MerchantWarehouse.com, one of the changes WiderFunnel made was to set expectations for a three-step process from filling in the application form.

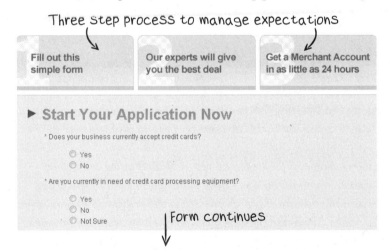

Three step process to manage expectations

Fill out this simple form

Our experts will give you the best deal

Get a Merchant Account in as little as 24 hours

▶ Start Your Application Now

* Does your business currently accept credit cards?
○ Yes
○ No

* Are you currently in need of credit card processing equipment?
○ Yes
○ No
○ Not Sure

Form continues

This helped clarify the prospect's expectations by specifying what would happen next. The expectations you need to set will differ depending on your fulfillment process and its potential anxieties for the prospect. You should think through the questions your prospects might have about the next steps and set their expectations.

To evaluate your pages for clarity, look at them from the perspective of your prospect and identify potential clarity breakdowns. As an example of this type of analysis, I searched for "e-commerce chat support" and came across the following landing page. It offers an example of common clarity problems.

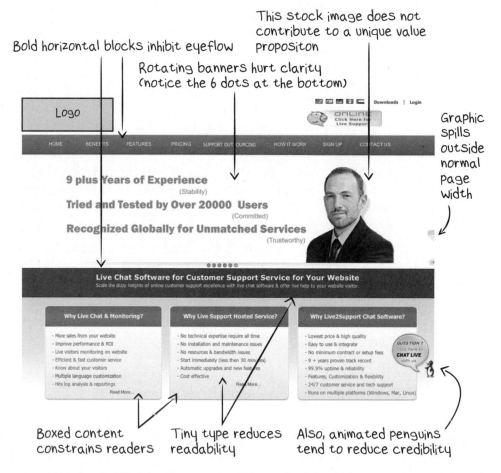

You may be thinking I'm shooting fish in a barrel. "Chris," you may say, "Why are you picking on these little companies with obvious conversion problems? Give yourself a challenge."

That's a fair comment. Some of the pages we test at WiderFunnel are owned by entrepreneurs and business owners who don't have teams of marketing specialists and communications experts. But many of our clients are in the Fortune 500 and have highly skilled marketing teams. There are opportunities to improve every communication, no matter the marketer's level of sophistication.

Conversion-lift opportunities abound in many larger organizations because of committee decision-making, competing time priorities, and the complexity of controlling the sheer volume of pages. Between corporate websites, product-specific websites, marketing campaign sites, and third-party pages, corporate marketers' attention is split in many directions.

As an example, SAP is a world-class company full of brilliant people. Because they're bright and knowledgeable, they know they have opportunities to improve through conversion optimization.

The following case study shows an example of a test WiderFunnel ran on one of SAP's landing pages. The clarity of the eyeflow, copywriting, and CTA were some of the most important aspects we changed to create the winning challenger pages.

Case Study: SAP's B2B Landing Page Optimization Lifts Lead Generation by 32.5 Percent—Within Strict Branding Guidelines

SAP® is the market and technology leader in business-management software, solutions, and services for improving business processes, and the world's largest business software company.

The Business Need

Pay-per-click (PPC) advertising is one of SAP's primary lead-generation tactics driving traffic to the site. Within this tactic, Christine Mykota, Director, Business Analytics Marketing, North American Ecosystem Group, had a landing page for a software trial download that was under-performing relative to her other pages and depressing the targeted lead-generation rate. Mykota believed best practices for landing-page optimization weren't being applied and that SAP needed a conversion-rate optimization strategy to improve its PPC results.

With a limited PPC budget, the option to buy more traffic wasn't available, so SAP management decided to test a conversion-rate optimization approach. Mykota knew that optimizing the conversion rate is one of the fastest and highest Return on Investment (ROI) ways for marketers to increase leads and sales.

The Challenges

Mykota had to clear four major hurdles before proceeding with the deployment of the strategy:

1. She needed to convince senior management of the potential ROI when asking for a budget increase to perform the test. Conversion optimization was a relatively new strategy for SAP, so senior management was rightfully skeptical—and had high expectations for a conversion improvement to be considered a success.

Continues

2. SAP has a well-known brand and works to continually strengthen it through brand standards. The website and landing pages have stringent design guidelines, limiting layout and creative changes that may be valuable to test. Corporate website design standards placed tough restrictions on layout and design, which limited testing flexibility. Examples of branding limitations included the following:

    • Pages had to include a standard corporate banner at the top, which took up valuable page space.

    • Pages could only employ a two- or three-column design, with standard widths for each column.

    • Only certain fonts and font sizes could be used.

    • Design elements had to stay within an approved brand color palette.

    • Images could only come from an approved list.

    • Buttons had to use approved colors and sizes.

3. New product launches called for tight timelines if testing and experimentation were to deliver improved conversion rates.

4. Mykota lacked internal resources to develop and execute conversion-rate optimization experiments. With neither the tools nor the experienced person-power in place, she needed to scope a solution that would deliver conversion-rate lift on time and on budget.

The Solution

SAP hired WiderFunnel to run experiments on the Crystal Reports trial download page. That desktop report-generating software is a relatively low-cost, high-volume product, and SAP targeted a 20–25 percent increase in conversions to justify the investment in the test.

WiderFunnel, using its Kaizen Method planning process, first took a macro view of all the Crystal Reports conversion funnel steps, target audience, and branding guidelines. In the case of SAP, the brand guidelines were particularly important, and WiderFunnel examined them to discover which page elements could be changed or were off limits. The resulting Kaizen Plan prioritized the company's testing opportunities and showed how landing-page changes would influence trial software download conversion rates.

Then, for each landing-page experiment, WiderFunnel followed the seven-step conversion testing process:

Step 1. LIFT Analysis of the Landing Page

The graphic standards restrictions forced the team to think creatively about new designs that could improve conversion rates. WiderFunnel evaluated page elements according to the LIFT Model. The LIFT Analysis of the landing page performed by WiderFunnel's conversion strategists identified the conversion problems.

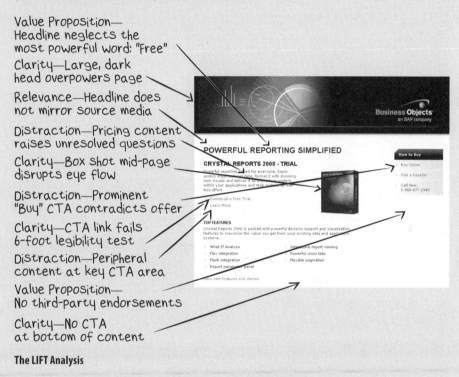

Value Proposition—
Headline neglects the
most powerful word: "Free"

Clarity—Large, dark
head overpowers page

Relevance—Headline does
not mirror source media

Distraction—Pricing content
raises unresolved questions

Clarity—Box shot mid-page
disrupts eye flow

Distraction—Prominent
"Buy" CTA contradicts offer

Clarity—CTA link fails
6-foot legibility test

Distraction—Peripheral
content at key CTA area

Value Proposition—
No third-party endorsements

Clarity—No CTA
at bottom of content

The LIFT Analysis

Step 2. Develop Hypotheses for Changes That Could Influence Conversions

The strategists converted those LIFT Analysis points into hypotheses that could be tested with SAP's live landing pages in a controlled A/B/*n* split test with multiple challenger variations. An important part of the hypothesis development is to identify which hypotheses to combine into challenger variations and which to isolate.

Continues

Case Study: SAP's B2B Landing Page Optimization Lifts Lead Generation by 32.5 Percent—Within Strict Branding Guidelines *(Continued)*

Step 3. Create the Test Design Document

WiderFunnel's strategists consolidated the hypotheses into two proposed challenger variations. They created a test design document to present the test structure, LIFT Analysis, and challenger page wireframes.

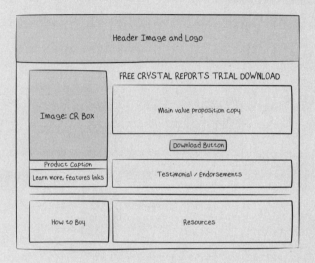

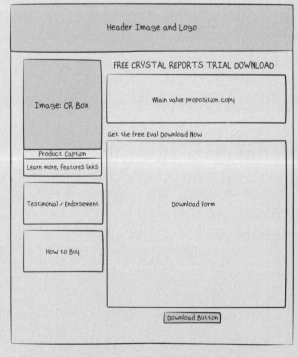

Step 4. Create Page Variations with Alternative Copy and Layout

Once Mykota and the SAP team had approved the test plan, WiderFunnel applied conversion design and copywriting to the two challenger wireframes.

Variation A: Stronger Call to Action

The WiderFunnel team's first landing-page variation employed changes intended to reduce distractions and emphasize the CTA. In certain instances, they had to receive special approval from the corporate branding team for ideas that pushed the envelope of SAP's design standards.

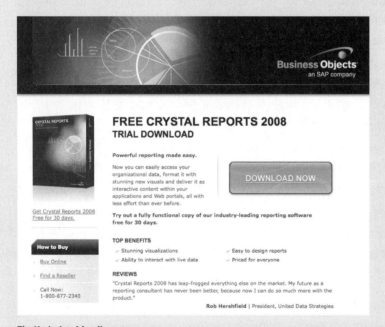

The Variation A landing page

Significant changes included the following:

- Improving the prospect's eyeflow on the page. Working within the corporate design standards, the team employed a two-column design but changed the position of the narrower column from right to left. This move allowed them to place the product hero shot on the left, where it improved eyeflow by leading prospects directly to the headline in the center of the page.

- Using a larger image. Although they wanted to try an alternative image, the team decided that change would violate brand design standards. Instead, they received approval to enlarge the existing image.

Continues

- Adding a caption link below the image, which took visitors to the trial download registration page.

- Writing a new headline. WiderFunnel wrote a headline that reinforced the message used in the search ad that brought visitors to the landing page.

- Consolidating information links. WiderFunnel reorganized the links on the control page to reduce distraction from the trial download CTA. Links for customer support, developer resources, training, and additional information about the product were moved to the bottom of the page, below the primary CTA.

- Relocating purchase links. WiderFunnel also moved a box containing links to facilitate immediate product purchases, either online, through the telephone, or through a reseller. That box was moved from the upper right to the left side of the page, just below the product hero shot.

- Enlarging the CTA button. WiderFunnel added a large orange download button (affectionately known as BOB: Big Orange Button). The existing page's CTA was a text link inviting visitors to download a trial. WiderFunnel believed that design was too small to attract visitors' attention.

  The proposed button was larger than allowed in the design standards, however, with a color that pushed the limits of the approved palette. So, Mykota had to press for the change with the brand marketing team. The brand marketing team approved the orange button.

Variation B: Integrated Registration Form

Both the control landing page and Variation A required prospects to click through to a separate registration form to complete the software trial download. This challenger tested the hypothesis that removing the extra step would improve conversions.

The headline, graphics, and layout of Variation B remained the same as in Variation A. But instead of a large orange button at the top of the page, the team added the registration form just below the headline and a brief product description.

The company's standard registration form had more than a dozen fields for prospects to fill out, along with several qualifying questions they had to answer. WiderFunnel initially designed a shorter registration form with only the important form fields—to no avail.

The brand marketing team denied the request to swap the existing form for a new one. As Mykota said, "So many folks use that form, there was no way we could change that."

Step 5. Technical Installation

For this test, WiderFunnel developed HTML stand-alone landing pages to be tested against the control. The test was set up as follows:

- Traffic was randomly and evenly divided between the three versions of the landing page.
- Each visitor was cookied and always shown the same page variation, regardless of how many times they returned to visit the website.
- WiderFunnel tracked conversion rates for each challenger page and the control.
- Only completed software trial downloads were counted as conversions.

Step 6. Data Collection

The controlled experiment was launched and run, testing the new page challengers against the control using live PPC search traffic. The test ran for 17 days until statistically significant results at a 95 percent confidence level were attained.

Step 7. Results Analysis

The test produced a clear winner and helped achieve an even bigger lift than Mykota had targeted:

- Variation A, with the large orange button, boosted conversions 32.5 percent over the control page.
- Variation B, despite maintaining the long form, delivered a 17 percent conversion lift over the control page.

The Result: Conversion-Rate Lift of 32.5 Percent

"I was very, very surprised," says Mykota. "I knew that we would have improvement, but I also knew that our branding restrictions and long form presented challenges. We've leveraged WiderFunnel's insights across the organization."

Even better, the test achieved a 154 percent ROI, convincing Mykota's previously skeptical boss. "Now she's a champion within the organization to look at landing-page testing and to do more of it."

Based on the test results, Mykota's team implemented similar design changes on other landing pages. In six weeks, they were able to achieve a 26 percent lift in conversion rates across all landing pages.

Now Mykota is confident that she can work with the brand marketing team on further tests that allow for flexibility within design standards—as long as the data can demonstrate an improvement.

Whether you're a world-leading company like SAP, are just getting your business started, or are somewhere in between, you can test to improve your clarity.

 Note: Do you have any other examples of clarity-enhancing tests and tips? Go to YouShouldTestThat.com/Clarity to start a conversation and download case study pdfs.

In Chapter 8, "Optimizing for Anxiety," you'll see how to tackle one of the drags on your conversion rate: anxiety. You'll test how to reduce anxiety by satisfying your visitors' need for privacy, usability, and fulfillment follow-through.

8 Optimize for Anxiety

*You only have to do a very few things right in your life
so long as you don't do too many things wrong.*
—*Warren Buffett*

Are you a Spiderman fan? I often wonder what makes some superheroes so easy to relate to. Perhaps many of us wish we had a secret identity to change into so we could kick ass, too.

Spiderman also has an appealing sixth-sense power: when danger is near, our hero Peter Parker can always tell because his "Spidey sense" tingles. His sixth sense alerts him so he can avoid surprise dangers. If you were like me as a kid, you may have wished for your own Spidey sense at school to warn you that a pop quiz was about to happen!

It turns out you *do* have a sense that's attuned to danger in your environment. And so do your customers. We scan the horizon for dangers and listen to our intuition telling us whether we're safe to proceed.

This is a good sense to have on alert when we're rock climbing or riding public transit, but it slows us down in our buying behavior. An anxious mind creates a closed wallet.

Successful consumer sales environments reduce anxiety. Take a walk through your local mattress or major appliance store, and look at the salespeople. I'll bet you won't see any tattoos, body piercings, or torn denim. There's nothing inherently dangerous in those things, but the store owners know that for some people, they would create anxiety.

In this chapter, you'll see how to avoid creating uncertainty in your prospects' minds. The most common concerns that users have about websites involve privacy, usability, fulfillment, and effort; you'll learn how to minimize each of these potential sources of anxiety and then find out how you can use anxiety in your favor to motivate your prospects to act.

 Anxiety Anything in the conversion funnel or missing from the pages that creates uncertainty in the prospect's mind. Ask yourself: "What are potential misgivings the visitor could have about undertaking the conversion?"

Privacy Anxiety

Privacy concerns have been front-page news in recent years. We've seen anonymous hackers take down the FBI website, Facebook's privacy policy smacked down by regulators, and sensitive government and corporate secrets exposed by WikiLeaks. Consumers are concerned about their privacy and the seeming inability of trusted organizations to keep private information just that—private. In this privacy-sensitive environment, it's more important than ever for you to justify the information you need to collect and assure your prospects of your trustworthiness.

The number of form fields you ask prospects to complete can affect your conversion rate. Asking for too much information (TMI) causes 12 percent of e-commerce shoppers to abandon their carts, according to Forrester research (North American Technographics Retail Online Survey, 2009). In addition, if you ask more questions than your prospects think are necessary, they'll give fake information. A study by Janrain showed that "88% of online buyers had at some point intentionally left registration information blank or used incorrect information when signing up for a new account at a website" (Consumer Perceptions of Online Registration and Social Login, Jan, 10, 2012).

One method you can test is to add help text explaining why you need to collect data or how to use fields, especially for sensitive information. On the Digg signup form, for example, supporting help text appears as the visitor progresses through the form. As the user tabs into the second password field, a step that can be confusing for some people, the help text explains why it's necessary.

Choose a username (no spaces) chrisgoward	
Choose a password ••••••	
Retype password 	Type in your password again for verification purposes.
Email address (must be real!) 	

Then, in the next field, the anxiety-producing email-collection step, Digg reduces anxiety with a simple privacy assurance message. Digg doesn't show all the help text at once, to avoid overcomplicating the look of the form.

Here's another option: can you move optional form fields to your thank-you page and provide additional benefit for completing them? WineExpress.com uses this method for its newsletter signup funnel. The first step presents a very simple two-field form.

By eliminating optional fields, the site optimizes its subscription conversion rate. Then, on the thank-you page, it gives the option for the subscriber to add their mailing address to also receive the print catalog.

Most companies include the print catalog option within the single form and probably reduce subscriptions because of it.

You can also test using thank-you pages to collect additional demographic and psychographic information to enrich your understanding of your customers. As long as you give a reason that benefits the prospect, many will give you the information. Compare that `WineExpress.com` example with a signup form for a well-known web-design newsletter.

Please enter your email address to receive a periodic digest of new articles in ▮▮▮▮▮▮. Your email address will not be shared with third parties or used for any purpose other than sending you articles from this series. Please fill out the optional fields to help us understand our audience better so we can deliver better content to you.

MAKE SURE TO CHOOSE AT LEAST ONE SUBSCRIPTION OPTION AT THE BOTTOM.

If your form needs this much instruction, it's designed wrong

(Required fields are bold)

Email Address *	
Industry *	*No dropdown? How should I define my industry?*
Job Title / Function *	
Role or Department *	Account Management
Company	*Many optional fields with no reason given*
Country	
Postal/ZIP Code	
What topics are you interested in reading about?	
Enter giveaway? (http://uxm.ag/q9)	○ Yes ○ No *Link to a contest adds significant distraction*
Response to giveaway question	*No idea what to enter here*
Subscribe to	☐ Weekly digest of articles and short news ☐ Daily alerts to new job listings *No default selection!*

Button pushed below the fold.

Subscribe to list

The many optional fields and confusing questions create all manner of anxiety and distraction on this form.

Here's another example from a well-known B2B company.

SIGN UP FOR THE ███████ **NEWSLETTER.**

You'll receive free weekly information on ████ news and events, demos, special offers, and more. By registering, you can easily save, organize, share, and manage your subscriptions.

Your Country/Region   * Required field(s)

*Office Location: [Canada ⇕] [?]

[handwritten] Subheads and boxes add to complication perception

Your e-mail and password ←

*Email Address: [_____] [?]

*Create Password: [_____] [?] ← *[handwritten] Password shouldn't be needed for newsletter*

*Verify Password: [_____] [?]

Subscriptions

*Would you like to subscribe to the ██████████ newsletter?

○ Yes   ○ No [?] ← *[handwritten] Unnecessary field. They're on the subscribe page!*

[handwritten] Very large legal message

* ☐ I acknowledge that I have read ████ Privacy Statement(+) (which is based on the country/region selection above) and consent to the processing of my personal data in accordance with the terms of the Privacy Statement. Based on my country/region selection above, my data will be controlled by ████████████

View Privacy Statement in another language: ████ Privacy Statement/French(+)
Legal Disclosure/Générique(+)

[**Register Me Now**]

The design and content of this form raise anxiety barriers by creating a perception of complication. Clearly, this legal department could use some restraint. They're harming the company's lead-generation results.

The fact that reducing the number of fields on a form increases its fill rate has been well documented. Many tests have confirmed this. Reducing your fields to the minimum required is an accepted "best practice" for increasing conversion rate.

But it doesn't always hold true. In tests we've run at WiderFunnel, we've seen many different form options win tests. Sometimes splitting forms into multiple pages has worked better than longer single pages, but in other cases a consolidated single-page form wins. We've even seen tests where *adding* certain fields has increased conversion rate.

In one form test example, during the run-up to the 2010 Winter Olympics, WiderFunnel worked with Elastic Path to optimize e-commerce sales on the Olympics merchandise store. One of the tests the Elastic Path team ran was on the checkout pages.

In an A/B/*n* split test, the team wanted to test against the original checkout with its four steps: Sign In, Shipping, Billing, and Receipt. The alternative test variation consolidated those four pages into a single-step checkout.

The single-step checkout out-performed the original multistep checkout with a 21.8 percent lift in sales. If you've got a retail site, You Should Test That!

Your privacy policy is also an area where you can reduce or create anxiety. For example, MarthaStewart.com offers free email newsletter subscriptions. On the signup page, way down at the bottom, is a small link to the privacy policy.

For now, let's ignore all the clarity and distraction problems the site has created by offering 18 subscription options and pushing the subtle gray Subscribe button to the bottom of a very long page. Once a visitor clicks the privacy link, they're in for a daunting read. At 3,700 words, the privacy policy creates anxiety for anyone interested enough to try reading it.

This is a common situation for corporations where overzealous legal teams create unnecessary hurdles for marketing teams to deal with. Even if you're in this situation and can't rewrite the privacy policy, you can frame it in a friendlier way. Test creating a summary of the privacy message for subscribers, like this:

Your privacy is important to us. We will never share your email address or other private information with anyone. Period.
You can always unsubscribe at any time.
If you'd like, you can read the full <u>corporate privacy policy</u>.

You can test opening that simple summary message in a lightbox with a link to the full policy for those interested enough to read the entire corporate policy. An even better option, if you can persuade the legal team, is to rewrite the corporate policy to use natural language or write a specific, short privacy policy for newsletters.

Only a small segment of your audience is likely to read your privacy policy. The rest will simply trust their gut reaction about whether the information you're asking for on your forms is justified.

In the next section, you'll see examples of forms that create anxiety with both usability and privacy concerns.

Usability Anxiety

Usability refers to how easy your experience is for your prospects to learn and use. The most common opportunities for improving usability relate to forms, website errors, and speed.

Form Usability

Do your forms make your prospects feel stupid? Poor form design, arcane error messages, and stark red error text all say, "Hey, Dummy, why can't you figure this out?!"

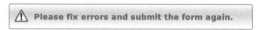

That's an unfortunate way to start a relationship.

Don't underestimate the confusion that forms can cause for your prospects. As a sophisticated web user, you're accustomed to forms and their purpose. You probably spend most of your day online. But think about all the other types of people who will be using your forms: plumbers, teachers, doctors, taxi drivers, waiters, and symphony bassoonists. Many of them won't be nearly as comfortable online as you are. Help your prospects avoid errors to reduce form anxiety for them and start the relationship more amicably.

Even on the clearest and most straightforward form, your users will make errors. You should design your forms to accommodate them in a friendly way. Allowing users to recover from errors easily will improve your conversion rate.

Signing up for a WordPress blog, for example, shows a low-anxiety method for highlighting form errors.

The field that needs attention is given pink shading and a red keyline with a helpful, even apologetic (!), error message. This error handling happens dynamically as the prospective subscriber is filling out the form. The prospect gets immediate feedback and the ability to fix errors during the form-filling process, rather than after the entire form is filled out.

L.L. Bean's product page forms give another good example of friendly error handling.

When the shopper chooses the item size and then clicks Add to Bag without choosing a color, a message appears over the button, directly in the shopper's line of sight, along with an arrow pointing at the spot to fix the error.

Compare these with the error handling on the web design newsletter shown earlier.

MAKE SURE TO CHOOSE AT LEAST ONE SUBSCRIPTION OPTION AT THE BOTTOM.

(Required fields are bold)

There are errors below

Email Address *   Test@

The domain portion of the email address is invalid (the portion after the @:)

Industry *   Marketing

Job Title / Function *   President & CEO

The error message, "There are errors below," is nonspecific and doesn't appear until the user has filled in the entire form and clicked the Subscribe button. With the entire form already filled out, the user needs to figure out which of the 11 fields have caused the errors. The error messages fail to help the user quickly identify the fields to fix, and there's no visual method of identifying the problem field.

As a final tip on the topic of form anxiety, please don't use CAPTCHA fields if the form is for important conversions. Companies often use CAPTCHA fields to reduce spam by detecting whether the form filler is a real person. But such fields are also confusing for real people who often make mistakes filling them out and get frustrated with the hassle. Many will give up if they can't get the CAPTCHA to work the first time.

Word verification: *

(verify using audio)

Type the characters you see in the picture above; if you can't read them, submit the form and a new image will be generated. Not case sensitive.

There are better ways to reduce your spam intake using software rather than making your prospects prove their humanity.

Form design justifies an entire book and, fortunately, Luke Wroblewski has written one that I recommend called *Web Form Design: Filling in the Blanks* (Rosenfeld Media, 2008). Reading it will give you all the detail you could want about form-interaction design and ideas to test.

Usability testing can be helpful for identifying form problems, too. Asking three or four people to complete your form will uncover any major roadblocks and can seed ideas for new test hypotheses. For more on the subject of usability testing, read Steve Krug's *Rocket Surgery Made Easy: The Do-It-Yourself Guide to Finding and Fixing Usability Problems* (New Riders, 2010) and Jeffrey Rubin and Dana Chisnell's *Handbook of Usability Testing: How to Plan, Design, and Conduct Effective Tests* (Wiley, 2008).

The important point to take away is that you can improve your forms to reduce anxiety and increase conversions. You Should Test That!

Website Errors

You can make all the conversion-optimization improvements imaginable, but if there are technical glitches on your website, all credibility is lost. Unlike forms, where your prospects may feel stupid, website errors make your company look stupid. Fixing website errors is low-hanging fruit in improving your conversion rates.

Make sure to include a thorough quality-assurance step in your website updates. You should do the following:

- Test all your pages on all major browser and operating system combinations.
- Don't forget to test interactions like form fields, hover effects, pop-ups, videos, and so on.

- Check your web analytics regularly for 404 page views, and make sure those are fixed.

- Test your website experience with JavaScript and cookie-acceptance turned off.

- Test your ad campaigns in the wild, and follow the conversion path from originating ad through to completed conversion.

- Use a proofreader who hasn't been involved in the project to compare the design and copy to the live test challengers.

If you do have technical errors, make sure you display friendly error messages, unlike the 404 page on this high-profile consumer brand's website.

Zappos, on the other hand, has a useful and fun 404 error page with buttons to the most common tasks: search bar, home page, and a help page.

Site Speed

Well-documented studies by Google, Yahoo!, Akamai, and Amazon show that page-load times affect site usage and conversion. Marissa Mayer of Google gave the example of Google Maps in her talk at the Web 2.0 Summit. When the company shrank the Google

Maps page size from 100 KB to about 75 KB, traffic increased 10 percent the first week and 25 percent more in the following three weeks. Google also found a 20 percent revenue difference when the main search-results page loaded in 0.9 seconds compared to 0.4 seconds.

Not only does site speed affect conversions, but Google also factors it in to AdWords quality score and organic search rankings. There's no downside to a fast-loading website.

Effort Anxiety

As you saw earlier with respect to filling out forms, perceived complexity and effort can create anxiety for your prospects. This principle applies to all of your communications, your website, and your landing pages too. If you can make your prospects' lives easier, they will make your life better by buying from you!

For example:

- Do your product category pages include relevant and easy-to-use filters?

  For e-commerce sites, much of the conversion improvement can be achieved by getting people to the right products easily. You should test filtering and sorting options to find the most relevant settings for your product mix.

- Do your product pages present the value proposition before the ordering details?

  As you'll see in the AllPopArt case study next, emphasizing value proposition over product ordering details can reduce anxiety and increase sales. You Should Test That!

- Are your offers easy to redeem?

  Using offer codes within promotional emails and website banners, for example, may be frustrating your shoppers. When they respond to an advertised offer, they may not notice that the code is needed and be annoyed when it's not automatically applied.

This offer could have been automatically applied without needing a code

Or, if you offer a live scheduled product demo, maybe your prospects would prefer a prerecorded demo at their convenience. If you were in your prospect's shoes, think about all the ways it would be easier to respond to the offer.

- Are the steps to purchase and use your products and services easy to understand?

One of the most common problems marketers have is forgetting what their prospects don't know. Have you told them how they should order? Do you recommend the best way to sample or preview the product?

In a test WiderFunnel ran for AllPopArt, we found that moving the product customization and ordering details below the fold increased sales substantially. For landing-page visitors, reducing the prominence of the product-customization form reduced the perceived complexity and minimized anxiety.

Case Study: AllPopArt Lifts Sales by 28 Percent and Revenue per Visitor by 42 Percent with Conversion-Optimization Testing

AllPopArt, a producer of handcrafted pop-art portraits and photos on canvas, used conversion-optimization testing on its product-page template and increased purchases by 28 percent and revenue per visitor by 42 percent.

Since opening its doors in 2004, AllPopArt has assembled an award-winning team of designers, illustrators, and professional framers to create one-of-a-kind custom portraits for thousands of customers worldwide. The company differentiates itself from competitors by focusing on craftsmanship, quality, and attention to detail. All artwork is hand-illustrated by U.S.-based AllPopArt artists using a mix of traditional media and sophisticated digital painting techniques. No artificial or premade software filters are ever used. And no illustrations are ever contracted out to anonymous designers.

The Business Need

With growing competitive pressures from China and India, AllPopArt keeps a close eye on the evolving needs of its customers. The company conducts surveys on an ongoing basis with both paying customers and website visitors at the pre-purchase stage. AllPopArt is proud of its high satisfaction level among customers; however, it also identified customer perceptions that may have been hindering purchase conversions:

- Half of the AllPopArt.com visitors didn't understand that an actual artist creates the artwork.

  AllPopArt's key differentiator wasn't clearly communicated, and many visitors failed to see all the features that made AllPopArt so unique compared to alternative options.

- Many website visitors believed the product was too expensive.

  Because a large number of website visitors didn't grasp AllPopArt's value proposition, it was no surprise that many found the price of the artwork to be high.

The Challenges

AllPopArt wanted to address these market issues by redesigning key pages on its website, but the company was concerned about the following:

- It didn't know which page to redesign first.

  Without an in-depth analysis of the company's website analytics, the AllPopArt team didn't know how to prioritize which pages had the best opportunities for improvement.

- The AllPopArt team didn't have in-house resources to design and implement conversion-optimization tests.

  The team was committed to using controlled, scientific testing before implementing new designs, but they didn't have the time or specialized skills to run the project on their own.

- They didn't want to risk increasing the purchase-conversion rate while inadvertently hurting revenues.

  The AllPopArt team knew they couldn't solely focus on increasing purchase conversions, because doing so could easily result in depressed overall revenues. Both the number of purchases and revenue per visitor were important metrics for the AllPopArt business.

  After an exhaustive search for the right conversion-optimization agency, one that would understand the company's challenges, the AllPopArt team hired WiderFunnel Marketing to solve their problem.

The Solution

WiderFunnel handled the AllPopArt conversion-optimization testing from end to end, beginning with an in-depth analytics review to identify key problem areas in the AllPopArt.com

Continues

Case Study: AllPopArt Lifts Sales by 28 Percent and Revenue per Visitor by 42 Percent with Conversion-Optimization Testing *(Continued)*

conversion funnel. In consultation with the AllPopArt team, WiderFunnel identified the product page template as a priority page to optimize and began planning a test.

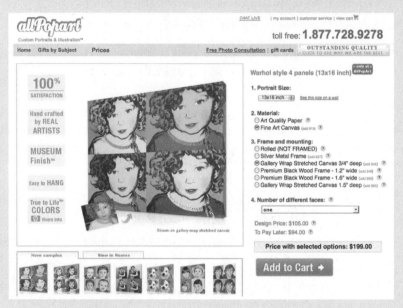

The AllPopArt control page

WiderFunnel designed and tested the following variations alongside the control (original) page:

- Variation A: "Lightbox & CTA." This design variation tested a number of changes, including more prominent call-to-action areas and clickable value propositions. The overall layout of the page remained unchanged from the control page.

- Variation B: "No +/- Prices." This variation was identical to Variation A, except that the price of each user-selectable option (such as frame type or materials) was removed and only the total price of the illustration was displayed. The test hypothesis was that removing the text would simplify the page content, improve clarity, and increase sales conversions.

- Variation C: "Horizontal Steps." This variation was a big departure from the other two. The product description and value propositions were brought to the forefront above the page fold, and user-selectable product options were moved below. Free shipping info was also more prominently displayed as well as thumbnails of samples.

The Results: 28 Percent More Purchases, 42 Percent Higher Revenue per Visitor!

Once the test received a sufficient number of visitors and conversions to reach statistical significance, the winning design was identified as Variation C. WiderFunnel analyzed revenue data to confirm that Variation C not only lifted purchase conversions by 28 percent but also lifted revenue per visitor by 42 percent!

For AllPopArt, this means they get 42 percent higher revenue from the same number of visitors to the company's product pages, at no extra cost. AllPopArt can increase its visitor cost per click and still receive improved return on marketing spend.

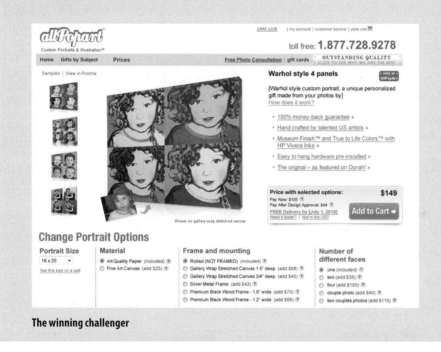

The winning challenger

Form fields are one of the least-loved things on the Web. In some cases, such as this AllPopArt example, reducing the prominence of a complex form can boost conversion rates. You Should Test That!

Fulfillment Anxiety

There's a barrier between you and your online prospects. They can't physically see you or your products. They can't tell who's on the receiving end of their requests for information or purchase. They also may anticipate feeling powerless to get responses to their grievances if things go wrong.

Fulfillment anxiety exists regardless of whether or not your online experience promotes it. You need to include messages that satisfy your prospects' need for assurance.

Security

The security assurance you need to provide depends on the types of private information you collect and store. One of the most common ways to assure your site visitors that their information is secure is to subscribe to a third-party security symbol like McAfee Secure or TRUSTe. In testing whether these symbols increase sales, I've seen mixed results. Some have reported seeing sales increases by adding the badge while others have seen no change or even decreases.

One of WiderFunnel's clients ran a test in which adding the McAfee Secure symbol in the site-wide shopping cart area reduced e-commerce sales by nearly 2 percent.

By over-emphasizing security, you can create even more anxiety. For visitors who aren't initially concerned about security, raising the issue can cause them to second-guess their safety. If you use security indicators, You Should Test That!

Fine Print

I came across a landing page recently with this headline:

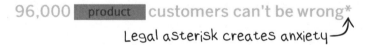

If you have to include a legal asterisk on your main message, you've immediately lost credibility. As it turned out, the disclaimer didn't need to hurt credibility. The footer said "*Customer count as of Q1 2012." They should ask themselves whether leaving that out would pose a credible risk.

Legal disclaimers in your marketing communications send a message to your prospects. Do you want them to think of you as trustworthy, honest, and approachable, or legalistic, inauthentic, and difficult?

You should get rid of legal disclaimers and find a way to include the full story in your copywriting. Tell your readers what they need to know in the copy, and you won't need to hide behind asterisks.

And if you do have to include legal copy, can you write it in natural language? In some organizations, the legal team is known as the "sales reduction department" because of their inflexible approach to customer communications. But there are other, progressive legal groups. Pushing for friendly legalese is worth the effort.

Brand Reputation

Your brand reputation and credibility can add to or reduce fulfillment anxiety. The prospect asks two brand-related questions when making a decision:

- Will this company deliver on its promises?

  If you have a known and trusted brand, your prospects are buying more than just your features. Your brand can reduce purchase anxiety and give prospects a value proposition advantage over your competitors.

- What will others think of my purchase?

  For a consumer, most purchases carry minimal reputation risks; but when a person makes a business purchase decision, they have to consider how the decision will be perceived by colleagues and bosses. Remember the old adage: "Nobody ever got fired for buying IBM equipment." If you're up against the industry-standard brand, you need to work harder to reduce purchase anxiety.

Third-party credibility indicators can help reduce anxiety for unknown brands, as discussed in Chapter 5, "Optimize Your Value Proposition." You should test emphasizing those indicators, especially if your brand isn't in a strong awareness and trust position.

If your industry has accreditations available, especially for services companies, you can also use their logos to lend credibility. For some target audiences, the Better Business Bureau can add credibility and reduce anxiety, too.

Delivery Promise

From the moment your prospect converts into a lead or customer, a virtual timer is ticking in their head until you deliver on your promise. You should set clear expectations for when they will receive fulfillment of your promise.

In the MerchantWarehouse.com example in Chapter 7, "Optimize for Clarity," you saw that we added a message setting the expectation that site visitors can get a merchant account in as little as 24 hours.

Amazon.com sets retail expectations well on its product pages by clearly showing availability and delivery dates.

Bold availability message   Delivery promise

Once you've set expectations, then you have to deliver on them or risk harming your brand.

Guarantees, Returns, and Unsubscription

Your prospects' biggest fear is post-purchase disappointment. To remove that anxiety, you need to answer the question, "What happens if I'm disappointed?"

Satisfaction guarantees can reduce fulfillment anxiety and increase conversions. If you have a guarantee, you should test how prominent its placement should be. In most cases, a guarantee works best as reference information in a secondary location.

Whether you use a guarantee symbol or a text link, you should link to more information. As you saw in the AllPopArt case study earlier in this chapter, WiderFunnel's new pages added guarantee information in a pop-up lightbox linked from a bullet list text link.

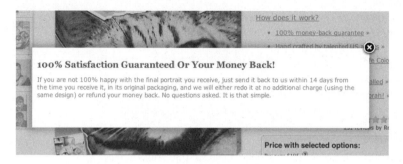

In WiderFunnel's tests, we've found that pop-up lightboxes work well for providing detail without the added distraction of taking the visitor to a different page.

L.L.Bean shows another example of additional guarantee information with a rollover message.

For subscriptions, you should make cancellation seem easy. Wordtracker demonstrates the one-step cancellation at the top of its signup page.

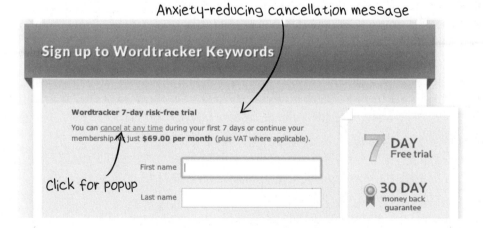

Clicking the "cancel at any time" link opens a pop-up lightbox with a screen-shot showing exactly how to unsubscribe in a single step.

If a picture is worth a thousand words, this example should eliminate all cancellation anxiety for the subscriber. You can add similar anxiety-reducing messages for your newsletter or blog subscriptions, too.

Turn Anxiety in Your Favor

Once a person owns something, that thing becomes more valuable to the person than it was before they owned it. This is called the *endowment effect*. A well-known study led by the Nobel laureate Daniel Kahneman showed that we overvalue what we own by nearly double.

Another study by Ziv Carmon, associate professor of marketing at INSEAD, and Dan Ariely showed the endowment effect increasing peoples' valuation of NCAA basketball game tickets by 14 times for those who had won a draw to be eligible to purchase tickets. The endowment effect can be a powerful cognitive bias!

The effect is connected to people's tendency regarding loss aversion and risk aversion. Imagine two scenarios where you need make a choice between two options:

- In one scenario, your choice could result in a bonus of $1,000 if you pick the right option, or nothing if you pick the other.
- In the second scenario, your choice could lead to a $1,000 fine that you have to pay, or nothing.

Which of those decision scenarios makes you feel more anxious?

If you're like most people, the potential loss of $1,000 creates much more decision anxiety than a chance for a $1,000 bonus. People's drive to avoid loss is more powerful than their drive for gain.

If your prospects are too comfortable in their current situation, they won't take the perceived risk of buying from you. The anxiety-causing risks outweigh their desire to gain the benefits of your product or service.

You can test using anxiety as motivation by framing your benefits in terms of loss avoidance. What would your prospect lose out on by *not* purchasing your product or service?

For example, in a search for business process management (BPM) consulting, one of the landing pages had this headline:

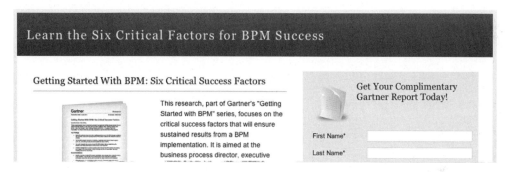

What would be the risks of not hiring this consultancy for BPM consulting?

An alternative headline and subhead could test an "avoiding failure" approach to create anxiety about not obtaining the right advice.

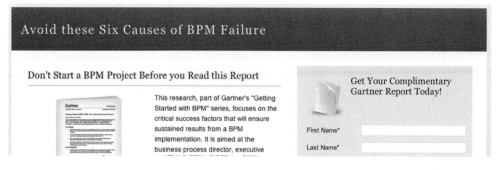

Try turning anxiety in your favor. You Should Test That!

Note: Do you have more to add to the conversation about optimizing for anxiety? Start a discussion at YouShouldTestThat.com/Anxiety.

In Chapter 9, "Optimize for Distraction," you'll see how to optimize for reducing distraction from elements like product options, competing messages, and images.

9 Optimize for Distraction

It was impossible to get a conversation going, everybody was talking too much.

—*Yogi Berra*

Steve Jobs built Apple into a $30 billion company with fewer than 30 major products. He was a master of focus.

He once said, "People think focus means saying yes to the thing you've got to focus on. But that's not what it means at all. It means saying no to the hundred other good ideas that there are. You have to pick carefully. I'm actually as proud of many of the things we haven't done as the things we have done."

In my early career as a campaign planner in ad agencies, I developed hundreds of creative briefs, some of which went on to produce award-winning ads. To me, the most important part of those briefs was what we called the *compelling idea* or *key message*. It was the one idea that, if we could get the target audience to believe it, would create desire for the product.

You can't create an ad with more than one compelling idea. It just wouldn't fly. Advertising messages need to focus on the one most important thing to stick in the prospect's mind.

The thing I did differently than anyone else at the time was to spend a lot of time finding that compelling idea. I explored the research, interviewed product managers, and wrote dozens of options that I winnowed down to the one idea.

Have you done that with your landing pages and conversion funnels? Do you know what your most compelling idea is?

Focus isn't easily achieved. In this chapter, you'll see how to create focus by eliminating the distraction of superfluous messages, options, images, and graphics.

Distraction Components of the page that redirect attention from the primary value proposition message and call to action. Ask yourself: "Are there elements on the page that could divert the visitor away from the goal?"

Two Distraction Points

Your prospects go through two stages of processing your landing page: the initial impression and the message-consumption stage. These two stages are distinct in their purpose and in the dangers for distraction.

Eye-tracking studies have shown that page viewers form their first impression nearly immediately, often within two tenths of a second. Within that first fraction of a second, the visual layout above the fold is the primary determinant of whether the visitor will continue reading or bounce off the page, and where their eyes will rest.

During the first-impression stage, information processing is entirely based on visual shapes and color. The visitor quickly determines whether the page is attractive or not, copy-heavy or sparse, welcoming or irritating.

After the first impression, the visitor takes up to three seconds to scan the page before their eyes settle on their first area of focus. The reader is looking for visual cues to understand how the page is organized and where the most important information is positioned. If there are too many distraction-causing visual elements, the visitor is likely to bounce off the page within a few seconds.

Once the reader chooses a focal point, the messages become the next distraction barrier. This message-consumption stage can range from several seconds to minutes as the reader scans and jumps around the information to choose which pieces of content are most interesting to read. While they're processing the page messages, distraction is introduced via competing messages, product options, images, and off-page links.

First-Impression Distraction

The importance of your above-the-fold layout and content can't be overstated. This part of the page is entirely responsible for the page's first impression. Even if your page takes a long-copy approach and the purchase decision is made after reading many screens of content, your prospect will decide whether to continue reading based on the above-fold first impression.

Even after the first impression, most visitors don't scroll very far. As you saw in the scrollmap example in Chapter 3, "Prioritize Testing Opportunities," most of your readers will only see the top portion of your page content. That is where you should spend the majority of your optimization effort.

Look through Your Prospects' Eyes

To find your points of distraction, you should evaluate your pages the way your visitors see them. If you have a graphic designer working on your page designs, they probably send you images of designs for your review and approval. Do you view the entire page on your screen to evaluate it? Most people make the mistake of reviewing the content in the context of the entire page. This is misleading.

Your visitors only look at your page one screen-height at a time. You should evaluate your pages in screen-height increments to understand whether there's enough reason for the visitor to scroll down to the next part of the content.

Don't forget to take browser toolbar height into account. On a 768-pixel height screen, for example, the viewable height is only about 600 pixels. Look at your web analytics reports to find the most common screen sizes for which to design. You can find this report in Google Analytics by going to Audience › Technology › Browser & OS. Then, beside Primary Dimension in the middle, click Screen Resolution.

The second number, screen height, is the most important.

You now see a report showing how much of your pages your visitors can see. For example, the majority of the WiderFunnel home-page content is viewable by 98 percent of visitors.

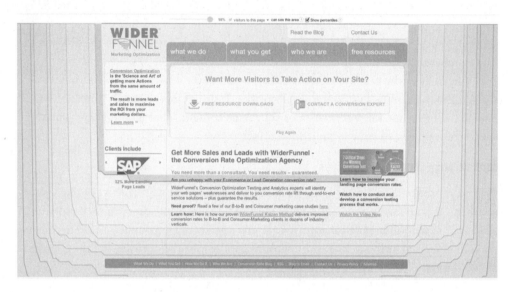

Note: This image is compressed to fit on the printed page. To view a full-size image with legible type, go to YouShouldTestThat.com/Distraction.

In Google Analytics, this report is in Content › In-Page Analytics. Click the Browser Size button to see which portions of the page are below the fold. You can adjust the percentage you're interested in by using a slider or clicking the shade gradations.

Looking at your important pages through this lens will help you see through your visitors' eyes. Look for the immediate distractions in that above-fold area.

Many landing pages have a deadly combination of visual and message distractions above the fold.

Distraction can be caused even by minor elements like background textures, asymmetrical designs, and complex graphic treatments.

I often squint my eyes during this stage of analysis to approximate the page's first impression and role-play where my prospects' eyes will be drawn. As you've seen in every stage of analysis in this book, you should try to put yourself in your prospects' shoes.

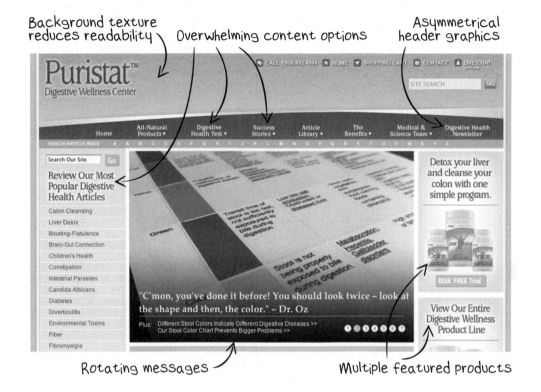

Background texture reduces readability

Overwhelming content options

Asymmetrical header graphics

Rotating messages

Multiple featured products

Too Much Content

The most common first-impression problem above the fold is too much content. You can distract visitors with too many columns, redundant content categories, too much text, and too many images.

Too much content crammed into the limited space above the fold doesn't give the viewer's eye an easy place to rest and begin the message-consumption phase. And if the starting point for reading a page isn't immediately apparent, the page is over-working your prospect.

This is a very common problem. Most marketers are terrified that they could be leaving something important off their communications. The temptation to add *just one more feature* is great, but it doesn't take long for your pages to become a wash of over-complication and distraction.

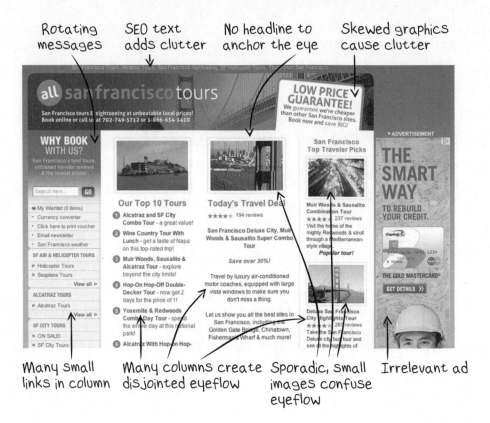

Rotating messages

SEO text adds clutter

No headline to anchor the eye

Skewed graphics cause clutter

Many small links in column

Many columns create disjointed eyeflow

Sporadic, small images confuse eyeflow

Irrelevant ad

An alternative page layout could solve these distraction problems. For example, it could have a featured product offer to anchor the eye, followed by two main columns to display available product categories and a list of popular tours. The right column could be given less visual prominence and contain contact and reference information.

Banner graphic
Guarantee

Value proposition headline to anchor eye

Featured most popular tour with compelling image
$XX.xx
Button
Email offer signup

Category tiles

Tour image
Tour description
$XX.xx

Value proposition
• Low prices
• Unbiased reviews
• Etc.

$XX.xx

$XX.xx

$XX.xx

Wishlist

The Color of Conversion

Few things are quite as personal as the interpretation of color. And few can stir such feeling and create so many arguments.

Remember the last time you debated with a friend whether a certain shade was a true orange color? Color conflict can be even more difficult to resolve within a business.

Google's lead designer, Douglas Bowman, famously left the company out of frustration with the company's tendency to test design and color decisions. In one example he gave, Google had been using different shades of blue in two of its products. To decide which one to standardize on, the company tested 41 shades between the products and found the one that maximized conversions.

To Bowman, that was a frustrating example of an overly data-driven culture. Although I'd agree with Bowman that this particular type of test may not be the best use of peoples' time, with the traffic volumes Google has access to, it's a viable solution to move past debates and opinions. As long as a consequence isn't to restrict creative initiative, test away, Google!

Color is important for conversion optimization, but not in the way many assume. There is no "best" color for conversion, but there is a best color treatment for each particular situation. In many cases, when it's difficult to pinpoint why a design is repelling, poor color choice can be at work.

Distraction: Pale yellow background color almost reminds of sweat stain. Ick.

Distraction: Prominent colored graphics distract from products

Value Proposition: Clashing colors—red, pink, gold and yellow—reduces credibility.

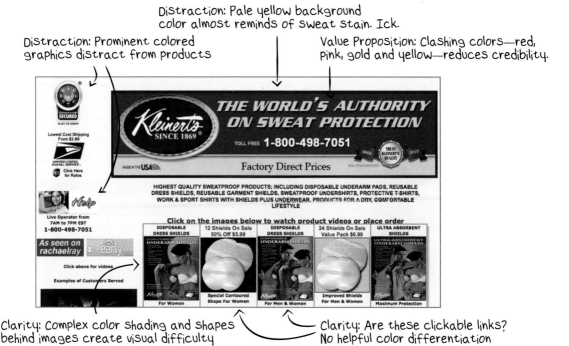

Clarity: Complex color shading and shapes behind images create visual difficulty

Clarity: Are these clickable links? No helpful color differentiation

The following pages highlight elements covered in this book that are best demonstrated in full color.

Heatmaps

Heatmaps show how page content influences where people focus on the page. They're just a few of the many possible methods for understanding user interactions and developing hypotheses for testing.

Eye-tracking studies show how people guide their attention. Here are eye-tracking heatmaps produced by Swedish eye-tracking tool company Tobii, with descriptions shown in Chapter 3, "Prioritize Testing Opportunities."

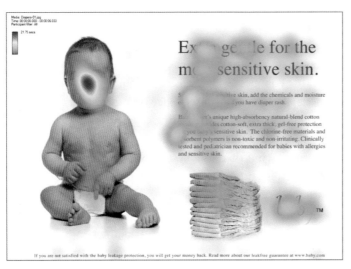

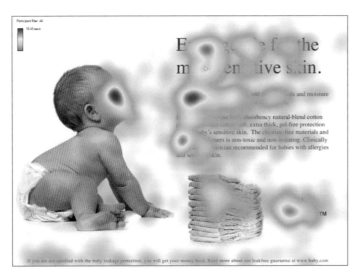

Chapter 3 also shows how click heatmaps can approximate a viewer's attention on the page. The heatmap of WiderFunnel's conversion-optimization service page, at WiderFunnel.com/solutions/conversion-optimization, shows that there's a lot of interest in the our process and landing-page optimization pages.

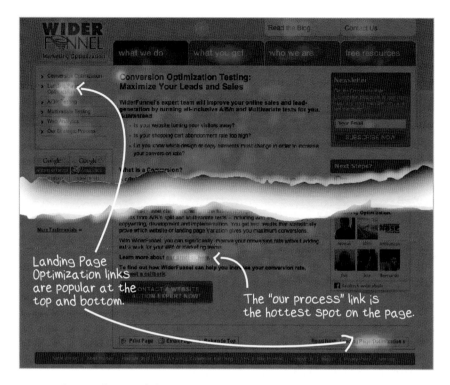

The scrollmap of the same page on the www.WiderFunnel.com site reinforces that a lot of people are reading through most of the content of this page, which is a good sign.

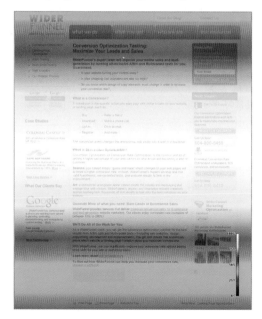

Chapter 3 shows how to use heatmaps and scrollmaps to come up with hypotheses that can be tested to improve your conversion rates and profits.

Clarity and Distraction

Color often plays a role in the conflicting forces of clarity and distraction. Here are a few website examples showing the impact of color.

Distracting Credibility Indicators

In Chapter 5, "Optimize Your Value Proposition," you saw that adding professional reviews, media mentions, and awards can boost credibility. If they're placed in color in the wrong position, though, they can also distract from your primary call to action (CTA).

Media logos in color can visually compete with your primary message and CTA.

37Signals minimizes distraction by placing logos in grayscale.

Visual Emphasis

Basecamp uses color to emphasize key points of its value proposition and CTA. The CTA could be enhanced even more by testing color and design treatment.

Color emphasis can visually tie benefits together.

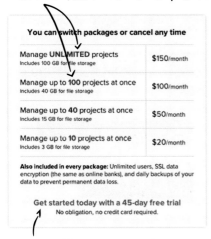

They could test using a button CTA here rather than just blue text.

In the case of a product page test for BabyAge, mentioned in Chapter 7, "Optimize for Clarity", WiderFunnel tested several challenger variations and increased sales by 22 percent. One of the design changes used a red color to enhance the visual clarity of discounted products. You can download the full case study at YouShouldTestThat.com/CaseStudies.

Improved color-message resonance

Buttons!

Too many people think there is one perfect button color. Here are just a few buttons from winning pages WiderFunnel has designed. As you can see, the best button color and design for each context vary greatly!

For a while we had a string of tests where we tested big orange buttons, and it became an acronym around the WiderFunnel office. We call him BOB. He works hard ;-)

Color Contrast

As shown in Chapter 7, low-contrast fonts and graphics reduce conversion rates.

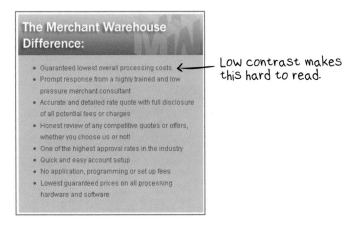

Low contrast makes this hard to read.

Overwhelming Content

In Chapter 7, one of the tips was that writing short paragraphs with large type size improves clarity. Poor type treatment affects more than just clarity. It can create first-impression visual distraction as well, as shown in Chapter 9, "Optimize for Distraction."

Small, low-contrast type in large blocks immediately discourages your prospect from even attempting to read your content.

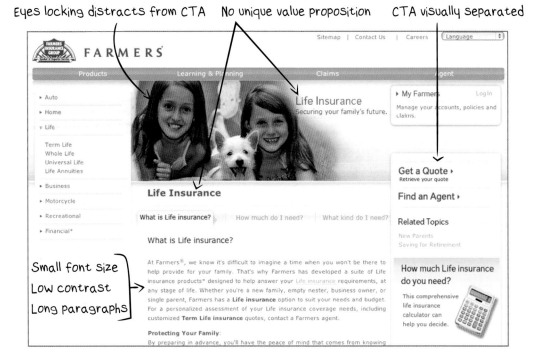

Complex Graphics

Graphics are used to direct the eyeflow toward the most important content. If the page is full of complex graphic elements, they compete for attention and make the page more difficult to digest. For more information, see Chapter 9.

Large Headers

Some websites consistently waste valuable pixels with large header images, logos, taglines, and navigation bars.

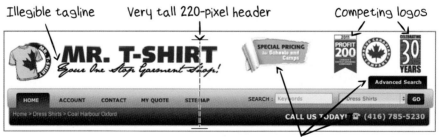

Challengers and Champions

Following are some of the screenshots from challenger variations of A/B/*n* tests. For full-color versions of all the case studies shown in the book, visit YouShouldTestThat.com/CaseStudies.

Electronic Arts Lifts Game Registration Conversion Rate by 128 Percent

EA's *The Sims 3*, a life-simulation computer game, used conversion-rate optimization testing to identify the most compelling value proposition—and boosted game registrations by 128 percent! Notice how the clear eyeflow and prominent, contrasting button color on the winning page left no doubt about the action the player should take. The full case study is in Chapter 5.

Control

Winner—128 percent conversion-rate lift

Nurse.com Lifts Subscription Sales by 15.7 Percent

Nurse.com provides continuing education (CE) training courses for nurses, which are required annually in most U.S. states. In a dramatic redesign A/B/*n* test, WiderFunnel created a page that lifted CE sales by 15.7 percent. By comparing the click heatmaps between the control and winning pages, you'll see how the new page's graphics created a clear eyeflow and focused attention on the single Get Access Now action.

Control

Heat map

Full page

The winning page improved the clarity and relevance of the page to significantly increase sales. For more detail about the business challenge and insights discovered, read the full case study at YouShouldTestThat.com/CaseStudies.

Control

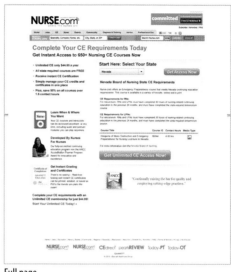

Full page

Heat map

BabyAge.com Lifts E-commerce Sales by 22 Percent

Leading online retailer BabyAge.com outsourced its website testing to WiderFunnel and increased its online sales by 22 percent with changes to its product page template. Notice how we reduced design distraction and increased the clarity of the product information. You can read the full case study at YouShouldTestThat.com/CaseStudies.

Control

Winner—22 percent sales lift

Hair Club Lifts Lead-Generation Conversion Rate by 20 Percent

Hair Club, a leading hair-restoration service company, increased retail lead-generation conversions by 20 percent with A/B/*n* testing that beat the previous "best practices" designs. You can find this case study in Chapter 9.

Control

Winner—20 percent conversion-rate lift

SAP Lifts Leads Generated by 32.5 Percent

A test on the SAP Crystal Reports landing page lifted downloads by using more compelling language, clarifying eyeflow, and including a prominent button design and color. The full case study is in Chapter 7.

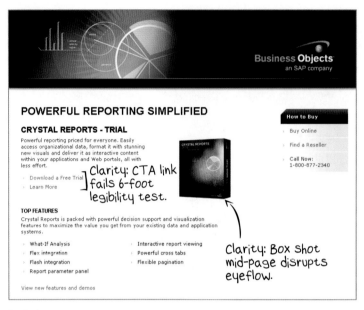

Control

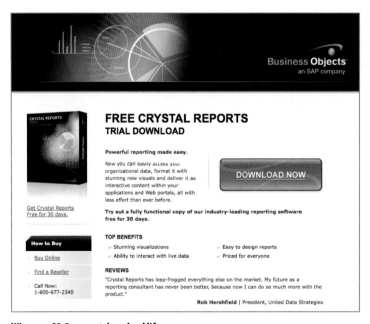

Winner—32.5 percent download lift

Travel Media Marketer Doubles Revenue with Site-Wide Conversion-Optimization Testing

WiderFunnel recommended and tested website changes that would significantly improve visitors' motivation to order travel guides. The winning page design used lighter colors, rewritten value-proposition content, and more prominent buttons. You can access the entire case study at YouShouldTestThat.com/CaseStudies.

Distraction: Large color blocks compete for attention.

Clarity: Low prominence for check-out button

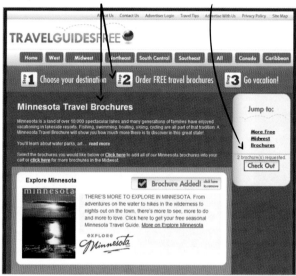

Control

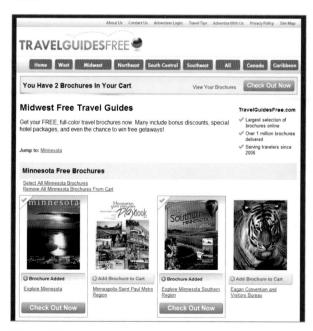

Winner—100 percent more revenue

Site-Wide Product Page Test Lifts Revenue Per Visitor by 42 Percent for AllPopArt.com

WiderFunnel tested four different product page designs in a site-wide template test for AllPopArt. You can access the entire case study at YouShouldTestThat.com/CaseStudies.

Distraction: Unclickable yellow tabs redirect attention.

Distraction: Color emphasizes additional costs.

Anxiety: Product option fields above the fold are uninviting.

Control

Winner—42 percent more revenue

Many alternative layouts could be tested that would reduce distracting content and have the potential to dramatically improve this site's sales. You Should Test That!

Daunting Text

In Chapter 7, "Optimize for Clarity," one of the tips was that writing short paragraphs with a large type size improves clarity. Poor copy treatment affects more than just clarity; it can create first-impression distraction as well. Large blocks of copywriting, especially when set in small, low-contrast type, immediately discourage your prospect from attempting to read your content.

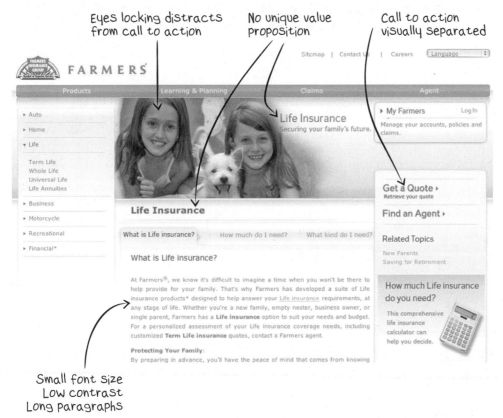

Eyes locking distracts from call to action

No unique value proposition

Call to action visually separated

Small font size
Low contrast
Long paragraphs

Especially above the fold, your paragraphs should be no more than three lines high. Font size and color can also affect clarity; see Chapter 7 for type-size and color-contrast tips.

Complex Graphics

Graphics are used to direct the eyeflow toward the most important content. If the entire page is full of complex graphic elements, they compete for attention and make the page more difficult to digest. Each graphical element—every line, shading, curve, and color—adds to the mental processing required to understand the page.

Just as concise copywriting improves your communication, so does eliminating unnecessary graphic elements.

Large Headers

The top part of your page is its most valuable space. Some websites consistently waste those valuable pixels with large areas for header images, logos, taglines, and navigation bars.

Low-contrast buttons Competing calls to action

Huge header area pushes
content below the fold. Low-readability type treatment

Looking at some page designs, you can imagine the size of monitor the designer was using. Designers should preview their work on a screen similar to the one their prospects will be using. For most websites and landing pages, your header should be close to 100 pixels in height and rarely more than 150 pixels.

Even worse is to have a large header combined with over-complex graphics!

Illegible tagline   Very tall 220-pixel header   Competing logos

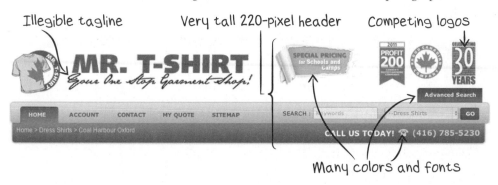

Many colors and fonts

Consider carefully whether additional graphics, logos, and design elements will support your conversions. Logos are designed to attract attention and will compete with your products and message.

Redundancy

If one call to action is good, two must be twice as good, right? Not if they create visual distraction or confusion.

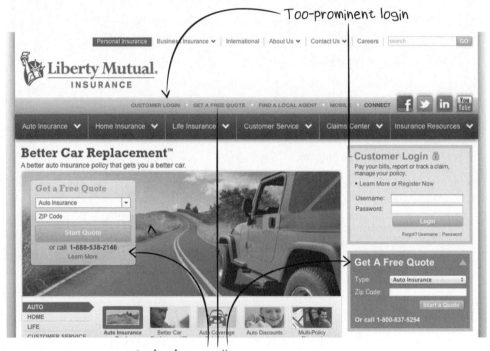

Too-prominent login

Redundant calls to action

It's better to create a focused eyeflow leading toward a single call to action. Repetition and overemphasis on secondary content, such as customer login areas, create an unnecessarily busy page.

By testing several variations of a newsletter signup pop-up form, Prime Publishing discovered that eliminating distraction dramatically lifted the subscription conversion rate. Check out the details in the following case study.

 Case Study: Craft Website Increases Email Capture by 22.3 Percent on Landing-Page Form

Prime Publishing was established in 1995 as a traditional niche book publisher. Recognizing the extraordinary marketing opportunities created by the Web, Prime Publishing reformulated its strategy to become a leading Internet media and marketing company. It now operates a rapidly growing network of niche content websites, online stores, blogs, and email newsletters, all primarily aimed at female audiences.

The 10 online properties Prime Publishing launched in the preceding two years focus on niche lifestyle topics such as crafts, crocheting, knitting, recipes, and healthy eating. Together, they're visited by more than two million people every month.

One of the company's web properties is `FaveCrafts.com`, a premier online destination for the crafting enthusiast. It offers a wealth of free content such as patterns, seasonal craft ideas, product reviews, and e-books.

The Business Need

FaveCrafts' advertising-supported business model relies heavily on capturing email addresses of first-time web visitors. The company has implemented an extensive demand-generation campaign, including paid search, to reach well-targeted audiences. It collects email addresses via various mechanisms such as a newsletter sign-up form and members-only content. This newsletter sign-up form is Prime Publishing's highest priority for conversion optimization.

The original form was simple, containing only one input field (email address). Its main value proposition was free access to crafting projects on the site. It was presented when a web visitor landed on the site.

The control landing page

Continues

Case Study: Craft Website Increases Email Capture by 22.3 Percent on Landing-Page Form *(Continued)*

Although the form had a very respectable conversion rate by general industry standards, the management team believed there was room for improvement and wanted to maximize the return on their paid-search marketing investment.

The Challenges

Over time, the company had made a few small adjustments to the FaveCrafts.com landing-page form in an attempt to improve the conversion rate. It had seen some successes, but none significant enough to meaningfully impact the bottom line.

The management team recognized that they needed a fresh pair of eyes to take the conversion rate to the next level. They knew their in-house conversion-optimization experience and resources were limited and felt that the best route would be to use the expertise of a specialized conversion-optimization agency to come up with strong test hypotheses and designs.

The Solution

The Prime Publishing management team approached WiderFunnel to develop a testing strategy for the FaveCrafts.com Crochet landing-page form. WiderFunnel developed the test plan, including hypotheses, wireframes, graphic design, and copy, and then customized test scripts and executed the test.

Based on WiderFunnel's LIFT Analysis of the original form, WiderFunnel created four redesigned challenger variations to run in an A/B/*n* split test, as follows:

Variation A: "Speed"

This challenger was a dramatic change from the control, with a different size, design, and copy approach. The overarching hypothesis of this challenger was that simplicity would result in more email addresses being collected because it's much less onerous for visitors to mentally process less versus more content.

The following changes were made:

- All imagery was removed to reduce clutter and distraction.
- The amount of copy was reduced to improve clarity of the value proposition.
- Ad copy keywords ("free crochet patterns") were repeated in the headline to improve relevance.
- Copy was left-aligned to improve eyeflow.

- The call to action (CTA) button was rewritten and made more prominent.
- The input field was enlarged and made more prominent.
- Step indicators were removed.
- The size of the form was reduced to a minimum.
- The color scheme was simplified.
- The Close button was moved to reduce distraction.

Variation B: "Patterns"

In this challenger variation, WiderFunnel again bumped up relevance to the incoming source media but, rather than removing all imagery, it tested one high-quality crochet-focused image. Other changes included these:

- An image caption with FaveCrafts' positioning statement was added.
- The amount of copy was reduced.
- Ad copy keywords were repeated in the headline.
- Benefit-oriented copy was written.
- Copy was left-aligned to improve eyeflow.
- The CTA button was rewritten and made more prominent.
- The input field was enlarged and made more prominent.
- Step indicators were removed.
- The color scheme was simplified.
- The Close button was moved to reduce distraction.

Variation C: "Community"

The layout approach of this challenger was similar to Variation B, but the image and caption were replaced with a photo of a group of women with crocheted items and a customer testimonial. The benefit-oriented copy was also adjusted to emphasize the value of belonging to a community of like-minded individuals.

Variation D: "Speed Larger"

This challenger took the same approach as Variation A but tested the impact of the form size on moving the conversion-rate dial. WiderFunnel added more white space around the content area and enlarged the lightbox frame.

Continues

Case Study: Craft Website Increases Email Capture by 22.3 Percent on Landing-Page Form *(Continued)*

The Results: Conversion Rate Lift of 22.3 Percent

Three of the four challengers generated a conversion-rate lift over the control. The winning design, Variation A: "Speed," lifted conversions by 22.3 percent! It was followed closely by Variation D: "Speed Larger," which delivered an 18.7 percent lift over the control.

Winning challenger page

With this test of the FaveCrafts landing-page form, the Prime Publishing management team discovered that minimizing distraction and maximizing relevance to ad copy were key factors in influencing conversions.

Message Distraction

There's a logical argument to be made for providing on your pages all the possible options prospects could want. It makes sense to assume that you'll serve a larger percentage of the audience by offering infinite variety for them to choose from.

But people's behavior doesn't always follow logic. (Some would argue that it rarely follows logic.) As Dan Ariely says in his book of the same title, we are "predictably irrational."

Remember the study of jam flavor selection in Chapter 4, "Create Hypotheses with the LIFT Model"? When the jam table in the store offered more selection, the store saw increased interest in the jam table but decreased sales.

When given too much choice, people freeze. And when given too many messages, none of them stick.

After the first few seconds on your page, your prospect has completed the first-impression stage and will have (you hope) decided to read some of the content. This is the point where the quality of your message and interaction becomes important.

Too Many Messages

You need to focus the messages on each of your pages for maximum effect. This isn't a new marketing concept. Professional communicators have known for many years that they have a much better chance of communicating anything if they focus on a single message. Politicians have the best results when they stick to their talking points and repeat their position (regardless of whether it answers the question at hand), advertisers' most effective ads promote a single feature, and mothers all over the world know the importance of repetition to get a single instruction to stick in the child's head.

The core problem you face is the limited mental processing power of your prospects. With background thoughts, concurrent tasks, fatigue, and interruptions going on, they simply don't have the bandwidth available.

Throw a baseball at someone, and he may catch it. Throw six, and he doesn't have a chance. All the messages may be relevant to your prospect, but he'll be overwhelmed long before he has a chance to consider each one.

The concept may seem simple: focus on a single message to get the message across. But it's surprisingly difficult to do.

Many forces are pushing you to add distracting messages. Competing stakeholders within the company need to promote their points of view on your pages. Multiple product lines need to be sold. And there's always the temptation to think that the prospect for widget x is also a good prospect for widget y, right?

Discipline is needed to focus on your primary message.

Irrelevant Content

Remember the San Francisco Tours page earlier in this chapter? One of the problems on that page is irrelevant content. The page displays an ad in the right column that doesn't relate to the company's tours. That ad creates a visual distraction that clutters the first impression and also distracts from the message as page visitors try to find relevant and interesting tours.

San Francisco Tours isn't the only one with this problem. Dell's home-office laptop page, for example, contains numerous ads and distracting messages that redirect attention away from the primary purpose of the page for the prospect: choosing the best type of Dell laptop for their needs.

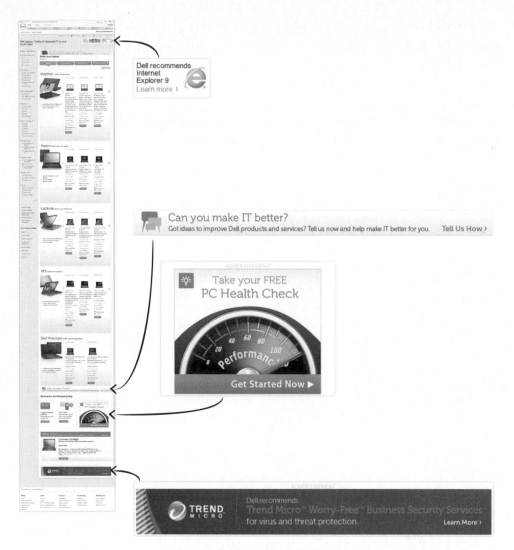

Although the companies are likely making some revenue from those ads, I would recommend testing whether they're providing a net benefit. The added distraction and reduced credibility from advertising may outweigh the advertising revenue stream. As you'll see in Chapter 11, "Test Your Hypotheses," if you're in this situation, you can test multiple income streams site-wide to determine the mix that maximizes overall revenue.

Too Many Options

An even more important question for Dell could be, is this long and detailed page of laptop specs the best way for prospects to choose their laptop? Maybe that long page with so many product options is overwhelming for shoppers.

Dell could test reducing the information and choices on the page and focusing shoppers' attention on the most important decisions to make first. Maybe fewer base laptop options could be shown initially.

Incidentally, if you're in a smaller company, you shouldn't assume that a big company like Dell, just because it's successful, shows the best way to present this content. Dell does a lot of testing, but it probably hasn't tested everything, and its situation also may not apply to yours. I've seen many examples of large organizations with limited testing resources and politics that make for poor decisions. Smaller companies often have the advantage of being able to make more pragmatic decisions without political interference.

Another example of product-option distraction is the common section that recommends up-sells and cross-sells.

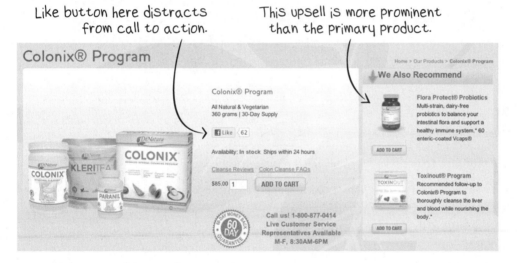

Your prospects have enough work to do to understand the main product. For e-commerce catalogs, you should test the optimal placement for cross-sells and up-sells that maximizes revenue.

Navigation Bars

I've often been asked whether landing pages should have navigation bars. Navigation can help when the page includes a high-involvement call to action or complex product decision. A navigation bar showing that there's a full website can also lend credibility to an unknown brand.

But navigation bars can also be distracting and, in some cases, overwhelming on landing pages.

A lot of e-commerce sites are removing navigation during checkout to minimize distraction. If you test that, make sure you track the average order value for each challenger as well as conversion rate.

Image Distraction

You may not have images that clearly support your value-proposition message. In many cases, it's better to go without than to use images that don't directly reinforce the value proposition, or that are overly distracting. Images have powerful effects and can be polarizing.

For example, WiderFunnel ran a test for OvernightPrints.com on a landing page where visitors could design and print their own business cards. In one of the test isolations, we saw the effect of showing standard stock imagery combined with the business card product, compared to showing the business card product image on its own. The page without the people in the left column outperformed the combined image.

Overnight Prints™

E-Mail Us Shopping Cart Track My Orders

PRODUCTS | PRICING | QUALITY | FREE SAMPLES | DESIGN GUIDE | FAQs | MY ACCOUNT   Español

Get 100 Premium Business Cards
for $9.95

- **The Fastest Printing Option You'll Find Online**
  Place your order today and we'll print, box and ship your business cards to you within just 24 hours!

- **High Quality Printing Without the High Price**
  Only Overnight Prints uses high resolution "offset" printing instead of digital printing. The result? You get brighter, crisper colors, graphics and text.

- **Thick, Professional Looking Paper Stock**
  You'll get the highest quality 15 point card stock with your choice of our popular matte finish or our premium "UV gloss" varnish for FREE!

- **Risk-Free 100% Satisfaction Guarantee**
  We guarantee you'll be satisfied with your business cards, or we'll gladly reprint your order or give you a full refund.

Pricing

Quantity	Single Sided	Double Sided
100	$9.95	$14.95
250	$24.95	$29.95
500	$34.95	$39.95
1000	$39.95	$49.95
2000	$79.95	$89.95
3000	$109.95	$119.95
5000	$149.95	$159.95
All Printed in 1 Business Day!		

Choose from 3 Easy Design Options:

Use the quick and easy **Express Designer**
Choose from thousands of professionally-designed background templates, add your text, and create your business cards in minutes.

Use the advanced **Interactive Designer**
Feeling creative? Use our step-by-step "point-and-click" design wizard to create your own custom business cards quickly and easily.

Use your own files and **Upload Your Design**
Upload your own business card design file, preview it, approve it, and place your order. We'll do the rest!

"I just received my first order business cards today. I am so impressed! The color and quality is simply amazing and the turn around time can't be beat. Your prices are also some of the best I found on the internet. I'll recommending you to everyone, as well as placing more orders. Thanks!"

Cherylynn

SATISFACTION GUARANTEE

Product Details

Color	Paper Quality	Coating	Quantities	Print Time
4:4 Printing	15pt Card Stock	Free Gloss or Matte	100 to 5,000	1 Business Day

PayPal   eCheck   Google Checkout   BBBOnLine RELIABILITY PROGRAM

Overnight Prints • (888) 677-2000

Overnight Prints International
Austria | France | Germany | Great Britain (UK) | USA

Removing the people lifted the conversion rate.

Overnight Prints™

E-Mail Us Shopping Cart Track My Orders

PRODUCTS | PRICING | QUALITY | FREE SAMPLES | DESIGN GUIDE | FAQs | MY ACCOUNT   Español

Get 100 Premium Business Cards
for $9.95

- **The Fastest Printing Option You'll Find Online**
  Place your order today and we'll print, box and ship your business cards to you within just 24 hours!

- **High Quality Printing Without the High Price**
  Only Overnight Prints uses high resolution "offset" printing instead of digital printing. The result? You get brighter, crisper colors, graphics and text.

- **Thick, Professional Looking Paper Stock**
  You'll get the highest quality 15 point card stock with your choice of our popular matte finish or our premium "UV gloss" varnish for FREE!

- **Risk-Free 100% Satisfaction Guarantee**
  We guarantee you'll be satisfied with your business cards, or we'll gladly reprint your order or give you a full refund.

Pricing

Quantity	Single Sided	Double Sided
100	$9.95	$14.95
250	$24.95	$29.95
500	$34.95	$39.95
1000	$39.95	$49.95
2000	$79.95	$89.95
3000	$109.95	$119.95
5000	$149.95	$159.95
All Printed in 1 Business Day!		

Choose from 3 Easy Design Options:

Use the quick and easy **Express Designer**
Choose from thousands of professionally-designed background templates, add your text, and create your business cards in minutes.

Use the advanced **Interactive Designer**
Use our step-by-step "point-and-click" design wizard to create your own custom business cards quickly and easily.

Use your own files and **Upload Your Design**
Upload your own business card design file, preview it, approve it, and place your order. We'll do the rest!

"I just received my first order business cards today. I am so impressed! The color and quality is simply amazing and the turn around time can't be beat. Your prices are also some of the best I found on the internet. I'll recommending you to everyone, as well as placing more orders. Thanks!"

Cherylynn

SATISFACTION GUARANTEE

In the next case study, which shows a landing-page test for Hair Club, we found that an old approach using sexy, aspirational images underperformed a design with less-distracting images.

Case Study: Hair Club Goes Beyond "Best Practices" and Increases Conversions by 20 Percent

Hair Club (www.hairclub.com) is the world leader in personalized hair-loss solutions, providing surgical and nonsurgical restoration treatments to men and women in more than 95 Hair Club Treatment Centers across North America. With over 30 years of experience, Hair Club is regarded as the gold standard in all hair-loss treatments available and has some of the world's most renowned and respected hair-loss physicians as members of its team.

The Business Need

Hair Club drives traffic to its website through fully integrated online and offline campaigns, centrally capturing leads for its network of Treatment Centers. A call to action for a free in-person consultation drives form-fill online conversions. Hair Club's sophisticated use of analytics ensures that web visitors are tracked through their entire lifecycle—from initial clickthrough to completion of consultation appointments to purchase.

Although Hair Club's paid search strategy was successful at driving highly targeted traffic to the site, the number of visitors who completed the online form was below expectations, resulting in a higher than desired cost per lead.

The Hair Club marketing team knew that improving the persuasiveness of the landing page was an obvious way to impact conversion rates drastically and quickly.

The Challenges

As an experienced, data-driven group, the Hair Club marketing team had already run several tests on various parts of the site and used time-tested web content such as professional photography, video, and copy.

The control landing page

Using "best practices" as a baseline, the team had identified some test elements for the landing-page optimization project but felt that a trial-and-error testing approach would be too time-consuming and, most important, would not deliver test results with a high degree of certainty. Hair Club recognized the need for an experienced conversion-optimization specialist to propose stronger testing hypotheses that would deliver statistically valid conversion-rate improvement fast.

The Solution

In March 2009, Hair Club worked with WiderFunnel to plan, develop, and execute a landing-page optimization strategy to lift form-fill conversions on its paid search landing page. Using the Kaizen Method, WiderFunnel reviewed and analyzed the following:

- Hair Club business goals and key performance indicators
- Overall website performance
- Previous test results
- Google AdWords campaigns
- Web analytics data
- The current landing page's design, copy, layout, and graphics

Continues

Case Study: Hair Club Goes Beyond "Best Practices" and Increases Conversions by 20 Percent *(Continued)*

Armed with a broad understanding of the Hair Club business and its conversion challenges, WiderFunnel recommended an A/B/*n* testing program as a starting point to lift form-completion conversions. WiderFunnel handled the conversion-optimization project in its entirety, developing a complete test plan—including hypotheses, wireframes, graphic design, and copy—and executing the test.

WiderFunnel narrowed the testing opportunities to three variations of the landing page, with the following main themes:

- Variation A: "Video Testimonials"
- Variation B: "Embedded Call-to-Action Form"
- Variation C: "Before & After Photos"

The Results: Conversion-Rate Lift of 20 Percent

Twenty percent more visitors completed the call-to-action form with Variation A (video testimonials) than with the control page design.

Winning challenger page

Variation B, which used a clean, best practice–based design, performed better than the control landing page but drove fewer conversions than the winning page.

Variation C, without video or an embedded form, underperformed all variations.

The winning challenger for Hair Club replaced rotating images of beautiful women in aspirational scenarios with rewritten descriptive copy about the service options. One of the standard beliefs in marketing is that "sex sells," but in WiderFunnel's testing, we often find that "sex is distracting!"

How can you reduce distraction on your important conversion-funnel pages?

- Can you reduce the number of product options you offer?
- Can you reduce the number of choices your prospects have to make on each page?
- Can you choose less-distracting images or remove images altogether?

You Should Test That!

Note: Join the conversation at YouShouldTestThat.com/Distraction to contribute your ideas and find more inspiration to optimize for distraction.

Continue reading to Chapter 10, "Optimize for Urgency," to learn how urgency affects your prospects and how you can test to create greater urgency.

10 Optimize for Urgency

*This old pro, a copywriter, a Greek named Teddy, told
me the most important thing in advertising is "new." It
creates an itch. You simply put your product in there as
a kind of calamine lotion.*

—Don Draper

On my way back to the office after lunch today, I realized
that my breath wasn't as fresh as it could be. The garlic in my
salad dressing had been a little stronger than I expected. But,
alas, when I reach for my customary pack of gum in my blazer
pocket, it's missing. I'm out of gum!

No problem. I know I can pick up another on my way
into the office building. As I reach the gum counter in the
foyer corner store, I quickly scan the options: Trident, Stride,
Juicy Fruit, and so on. I spend no more than a few seconds
before grabbing one and heading to the counter.

With little consideration, I pick up a package that subconsciously seems to have the right balance of graphics and
white space with a blue or black color that indicates a flavor
I'll like. Then, after paying, I head to the elevator for my next
meeting.

Urgency shouldn't be confused with importance. This
decision wasn't particularly important, but it was urgent.
Urgency relates to the shortness of the decision cycle. How
soon will the decision be made? A decision with high importance can actually lengthen the decision cycle or delay a
decision.

In this chapter, you'll learn about the impact that internal and external urgency have on your conversion rates and
how you can influence urgency.

Urgency The degree to which your prospect feels a need to act now, based on their internal drivers and the external influences you introduce, is your urgency factor.

Ask yourself: does your page give a feeling and reason that the call to action needs to be taken now?

Internal Urgency

Okay, so maybe you're thinking the gum purchase is a banal example, but life is made up of trivia just like it. You may be solving similar everyday needs for your prospects and should understand their purchase experience.

This scenario is a demonstration of high *internal* urgency. In that mindframe, I'm less influenced by variations between the options. If I hadn't had such internal urgency to solve a need, I could have made a more considered purchase. Perhaps a sale or a new flavor display or a sampling offer could have enticed me to buy if I'd already had a pack of gum in my pocket.

Internal urgency is dependent on the nature of your prospect's need. It's the preexisting time pressure they feel to find a solution regardless of the options or offers available. Internal urgency is based on your prospect's preexisting needs and desires. How quickly do they need to solve their need?

Your prospects have high internal urgency when they:

- Have made a decision to solve an immediate need
- Have narrowed the range of options
- Have the budget available
- Have authority to spend the budget
- Are ready to make a decision now.

Understanding your prospects' internal urgency scenarios will help you to create more relevant experiences and offers that move them to act.

Seasonality's Effect on Urgency

If your business has seasonality cycles, seasonal urgency may be influencing your test results. Urgency can be a powerful motivational factor that can lead to misleading test outcomes.

In the short term, high urgency during a test can produce higher leads and sales, a result that seems great. The risk is that you may miss out on a potentially larger long-term conversion-rate lift if you stop your tests prematurely.

In one test WiderFunnel developed for a retail e-commerce client that sells a lot of gift items, the goal was to increase sales from their landing pages. The challenger variations we tested didn't change the offer or products featured. Only the layout, design, and copywriting were changed.

We ran the test during two time periods—December and January—which allowed us to observe the effect of seasonal urgency. Each of the periods included approximately the same number of conversions to control for the degree of test accuracy.

The results for each of those periods were quite different. The conversion-rate delta (or "difference") was much smaller during the high-urgency December gift-giving season than in January.

The following graphics show the relative conversion rates between the control and challenger variations. The bars represent the range of estimated conversion rates for each challenger. In Chapter 12, "Analyze Your Test Results," you'll learn the technical meaning of the bars and how to interpret them. The most important thing to know is when the bars between two variations overlap; we can't yet tell if they have a statistically significant conversion-rate difference. The bars that are mostly overlapping are statistically identical in performance.

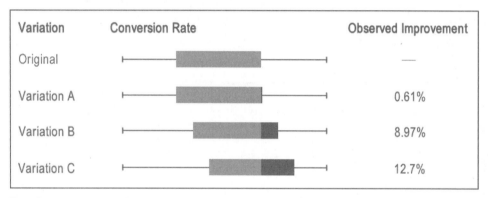

December

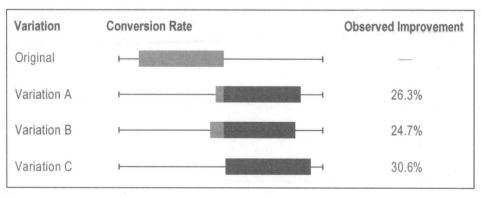

January

Although the same challenger variation won or was leading in both time periods, the conversion-rate lift was higher in January. The observed lift in December was 12.7 percent versus 30.6 percent in January. December's results also didn't achieve statistical significance with the same volume of conversions that did achieve significance in January. There was a slight difference in the order of the variations' performance, but that difference wasn't statistically significant either.

The takeaway is that when there was high internal urgency, such as during a gift-giving season, the layout, design, and copy changes had a smaller effect than during the low-urgency period.

Seasonal urgency affects conversion optimization tests by doing the following:

• Reducing the relative impact of design changes

• Increasing conversion rates for all test variations

• Showing different winners during different seasonal periods in some cases

The implication is that abnormally high urgency periods reduce the sensitivity of your tests and may result in different winners. If you run tests during high-urgency seasons, you'll need to collect more data to achieve statistical significance than in lower seasons. You should also try running your tests in both high- and low-urgency seasons to detect differences.

In a test WiderFunnel developed for Environics Analytics, we saw the distinct effect of urgency on the conversion rate for webinar signups as the webinar approached. Check out the details in the following case study.

Case Study: B2B Marketer Gets 290 Percent More Webinar Preregistration Leads with Conversion Optimization

Environics Analytics helps businesses reach their customers more effectively by building consumer market insights. The company's analytical services give a detailed view of the marketplace and deliver market-driven solutions specifically created for each client.

ENVIRONICS
A N A L Y T I C S

To deliver these solutions, Environics Analytics' highly specialized team combines understanding of business challenges with proprietary techniques and comprehensive data.

The Business Need

Every five years, Statistics Canada releases the results of the Canadian census in installments. As they normally did when these data sets were released, Environics Analytics' senior vice president and chief demographer presented a webinar to provide demographic insights to the company's customers and prospects.

This webinar represented a significant awareness and business development opportunity—and a critical component to Environics Analytics' inbound marketing strategy. Another opportunity like this wouldn't occur for several months, and the company needed to maximize attendance.

The Challenges

Environics Analytics had run similar webinars in the past, and although traffic to the website was significant, webinar registrations were disappointing. Too many website visitors were leaving the website without registering.

The Environics Analytics team knew they needed to improve their webinar registration conversion rate. They believed improvements to the webinar ad on their website could improve registrations, but they weren't sure which changes to make. Without an experienced conversion optimization team on staff, they risked making changes that could further harm registrations.

The Solution

Environics Analytics hired WiderFunnel to plan, develop, and drive a conversion-optimization testing plan for the webinar. WiderFunnel developed a controlled scientific experiment in which alternative content was presented to website visitors in order to determine which presentation would optimize the website's webinar registration conversion rate.

Using its seven-step testing system—including the LIFT Model—to analyze the page, WiderFunnel developed a test plan to maximize registrations and improve registration results from the original control ad.

Continues

Case Study: B2B Marketer Gets 290 Percent More Webinar Preregistration Leads with Conversion Optimization *(Continued)*

What's New

September 12th is Census Release Day

Dr. Doug Norris
Senior Vice President and
Chief Demographer
at Environics Analytics

Release 3 of 8, this release includes data for dwelling and household characteristics.

Please join our next WebEx Seminar September 19th, 2007 @ 1pm ET with Dr. Doug Norris as he discusses his insights about the third installment of the new 2006 Canadian Census released by Statistics Canada.

Check out our Webcasts page for a listing of past interviews and presentations.

The control home page webinar ad

The test plan defined how the test would be structured, including the following:

- LIFT Analysis, which identified significant harmful clarity, urgency, and relevance factors that were affecting the conversion rate

- Test structured as an A/B/*n* experiment with one variation against the control to rapidly achieve statistically significant results within a short testing timeframe

- Hypotheses to be included in the experiment challenger ad variation

- The recommended testing and optimization software to achieve reliable results.

The Results: 290 Percent Webinar Preregistration Conversion-Rate Lift!

The results of the experiment showed a remarkable conversion-rate lift from using WiderFunnel's design challenger.

New Web Seminar

Dr. Doug Norris
Senior Vice President
Chief Demographer
at Environics Analytics

Census Release: Hear the Latest Insights from our Chief Demographer

The latest Census release includes valuable information on dwelling and household characteristics including families, marital status, household size and type as well as how children fit into Canada's evolving family structures.

Join us for our free live Web Seminar, where Dr. Doug Norris will share with you his insights about the third installment of the new 2006 Canadian Census released by Statistics Canada.

When: September 19th, 2007 @ 1pm ET

Reserve Your Spot Now

Winning challenger webinar ad

Pre-Seminar Registration Results

On the day of the webinar, two hours prior to the start, the challenger had already achieved a statistically significant test result showing nearly triple the preregistrations of the original!

Test Variation	Conversion Rate
Control	3.2%
Challenger	12.5%
Conversion-rate lift	**290%**

Final-Hour Urgency

The WiderFunnel strategists continued the experiment until the webinar began, and they found an interesting result. The conversion rate for both the control and the challenger spiked dramatically in the final hour before the webinar.

WiderFunnel's challenger variation still increased the conversion rate by 27 percent, but time urgency decreased the performance difference between the variations.

Test Variation	Conversion Rate
Control	19.5%
Challenger	24.9%
Conversion-rate lift	**27%**

The strategists' analysis showed that as the webinar began, the urgency for visitors to join the seminar increased. The result was that more prospective viewers in both the control and challenger test groups overcame any conversion-inhibiting barriers in the page design. The conversion rate for both the control and the test spiked—with the challenger version remaining the highest-converting version in the test.

In the end, the WiderFunnel–designed challenger version of the promo ad gave a tremendous lift to Environics Analytics' webinar preregistration conversions, nearly tripling the registration conversion rate.

As an organization that values web seminars to enhance the sales relationship, Environics Analytics gained from the experiment by now having a new default design the company can use to run further experiments to continually improve. The fluctuation in the late-stage conversion rate also reinforced the importance of the urgency component for conversion optimization, one of the six key conversion factors in WiderFunnel's LIFT Model.

Create Internal Urgency

You can build internal urgency by creating a need. The tone of your content can create perceived needs and desires outside of the features and benefits of your product or service.

Use an Emotive Appeal

"Sell the sizzle, not the steak."

This expression is a commonly held belief in marketing. The concept of creating an emotive appeal can work very well for some circumstances and target audiences. An emotive appeal uses descriptive copy and evocative imagery to paint a picture of the benefits your prospect will experience. An effective emotive page creates an aspirational picture that resonates with the prospect's desires.

In the next case study, you'll see how much better the Sytropin HGH Spray product sold using an emotive approach. On the other hand, in Chapter 9, "Optimize for Distraction," you saw the example of Hair Club's landing page, where an emotive appeal didn't work as well as a more static explanation of the available options. Several variables changed in each of those tests, but the general takeaway from many of WiderFunnel's tests is that testing between an emotive and a factual approach can be valuable. Does a blatant emotional appeal work for your target audience? You Should Test That!

Sytropin found that creating internal urgency through an "emotive" approach rather than a more factual-based "credibility" approach resulted in significant sales lift.

Case Study: Sytropin, a Nutritional Supplement Sold Online, Realizes a 50 Percent Uplift in Sales Conversions

Sytropin is a high-grade human growth hormone (HGH) supplement available without a prescription. An alternative to costly injections dispensed at doctors' offices, Sytropin oral spray brings HGH within reach of most budgets. Individuals concerned about lack of vitality and energy, athletic performance, and aging are typical users of HGH.

Sytropin is a product of Speedwinds Nutrition, a Portland, Oregon–based business focused exclusively on developing top quality nutritional supplements.

The Business Need

Sytropin customer traffic comes from a mix of paid search, organic search, and referral demand-creation strategies. Although a significant percentage of website visitors came from paid search campaigns, Sytropin management was concerned about the low sales conversion rate of these visitors.

In the Sytropin management team's view, achieving sales targets by increasing the search marketing budget to boost the amount of traffic reaching the website was not only costly but unnecessary. The Sytropin team felt that a more cost-effective solution would be to get more paying customers out of the same number of site visitors by increasing the purchase conversion rate.

To increase the site's purchase conversion rate, the Sytropin team had already reworked the landing page and conducted extensive testing—both A/B/n and multivariate. Visitor-to-buyer conversions had increased, but Sytropin had reached a conversion-rate plateau and needed help.

Sytropin control page

The Challenges

As an e-commerce site with a single product, Sytropin.com had a number of conversion optimization challenges to tackle, including the following:

- Driving enough traffic to its landing page to reach statistically significant test results in a timely manner
- Limited opportunities to cross-sell or up-sell
- Generally high visitor anxiety toward the product category

Sytropin management recognized the need for an external conversion optimization specialist who could confidently develop a robust testing strategy to convert more paid search visitors into customers and, ultimately, provide a better return on the current advertising investment.

Continues

The Solution

Sytropin management engaged WiderFunnel to plan, develop, and execute a landing-page optimization strategy to lift purchase conversions on the Sytropin paid-search landing page.

Although the Sytropin landing page had been the subject of multiple tests in the past, WiderFunnel recommended an A/B/*n* testing program as a starting point to set an improved baseline for further refinement. The WiderFunnel team developed a complete test plan—including hypotheses, wireframes, graphic design, copy, and development—and executed the controlled test.

WiderFunnel narrowed the testing opportunities to two variations of the existing landing page:

- Variation A: "Emotive" theme with aspirational imagery and copy

Continues

Emotive challenger page

- Variation B: "Medical" theme with a product-focused approach

Credibility challenger page

The Results

The top-performing design, the "Emotive" theme, delivered a 50 percent uplift in purchase conversions over the control landing page. For Sytropin, an aspiration-based theme proved to be highly effective at increasing website visitor engagement and at turning more browsers into paying customers. This theme includes benefit-oriented copy, images reflecting the target market engaged in aspirational activities, and a large call-to-action button placed visibly above the fold.

Although single-product e-commerce websites such as Sytropin's present unique challenges for increasing conversions, an experienced conversion-optimization specialist can draw on insights from many previously conducted tests to develop a strategy that makes dramatic increases in sales possible quickly.

Rationalize

Remember that your prospects buy emotionally and defend the purchase rationally. Once you've created an emotional need to buy, you need to give them rationale to support it.

Your prospects have a discussion in their heads when considering a purchase. Their self-argument is waged between the reasons to buy and the reasons not to buy. You can help by giving them the rationale to buy now. Think about the reasons they shouldn't delay the purchase. Here are some examples of creating a rationale for urgency:

Photobooks   How many summers will you have with your children? Can you afford not to create a photo book to remember this year?

Exercise Equipment   Don't lose your youthfulness. Each day you don't exercise is another day of damage and degeneration to your heart, lungs, and muscles. Order your [insert exercise gadget] today to reverse the downward spiral.

Children's Book Subscription   If you're like most, you have only a few short hours per week to spend with your children. Shouldn't one of them be spent reading a good book together?

Conversion Optimization   Every day you delay improving your website conversion rate is a day of lost revenue. What if you're losing 10, 20, or 50 percent of your revenue every day?

Using an emotive appeal plus a rational support argument to back it up is a potent one-two punch of persuasive magic.

External Urgency

External urgency is where you can have even more influence than via internal urgency. You create external urgency with the offers you show to prospects. Giving them a reason and emotional pull to buy now will lift your conversion rates.

The Offer's Effect on Urgency

In a test WiderFunnel ran for an online apparel store, we showed the direct effect offers have on urgency. The test was run on the site's product category site-wide template. Visitors to any of the category pages were entered into the test and saw a consistent variation of that template throughout the site. In this case, the challenger variations changed the layout of the product listings, filtering options, and user interface elements only.

The test included four variations plus the control. After successfully finding a new champion variation, we ran a follow-up test with only the winner and the original control, to verify the result.

Partway through the follow-up test, the company ran a special limited-time promotion. The test results over time, which show the aggregate conversion rate for each variation, tell an interesting story.

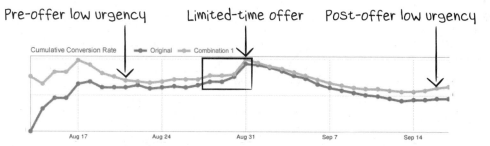

During the low-urgency periods before and after the limited-time offer was in market, the performance delta between the control and the challenger was much greater. During the high-urgency offer period, the conversion rates for the variations converged just as we saw earlier in the seasonal urgency example.

The layout, eyeflow, and interaction changes that made the conversion experience much better during normal shopping periods had less of an effect during high-urgency periods. When shoppers had high internal urgency, they were motivated to overcome usability and informational barriers to find the products they needed.

Remember the analogy of the jar of marbles in Chapter 2, "What is Conversion Optimization"? In both of those urgency examples, the visitors had so many urgency marbles dumped into the jar that they didn't need as much clarity and relevance to push them over the conversion line.

Let's look at ways to enhance urgency.

Create Offer Urgency

People want what they can't have. I had this principle reinforced for me early on, when I was trying to find tenants for a rental suite in our first home. I discovered that potential tenants were much more interested in filling out an application when they "bumped into" others coming to look at the suite.

Little did they know that I had carefully planned these chance encounters with other prospective tenants. I began booking all the appointments at the same time and sometimes ended up with a bidding war between interested applicants. Whenever our rental suite was available, it became the hot place in town to rent.

Scarcity creates an urgency to have what we're missing. As Robert Cialdini said in *Influence: The Psychology of Persuasion*, "As a rule, if it is rare or becoming rare, it is more valuable."

Limited Access

Scarcity is used in many types of offers, such as for technology startups. Facebook was famously available only to college students at first, then by invitation only to a wider audience. Gmail was invitation-only when it launched. Pinterest used a Request an Invite call to action to help it reach 10 million registered users and beyond.

You need an invitation? It must be good!

The "Limit 5 per customer" offers you see in grocery stores are a similar way of creating a sense of scarcity. If you can create a limited-access offer for your products or services, You Should Test That!

Limited-Edition Products

You might think Tiffany & Co. has done enough to create demand for its products that it doesn't need to use tactics like this. But the company creates demand for its brand precisely because it knows how to use persuasion tactics that create urgency. Check out Tiffany's limited-edition 1837 product line.

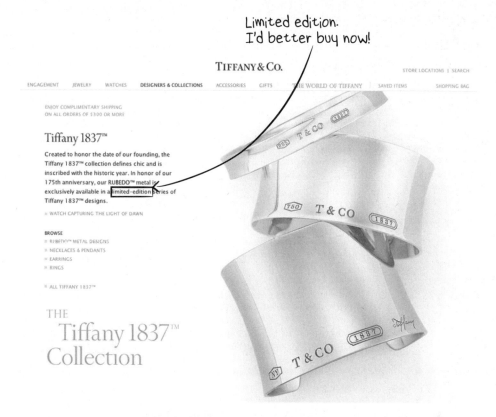

Can you create a special edition of your product or service that's only available in limited quantities? You Should Test That!

Highlight Purchases

You can emulate my tenant rental experience by making visitors "bump into" others making purchases. Hotels.com reminds visitors on the hotel details pages that hotels are being booked right now. This subtle pop-up appeared in the bottom corner of the browser while I was looking at a hotel for a weekend getaway recently.

> This hotel has been booked 2 times in the last 24 hours

Woot.com gives detailed information about how fast its daily deals are selling.

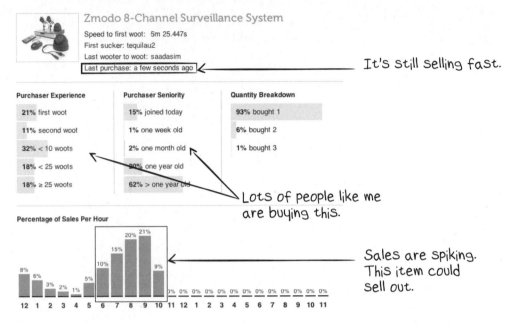

Zmodo 8-Channel Surveillance System

Speed to first woot: 5m 25.447s
First sucker: tequilau2
Last wooter to woot: saadasim

Last purchase: a few seconds ago ← ——————— It's still selling fast.

Purchaser Experience	Purchaser Seniority	Quantity Breakdown
21% first woot	**15%** joined today	**93%** bought 1
11% second woot	**1%** one week old	**6%** bought 2
32% < 10 woots	**2%** one month old	**1%** bought 3
18% < 25 woots	**20%** one year old	
18% ≥ 25 woots	**62%** > one year old	

Lots of people like me
are buying this.

Percentage of Sales Per Hour

Sales are spiking.
This item could
sell out.

You may not need to go that far. This type of info fits well with Woot's brand. But do you have a way to present the demand for your products to create urgency? Maybe you can display how many people are considering a purchase, as Bookedy.com does for its London travel tours.

I'm not alone in considering this. Looks like it's popular.

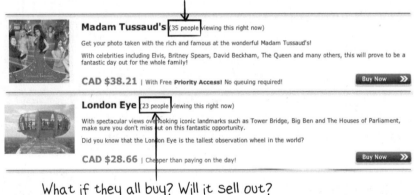

What if they all buy? Will it sell out?

Use Fear of Loss

The research about loss aversion that you saw in Chapter 8, "Optimize for Anxiety," demonstrated how powerful the fear of loss can be in creating anxiety. Similarly, you can use fear of missing out to create urgency.

Daily-deal sites have been using scarcity for years in the form of limited availability of a single item each day. Woot.com, which has since been acquired by Amazon.com, was one of the earliest to use this tactic. Amazon's Lightning Deals offer continues this idea by using several scarcity tactics on a deals page.

Previously expired products prime fear of loss.

Countdown timer

Limited quantity

Next product coming soon creates urgency.

Respond with Urgency

The speed of your response to your prospects' inquiry creates or stifles their sense of urgency. They're taking clues from your salespeople about the urgency to make a decision. If you treat the decision as time-sensitive, they will view it with greater urgency.

Research by Dr. James B. Oldroyd, faculty fellow at MIT, investigated the best times to respond to sales leads. Through a survey of over 600 companies, commissioned by InsideSales.com, Dr. Oldroyd found that sales reps had a *100x greater chance* of successfully contacting a lead if the first call was within 5 minutes after the lead form was filled out rather than 30 minutes. And if the sales rep didn't call for 5 hours, their success rate decreased by *3000x*!

We have clients who have measured significant increases in conversion rate to sale when follow-up calls are done within a minute compared to within five minutes. For lead response, time is of the essence.

This result makes sense if you think about your prospects' experience. They have taken the effort to fill in your form to inquire about your products or services. They have your solution in their mind and are sitting in front of their computer, probably with their phone beside them. In five minutes, they could be working on another task, talking to a colleague, or down the hall in the restroom. If you can catch them while their internal urgency is high, you'll give yourself a much better chance of moving them to the next stage.

 Note: Do you want to discuss other ideas about optimizing for urgency? Check out YouShouldTestThat.com/Urgency to start a conversation and find more inspiration.

Continue reading to Chapter 11, "Test Your Hypotheses," to find out how to set up experiments and avoid common testing mistakes.

11

Test Your Hypotheses

In every block of marble I see a statue as plain as though it stood before me, shaped and perfect in attitude and action. I have only to hew away the rough walls that imprison the lovely apparition to reveal it to the other eyes as mine see it.

—Michelangelo

This book has already presented you with lots of ideas to improve your marketing. As you've read through the chapters, you've probably recognized problems affecting your own company's communications.

You may be tempted to make changes immediately without testing them. "Some of these things obviously need to change," you'll tell yourself. You may be right.

Or not.

If you take anything away from this book, I hope it's an understanding of the importance of testing. The only way to know what really works is to gain experience from many tests. From seeing many results, you can discover human behavior patterns from similar test situations and continuously improve your conversion intuition.

This chapter is all about building a test plan and putting your good ideas into action. In Chapters 4 ("Create Hypotheses with the LIFT Model") through 10 ("Optimize for Urgency"), you learned how to analyze your pages and create powerful hypotheses for testing. Now you need to put those ideas into a structure that you and your team can follow to run your tests.

Starting with a test plan can save you from being surprised by organizational or technical barriers or, worse, losing support after wasting time on directionless tests.

A test plan solidifies the goal for your test, outlines the structure of the experiment, locks down a valid control, and avoids common mistakes. In this chapter, you'll learn how to build a test plan that you can follow to get dramatic conversion-rate and revenue lift.

Set Test Goals

The first decision in your test plan is to set the goal or goals for your test. The goals for each of your tests should match the overall conversion-rate optimization goals you identified and prioritized in Chapter 2, "What Is Conversion Optimization." Individual tests may focus on one or more of your conversion-optimization goals, depending where the test page is in your conversion funnel.

Types of Goals

You can set a wide variety of goals. Following is a brainstorming idea list of typical goals. Remember that your conversion optimization goal should be as close to revenue as possible.

Lead-Generation Goals

If lead generation is your overall purpose, the goals might include any of the following specific user actions:

- Request a quote
- Request an in-person demo
- Request a phone call
- Request a situation analysis
- Request market information
- Book a meeting
- Ask a question
- Complete a contact form inquiry
- Download software
- Sign up for trial offer
- Request a printed brochure
- Request a catalogue
- Download an online brochure
- Download a whitepaper
- Download an e-book
- Download a worksheet
- Download a case study

- Create an online quote
- View an overview video
- Take a quiz or poll
- Join a contest
- Fill out a needs-analysis questionnaire
- Use a needs-analysis wizard
- Use an interactive savings or ROI calculator
- Click to call
- Click to chat
- Make a phone call
- Register for a webinar
- Register for a conference
- Sign up for a newsletter
- Sign up for a blog subscription
- Sign up for an RSS feed subscription

E-Commerce Goals

For e-commerce, your goals might be based on any of these common metrics:

- E-commerce purchase conversion rate
- Average order value
- Return on ad spend
- Revenue per visitor

Or they might include any of the following user actions:

- Request a catalog
- Ask a question
- Click to call
- Click to chat
- Sign up for a newsletter
- Sign up for a blog subscription
- Sign up for an RSS feed subscription
- Add to cart
- Save to a wish list
- Sign up for auto-reordering
- Add accessories (up-sell)

Affiliate Marketing Goals

For affiliate marketing, your goals might include a specific revenue-per-visitor value, along with any of the following actions:

- Click through to an affiliate site
- Fill out a needs-analysis questionnaire
- Use a needs-analysis wizard
- Use an interactive savings or ROI calculator
- Create an online quote
- Sign up for a newsletter
- Sign up for a blog subscription
- Sign up for an RSS feed subscription
- Find a service provider
- Find savings in your area

Subscription Goals

Subscription goals might include any of the following actions and metrics:

- Sign up for a free trial subscription
- Upgrade subscription
- Paid subscription signups
- Average subscription signup value

There are many more goals you can track, depending on your business model. For each test, choose the one that drives the most revenue. Once you have identified the goals for your test, you'll be ready to set up your conversion-optimization experiment and get testing.

Use Clickthroughs with Caution

One of the most common metrics used for judging marketing effectiveness is the click-through rate (CTR). Many people use it to measure their banner ads, paid search listings, and even internal promotions within their websites.

The problem is that when marketers use CTR as the primary success metric, it's misleading. Measuring the effectiveness of your ads independently of the rest of your conversion funnel doesn't tell you much about how well your ad performed. It only tells you that people click the ad. But they may have clicked the ad for many different reasons. Maybe they were just curious or confused by the ad. A click alone doesn't measure your prospects' intent to purchase.

Ben Louie at PlentyOfFish (www.pof.com) shared a humorous example that demonstrates how CTR measurement could lead to misleading results. He ran a banner-ad test that promoted Electronic Arts's *Need for Speed* video game. The test included one of EA's professionally designed banners with the EA logo, a concise value proposition, and a photo of one of the race cars from the game. We'll call this the control ad. The other was, as Ben described it, "Some [bleep] ad I made in five minutes in Microsoft Paint," which we'll lovingly call the challenger.

Control   **Challenger**

Care to guess the result?

Based on the success measure of clickthrough rate, the challenger more than doubled the control. The control had a 0.049 percent CTR and the challenger got a 0.137 percent CTR. That's a *180 percent CTR lift!*

But which ad generated higher sales and revenue? Maybe the challenger would also have produced more players and subscribers for the *Need for Speed* game. Or, maybe more of the challenger prospects clicked out of curiosity or looking for a laugh. Maybe they didn't convert, and the control produced more revenue.

We don't know. This test wasn't tracked through to conversions or revenue.

Ben ran this test and publicized it in a somewhat tongue-in-cheek way, and he assures me that most of his tests are tracked through to more important conversion goals. But it's a vivid example of the importance of choosing the right goal to track.

Measuring with CTR has done more harm than good for online advertisers. Whenever possible, your conversion-optimization goals should show purchase intent or, even better, represent real revenue.

Once you have decided on your most important conversion goal for your experiment, you have to translate that into a technical goal trigger that will be tracked by the testing tool.

> **Do you speak "tech"?** Setting up conversion-goal triggers can be the most technically involved part of creating tests. At the risk of losing your interest, this section will give you the most important technical goal-tracking points to understand. Don't worry if it's too much "tech speak" for you—your developers, IT department, or conversion consultant can help you through any of the more technical aspects of testing. This section will equip you to communicate the requirements effectively with them.

Goal Triggers

The goal you track must be represented by a specific action the visitor takes on the website, like a button click or a visit to a page. Think about an action on the site that the visitors will do only once they have completed the goal. Experiment goals can be calculations like average order value, but they still must be triggered by something simpler, such as the viewing of a purchase-confirmation page. In most cases, calculated goals should be secondary to direct revenue-generating conversion rates and are for more advanced test strategies.

In an e-commerce purchase, the goal trigger could be placed on the post-purchase thank-you or purchase-confirmation page. A quote request, contact form, or download will likely have a similar thank-you page.

In most testing tools, you have a technical action that triggers a conversion goal. The tool may give you a snippet of code called a *goal script* that triggers your conversion goal, or a setting within the tool interface that defines the user action. You want to trigger that goal at a point that can only occur after a visitor has completed the goal.

After requesting a travel guide from www.GoHawaii.com, for example, I was shown a thank-you page. If the Hawaii Tourism Authority had been running a test to increase their guide request conversion rates, they would identify this page as the conversion-goal trigger.

Filling this lead-gen form leads to this thank-you page.

The goal should be triggered on viewing this page.

In some cases, you may want to recognize clicking a link as a goal rather than a post-action page view. For example, clicking a Like button or a click that leads to a page on a different website (or at least a different domain name) may require a click goal. Your developer can modify your technical goal setup so that it's triggered when visitors click a link rather than when they visit a thank-you page.

If you have a testing tool that is installed site-wide (or not installed with JavaScript at all), you may be able to do your goal setting in the tool's interface rather than modify the page code. Check with your testing tool vendor or conversion consultant for specific instructions for triggering conversion goals.

However your goals are set up technically, make sure you understand exactly how they're triggered. Being certain about this technical setup will give you more confidence when analyzing the test results.

The One-Goal Goal

In Chapter 9, "Optimize for Distraction," you learned that having too many options, messages, and goals distracts your prospects from understanding your primary message. Giving your prospects choice in how to respond may seem like a good thing to do. But the evidence is clear that more choice isn't always better. Too many calls to action and goals reduce overall conversions.

When you're setting your conversion goal, can you whittle the options down to just one? If you can, you'll give yourself a much easier time in analyzing the results later. An unambiguous winning result is more fun than holding debates over relative goal value when a test is complete.

Maybe you have secondary goals that you also think are important to support your primary goal. That's fine, but they don't all have to be tracked as conversions for the sake of your optimization tests.

Remember what you learned in Chapter 2 about the difference between conversion-optimization goals and web-analytics goals: if your supporting goals and micro-conversions are truly supporting your main goal, they'll be captured in the results of your test when the primary goal's conversion rate is lifted. They don't need to be tracked as test goals.

For example, WiderFunnel had a client whose primary goal on their retail catalog website was e-commerce sales. They also tracked "add to cart" and "time on site" as key performance indicators in their web-analytics tool. Initially, they wanted to track those supporting metrics as conversion-optimization goals within our tests as well.

The question we asked was, "How would the outcome change if one of these supporting goals outperformed for a challenger where the primary goal underperformed?" If a challenger variation were to double the add-to-cart conversion rate, but final sales were cut in half, that wouldn't be considered a win, would it? The client agreed to track only sales for the tests, and we also tracked the micro-conversions as secondary goals outside of the testing tool. The client ended up with both a significant lift in sales and an understanding of how micro-conversion behavior was affected.

You shouldn't include supporting goals for your conversion optimization. Whenever possible, focus your tests on the single primary goal for your test pages. If you do have more than one revenue-related end goal, you'll need to set up multi-goal conversion tracking.

Multi-Goal Tracking

In many businesses, sales don't tidily fit into a single conversion scenario. You may have several types of conversions on your website that are tied to revenue. You may even have offline sales channels to consider. Multi-goal tracking allows you to measure all the revenue-driving conversions and optimize for overall revenue.

For each of your goals, online and offline, you need to assign a value. You can use the relative goal values you set in Chapter 2 for this.

Phone Call Conversions

At WiderFunnel, we often set up multi-channel conversion tracking for companies that drive their online marketing to offline conversions. By tracking phone calls and online leads independently, you'll find some challengers that attract your prospects to different channels and can maximize overall lead value.

Phone call conversions produce some of the most valuable leads for companies that use a lead-generation strategy. You may find, as many of WiderFunnel's clients have, that your sales conversion rate and average order value are higher for inbound phone calls than for online form leads.

To track phone calls, you need to assign unique phone numbers for each test variation. Several companies provide tracking phone numbers, such as Ifbyphone (www.ifbyphone.com), Mongoose Metrics (www.mongoosemetrics.com), and ClickPath (www.clickpath.com). The unique numbers should be added to each page and updated throughout the website for each test participant.

Remember to also use a new unique phone number for the control page. If you don't, you'll inflate conversions for the control; that's because some callers will have the number written down, cached in their browser from before the test began, or will be part of a test-exclusion segment.

In an ideal world, your phone call conversions would be counted only when sales occur. But, as you know, this isn't an ideal world. This revenue tracking by test variation is often challenging for organizations whose inbound call center's customer relationship management (CRM) system isn't able to attach the phone number to the lead. If manual entry of phone numbers would be required in order to track revenue, don't track it. In my experience, the inaccuracy of manual phone number entry is much greater than that of estimating phone lead value.

If you can't track phone calls to revenue, you may want to count only phone calls over a certain call length as conversions. Then you can estimate the value of those leads based on your phone call to sale conversion rate and average order value during the test period.

There are added complications to multi-channel conversion testing that you should be aware of. Your testing tool probably won't have built-in integration with the phone-tracking providers. Online and offline conversions will need to be exported separately and combined in a spreadsheet. Then the various conversion points will need to be normalized, combined, and calculated for statistical significance. You may find it reassuring to bring in a consulting firm with experience in this type of multi-channel testing to help so you can trust the results.

Multiple Online Conversions

To track multiple online goals, your testing tool needs to allow you to track goals independently. Ideally, it should let you set goal values; but if it doesn't, you can calculate the weighted values in a spreadsheet once the test is complete.

Be sure to set up revenue tracking for e-commerce sites as well. Increasing average order value can be just as effective as the sales conversion rate, and you'll want to be able to include that in your results analysis.

Keep It Simple, Smartypants

Even though I've just covered the ideal-world scenarios for tracking accurate conversions to revenue, I urge you to practice the KISS principle when getting started with goal setting. I don't want you to fall into the trap we've helped many companies out of—being frozen by an over-concern for goal accuracy. They're so concerned with precision that they stop everything until they're 100 percent convinced that their test results would stand up to a doctoral thesis committee. Determining relative goal values down to the fifth decimal point isn't necessary or productive.

Start with what you can get. If it takes you more than a week to determine your goal values, stop and simplify.

Remember, all tests have inherent inaccuracies, but any test is more accurate than running on gut feeling. A strange phenomenon happens when you introduce the concept of testing. Often, people become fixated by the numbers and statistical certainty and forget that *any* accuracy level is better than not testing.

In Chapter 12, "Analyze Your Test Results," you'll learn how to evaluate multiple weighted conversion goals, including revenue metrics.

Along with selecting your goals, you'll need to determine the type of experiment to run. But first it will help to understand how to choose your test page.

Choose the Test Area

Test-page opportunities can take several forms and may not look like pages at all. What I call a *test page* may be a single page, a site-wide page template, a repeating section that appears on many pages, a microsite, or a series of pages (that is, a defined conversion funnel or split-path test). Each of these types of opportunities can be tested and has different characteristics to consider.

What's a Microsite? Often, when marketers want to create a distinct look and feel for a specific campaign or product group, they create a microsite. It's essentially a small website, usually 3–10 pages, on its own domain. It's often not connected to the main company website and may only have marketing campaign traffic directed to it. Microsites are usually focused on a single goal, have expensive traffic, and are totally within the control of the marketing department, making them great candidates for conversion testing!

Templated Pages

Template-driven pages make up most website content pages. You'll know the page you want to test is template-driven if it looks similar to other pages on your website. It may be updated through a CMS system or e-commerce platform.

At WiderFunnel, we often test layouts at the page-template level to find the best layout and site-wide content. Testing template pages typically involves hypotheses related to eyeflow, layout clarity, and overall company value proposition. These types of tests tend not to be focused on testing the value proposition of individual products.

We love these types of tests and often see some of the most rewarding results with them, because they reach most of the website visitors at once. There are several reasons to consider testing site-wide page templates:

- Layout tests complete much more quickly because most visitors to the site see the template pages and are entered into the experiment.

- Visitors' experience on the site is more consistent if all pages on the same template have the same layout variation.

- The learning from the aggregate templated pages is more applicable to the entire website than trying to apply learning from an individual page to all other similar pages.

- You can test more dramatic eyeflow and layout approaches than you can if you test individual pages within the website, because you don't have to worry about inconsistency across the site if visitors see a different variation for each page.

- Testing your site templates is used to redesign your site using an evolutionary site redesign (ESR) approach where the site design evolves based on tested changes that improve business results, as opposed to a traditional abrupt site-redesign project.

The downside of template tests is that it's more difficult to vary individual product messaging. When your test includes dozens, hundreds, or even thousands of pages, you can't create unique content variations for all of them.

Individual Static Test Pages

On the other hand, if you want to test content that is unique to individual high-traffic pages, you have a good reason to test on a single page rather than a template. For example, on a product or service page, you may want to find the features and images that work best, which can only be tested at the individual page level.

Single, static, stand-alone pages are the most straightforward test pages. These are usually marketing landing pages that sit outside of your website's content-management system (CMS). The Hair Club case study in Chapter 9 is an example of a static campaign landing-page test.

When testing individual landing pages, you can test more specific content related to that product, service, or topic. Your test design is less constrained to fit into a corporate website or be integrated with dynamic content.

The downside of testing on a single landing page is that your traffic level will usually be lower than with a site-wide test. In that case, your landing page test will need to run longer than website tests to complete with statistical significance.

Individual Pages with Dynamic Content

A hybrid type of testable page can appear when your individual page includes dynamic content or has database interactions. Dynamic elements can include server-side form interactions, product and price updates from a database, social commenting sections, and dependencies on a CMS.

Individual pages with dynamic content may still give you the flexibility to test dramatically different design, layout, and content than you can within a website structure. The technical setup may be a little more complicated, and you'll need a developer involved to connect the test sections with database content.

Site-Wide Section Tests

You can also test elements within your website that affect more than just a single template.

Stylesheet Test

Modern web design follows the principle of separating content from design. This structure allows you to create content without worrying about the design becoming outdated. The content is independent of the look and feel and, theoretically, can be easily updated as the design is updated in the future.

Cascading Style Sheets (CSS) is the web equivalent of the stylesheets you may be familiar with from Microsoft Word or other document publishing software. With CSS, the web developer identifies the types of content on the site and then defines the attributes of each of those types.

For example, each piece of body copy on the site is labeled as such. Then, when the designer decides that the body copy should change from 10px Verdana font to 12px Helvetica, only one CSS file needs to change to alter the look of every piece of body copy site-wide.

Doing a stylesheet swap test is an easy way to test design and layout elements throughout the site. You can change anything that is defined by your CSS file, from type size and headline treatment to column placement and page color.

Many websites are still not fully CSS-driven, however. If yours isn't, a CSS test may not give you much flexibility. You'll need to target specific site-wide areas to test the entire site experience.

Navigation and Header Test

Your site's navigation structure is an important part of your information architecture. It can help or hinder your prospects' ability to find what they're looking for. Are the navigation labels clear? Do they use words that are relevant to your prospects? Rather than debate with your colleagues over semantics, You Should Test That!

Navigation and header areas are often overlooked opportunities for value-proposition positioning as well. You may find that assurance messages in the header remind prospects of your key messages when they need it. Those messages can improve your conversion rates, even if your visitors don't click them often.

Persistent Call-to-Action Areas

Do you have consistent areas in your website template that include a call to action? It may be promoting quote requests, newsletter signups, whitepaper or e-book downloads, or social media connections. Many websites do, especially for sites that generate leads.

I've coined the term persistent call-to-action areas (PCTAs) for these. Testing PCTAs can be a powerful way to target nearly convinced prospects and move them to act. These site-wide sections can produce significant test results. The following case study shows a PCTA test that doubled conversions for one company.

Case Study: Conversion-Optimization Testing Drives a 106 Percent Increase in Bookings for RV Rental Company

CanaDream, in business since 1995, has become one of the largest recreational vehicle rental and sales companies in Canada, catering mostly to an international clientele eager to experience the country. With a fleet of over 750 quality motor homes available through a network of eight rental locations across Canada, CanaDream has positioned itself as a top-of-the-line supplier of Canadian leisure travel. Custom-built vehicles and superior customer service represent the foundation of its competitive advantage—an advantage recognized internationally.

CANADREAM®

The Business Need

CanaDream customers book their RV vacations through one of three channels: via accredited wholesalers, directly via www.CanaDream.com, or over the telephone.

The CanaDream team knew their website booking conversion rate was below the industry average and that they needed to generate more direct bookings. CanaDream needed to find a way to increase conversions online and by phone.

The Challenges

As a business in a very competitive marketplace, CanaDream understood that the website had to work hard at differentiating the company's unique value proposition for web visitors, but it wasn't doing the job: visitors couldn't easily understand their rental options and all the benefits they would receive from booking with CanaDream.

Moreover, on-site surveys conducted by the CanaDream management team indicated that visitors couldn't easily find pricing for their trips, despite the PCTA area that existed on all pages.

The Solution

CanaDream turned to WiderFunnel to improve the performance of the www.CanaDream.com website. CanaDream management contacted WiderFunnel to help them make changes to the website that would immediately improve the RV booking conversion rate.

WiderFunnel used its Kaizen Method to plan and execute the CanaDream conversion-optimization strategy. Steps undertaken included the following:

- In-depth web analytics audit of the entire www.CanaDream.com website to understand and evaluate business goals and key performance indicators (KPIs), website metrics, visitor experience, and purchase flow
- Review of identified conversion issues and prioritization of pages to test

Continues

Case Study: Conversion-Optimization Testing Drives a 106 Percent Increase in Bookings for RV Rental Company *(Continued)*

- Analysis of priority high-traffic pages using the LIFT Model to analyze pages along the six conversion dimensions:

  1. Value Proposition

  2. Relevance

  3. Clarity

  4. Anxiety

  5. Distraction

  6. Urgency

- Create scientific marketing hypotheses

- Wireframing of all test variations

- Design and copywriting

- HTML/CSS build and quality assurance

- Technical installation instructions

- Test round launch

- Results monitoring, analysis, and recommendations

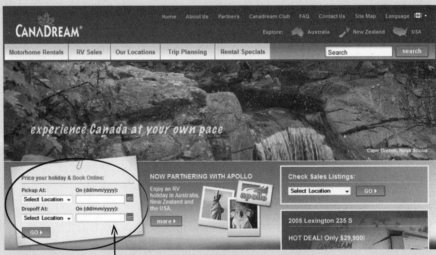

The PCTA area on the home page

The LIFT Analysis revealed several areas that were contributing to poor conversion rates. One was the persistent call-to-action area. As the critical gateway to the conversion funnel, the PCTA had a major negative influence on overall site revenue generation.

To solve this website problem and improve the conversion rate, WiderFunnel took into account the traffic levels on the page and developed two variations of the PCTA based on the hypotheses from the LIFT Analysis. The team tested the variations plus the control with live visitors to the CanaDream website.

WiderFunnel ensured that each visitor saw only one variation in the experiment regardless of how often they visited the site, and that each visitor was tracked through to online or phone-call booking.

Variation A: "Update"

This PCTA variation tested a new layout and graphic design approach that addressed the major eyeflow problems observed on the control. Changes made included the following:

- Increased the prominence of the headline
- Aligned input fields to ease eyeflow
- Changed the shape of the disrupting angled background area
- Increased the prominence of the call-to-action button
- Changed the call-to-action button copy to match the form headline

Variation B: "Urgency"

In addition to the changes in the first variation, WiderFunnel decided to isolate a key hypothesis related to the need for relevance and urgency messaging in the PCTA area. By changing the headline and button copy, the team was able to understand how important this type of message is to CanaDream's booking results.

Once the experiment received a sufficient number of visitors and conversions to achieve 95 percent statistical significance, WiderFunnel analyzed both data sources to identify the best-performing variation.

The Results: A 106 Percent Boost in Bookings

Both experiment variations outperformed the control page in terms of bookings. The winning variation, "Urgency," more than doubled the online and telephone booking conversion rate. CanaDream now gets 106 percent more bookings with the same traffic!

Continues

Case Study: Conversion-Optimization Testing Drives a 106 Percent Increase in Bookings for RV Rental Company *(Continued)*

Winning challenger PCTA

Choose the Test Type

I'm often asked, "For conversion-rate optimization, should I run an A/B/*n* test or a multivariate test?" The short answer is, "Yes!"

Of course, I know the real question being asked is, "Which method should I emphasize?" There is an ongoing debate between proponents of multivariate (or multi-variable or MVT) testing and A/B/*n* testing over which method gets better results.

Consider Traffic Volume

The monthly traffic volume on your test page will be a big part of the test type decision. Lower-traffic sites need to consider more carefully how many challengers are run in each test round.

I'm often asked how much traffic you need to run tests. Although testing the duration to achieve statistical significance is notoriously unpredictable, as a general rule of thumb, you'll need between 100 and 400 conversions per challenger. We've had tests complete with fewer and some that have needed 10 times more, though.

Multivariate Testing

Some people, especially some software vendors, believe conversion-optimization testing and multivariate testing to be two ways of saying the same thing. In their view, the technology and statistics behind the tests provide the value, and therefore the more complex multivariate testing should deliver the best results. I disagree, based on WiderFunnel's results: multivariate testing does play a role in your conversion-optimization strategy, but it shouldn't play the leading part.

In Chapter 2, you saw how testing works by redirecting prospects to different challenger pages or swapping a single section for each variation. The difference between A/B/*n* testing and MVT is that MVT swaps content within multiple sections on the same page and compares all the possible combinations. With MVT, each variable is tested against each of the other variables.

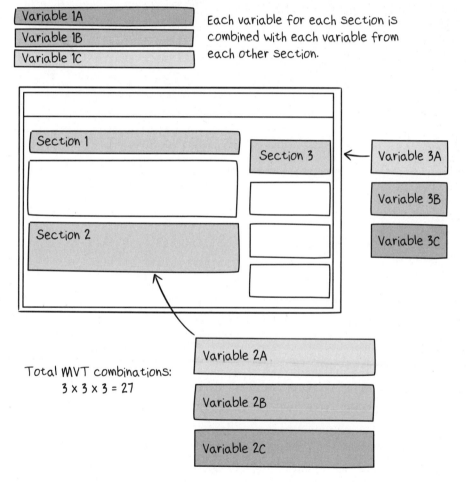

Each variable for each section is combined with each variable from each other section.

Total MVT combinations:
3 x 3 x 3 = 27

In the case of a test setup with three sections and three variables in each, adding one more test variable in just one of the sections would increase the test combinations from 27 to 36:

3 x 3 x 4 = 36

Taguchi? Gesundheit!

There are two competing strains of MVT: full factorial and fractional factorial.

With full factorial tests, all possible combinations of the variables you plan are combined with each other and tested.

Fractional factorial methods, such as the Taguchi method, reduce the number of variations while still hoping to achieve similar learning. The software tests only some of the combinations and makes assumptions about how the nontested combinations will perform.

Fractional factorial mathematics were developed for manufacturing processes, and their value for predicting human behavior is debatable. The intricacies of the fractional factorial method depend on the testing tool you choose, so choose wisely and always run follow-up A/B/n tests of the projected winning combination.

For the purposes of illustration in this book, we assume full factorial MVT is being used.

There are distinct advantages to MVT, namely the abilities to do the following:

- Easily isolate many small page elements and understand their individual effects on conversion rate
- Measure interaction effects between independent elements to find compound effects
- Follow a more conservative path of incremental conversion-rate improvement
- Facilitate interesting statistical analysis of interaction effects

But multivariate testing also has downsides:

- MVT usually requires many more variable combinations to be run than A/B/n.
- MVT requires more traffic to reach statistical significance than A/B/n.
- Major layout changes aren't possible.
- All variations within each swapbox area must make sense together, which restricts the marketer's freedom to try new positioning approaches.
- MVT either gives approximated results (if using Taguchi or a similar test design) or requires exponentially more traffic (if using full factorial) than A/B/n.

A/B/n Testing

A/B/n testing is much less dependent on advanced technology. It often doesn't take full advantage of a testing tool's capabilities and is therefore much less interesting for technology vendors. After all, there may not be a need for high licensing fees on testing tools if you can get the same results without spending much on the technology.

Advantages of A/B/*n* testing are as follows:

- The conversion strategist isn't constrained by which areas of the page to vary.
- You can test more dramatic layout, design, page-consolidation, and value-proposition variations.
- Advanced analytics can be installed and evaluated for each variation (examples include click heatmaps, phone call tracking, analytics integration, and so on).
- Test rounds usually complete more quickly than with MVT.
- Often, you can achieve more dramatic conversion-rate lift results.
- Individual elements and interaction effects can still be isolated for learning.

Here are the disadvantages of A/B/*n* testing:

- The test rounds must be planned carefully if a goal is to measure interaction effects between isolated elements.
- Any Taguchi or design-of-experiment setups must be planned manually.

We take a software-agnostic approach at WiderFunnel, so we don't need to promote software features unless they will produce better results. We find that we can get better results for our clients by not constraining ourselves to the features of a particular testing tool. This approach gives us the freedom to recommend the type of test plan that will get the best results.

My Recommendation: Emphasize A/B/*n* Testing

The comfort MVT gives is enticing. But I'm a businessperson, and I recognize the significant opportunity cost of running the prolonged tests that often are unavoidable with MVT.

At WiderFunnel, we run one multivariate test for every 8 to 10 A/B/*n* test rounds. In most cases, our first test rounds on a web page or conversion funnel start with A/B/*n* testing of the major elements (such as value-proposition emphasis, page layout, copy length, and eyeflow manipulation). In a third or fourth test round, we may want to investigate interaction effects using MVT, usually only on pages with more than 60,000–100,000 unique monthly visitors.

Thirty Reasons to Use A/B/*n* Testing

Here are 30 fun reasons to use A/B/*n* split testing! Use this list in your next company meeting to convince stakeholders to support your A/B/*n* testing proposal:

1. Conversion-rate optimization doesn't exist without controlled, statistically valid testing.
2. A/B/*n* testing finds out how people actually act rather than how they think they act, which is what you get from focus groups and user testing.

Continues

3. A/B/*n* testing confirms or disproves the hypotheses gathered from eyetracking, click heatmaps, surveys, and all other qualitative data gathering.

4. A/B/*n* testing is quantitative, and the probability of error is known (and when was the last time your other marketing tactics told you that?!).

5. A/B/*n* testing lets you test radical redesign variations, which can be a great starting point for most landing pages and site templates.

6. You can test different layouts of site-wide page templates on dynamic, CMS-driven pages with A/B/*n* testing.

7. A/B/*n* testing usually delivers more dramatic conversion-rate improvements than are possible with MVT.

8. A/B/*n* testing is *not* limited to just two variations.

9. A/B/*n* testing allows you to isolate individual hypotheses to build your customized "best practices" playbook.

10. You can't imagine how bad your web pages and site templates really are until you start A/B/*n* testing them.

11. A/B/*n* testing allows entirely different messaging approaches that can lead to strategic marketing insights.

12. Insights from A/B/*n* testing can be used to improve your other online and offline marketing messages.

13. You can track multi-channel conversions with A/B/*n* testing, including online lead generation, affiliate revenue, e-commerce, and phone call conversion optimization.

14. A/B/*n* testing allows for easier in-depth analytics than MVT, so you can develop further test hypotheses for follow-up test rounds.

15. A/B/*n* testing allows alternative conversion funnel tests.

16. A/B/*n* testing lets you condense and expand multi-step forms.

17. A/B/*n* testing can be used for landing-page optimization, website conversion optimization, email testing, and evolutionary site redesign (ESR).

18. A/B/*n* testing can be used to run a customized MVT test using any test design.

19. A/B/*n* testing allows you to isolate only interesting potential interaction effects without wasting traffic on the inconsequential.

20. A/B/*n* testing doesn't limit your test design options as MVT does.

21. A/B/*n* testing gets results faster than any other method, whereas MVT is greedy for traffic.

22. A/B/*n* testing doesn't tempt you to end the test before statistical confidence has been achieved as much as MVT does.

23. You can easily prune underperforming variations in A/B/*n* testing without restarting the test round.

24. A/B/*n* testing is easy to spell.

25. A/B/*n* tests can quickly be rerun and confirmed for extra assurance.

26. A/B/*n* testing results make both the CMO and the CFO happy.

27. The business results from A/B/*n* testing look great on your resumé.

28. A/B/*n* testing allows you to test your marketing strategy and core value proposition.

29. A/B/*n* testing delivers conversion-rate and revenue improvement for all types for companies.

30. A/B/*n* testing is fun!

Alternative Path Tests

For defined conversion funnels, you may want to test different multi-page paths rather than single pages. This split-path (or alternative flow) testing is a type of A/B/*n* test where, instead of just altering a single page, you change multiple sequential pages. Examples include multi-step checkout paths, multi-page forms, and product recommendation wizards.

Alternative path testing allows you to maintain consistency of design elements throughout the path and change the number or sequence of steps. In a simple example, if you were to test a checkout path and wanted to test the button color in the cart, you should change the buttons on all pages in the checkout to match. Alternatively, testing individual pages would produce inconsistency throughout the path that could decrease sales and outweigh any improvement from the change.

Once you've chosen your test target page and type of test, you're ready to create your challenger variations.

Isolate for Insights

There are three overarching purposes for conversion optimization: lift, learning, and insights.

The first purpose, lift, is to gain conversion-rate and revenue increase. This is why most companies are attracted to testing. They've seen the case studies about the great test results other companies get, and they want those results, too! If I could give you a 10 percent, 20 percent, 50 percent or higher conversion-rate lift, you'd want that, right?

The second purpose, learning, is where you understand which changes have the biggest positive effect. This is the reason you plan tests with single variable isolations. Some people aren't initially interested in this part. Many people think that a page is optimized after you've tested it once and seen a good conversion-rate lift. They don't understand how important the ongoing process of learning and iterating is to achieving long-term results. Everything a company learns can be built on and leveraged in other areas.

The third purpose, insights, is where you plan for learning that gleans insights about your customers and prospects. These insights happen when you discover the "why" behind the results you observe. When you see a pattern that implies a motivational driver or usability principle, you can use it to create many more test hypotheses. We'll talk about this more in Chapter 13, "Strategic Marketing Optimization."

The learning and insights outcomes are dependent on test isolations. Isolations allow you to learn which changes are influencing the test results.

For example, on the WiderFunnel blog, we've tested using a call to action at the bottom of each blog post.

Get a Free Landing Page Evaluation

Discover the major areas hurting your conversion rate and learn how to calculate your own Conversion Optimization ROI. (To qualify, you need to have at least 30,000 unique visitors per month)

Get a FREE Landing Page Evaluation Now!

We could run a test on this section to isolate whether this is the best offer. One alternative could be to test changing the offer message to say "Request a Free Demo (with Case Studies)."

Request a Free Demo (with Case Studies)

Discover the major areas hurting your conversion rate and learn how to calculate your own Conversion Optimization ROI. (To qualify, you need to have at least 30,000 unique visitors per month)

Request a FREE Demo Now!

That test variable would isolate which of those two offer wording options is the most effective. There are several hypotheses within this test, so it's not a pure isolation. The words "Request" and "Get" differ between the two challengers, for example, along with the "(with Case Studies)" add-on. It's not a pure isolation, but it still could point toward a potential insight about the type of wording that works best for our future clients.

Or, we could try matching the headline color with the button by changing the headline to orange. That would be an example of a pure isolation of a single color variable. A headline color isolation like that isn't likely to deliver a profound customer insight, though. Isolations that give you insights into the best messaging and user interfaces are more useful.

At WiderFunnel, we strategically build isolations into the tests that aim to generate customer insights. In the case study shown in Chapter 5, "Optimize Your Value Proposition," for the Electronic Arts *The Sims 3* team, for example, the isolations of offer positioning pointed to valuable insights about the types of offers that work for the game's players. *The Sims 3* team was able to use those insights in their other marketing activities.

How to Get ~~Good~~ Great Results

Deciding to test your marketing decisions is one small step toward achieving great conversion-optimization wins. The rest of the path is littered with obstacles and pitfalls. Here are six tips that will give you a better chance of achieving the results you need.

Test Boldly

It's always fun to share in our clients' excitement when they first start testing. We'll spend a few weeks with them planning and creating their first test, and then, when we're ready to launch, the anticipation is palpable! When we pull the trigger and launch the test, the reaction of most is to immediately look at the results report.

But there's nothing there yet. Results take time.

Fortunately, we plan for tests to complete within two to three weeks whenever possible. Sometimes they take longer for low-traffic sites, but our goal is to run fast test iterations.

One of the most common complaints I hear from those who come to WiderFunnel after testing on their own is that their tests take too long to complete. They begin with that same excitement when launching a test, but it slowly turns to frustration as their tests seem to limp along endlessly.

One of the underlying problems with many tests is that they only vary minutiae on the page. Many people falsely believe that conversion optimization is used only to test small tweaks to landing pages. This leads to frustration as they test minor variations of words, colors, and button design and expect dramatic results. By testing insignificant challengers, you'll be in for a long test that may never complete with statistical significance. The case studies throughout this book show examples of the types of bold test challengers that can produce significant conversion-rate improvements.

So, as you analyze your pages, think about bold changes you could make. When you come up with something entirely different, You Should Test That!

Test Fewer Variations

Bloated tests are a common problem that causes tests to run too long. The duration that your tests need to be in market is directly affected by the amount of traffic and conversions each challenger variation records. This means that increasing the number of challengers from four to eight doubles the time your test will take to complete.

It's better to run two tests with four challengers each than one test with eight. Each test round will complete more quickly, and the second test can take into account what was learned from the first.

Minimizing the number of challengers you run isn't as easy as it appears at first. It takes discipline to stick with your plan of testing only a certain number. There are so many good ideas to try!

Avoid Committee Testing

Committee-run testing is notorious for producing diluted ideas and bloated test plans. When everyone has to agree on all variations being tested, many of the novel ideas are weeded out because they don't "make sense." Often the most interesting insights come from those winning challengers that were more risky or that few predicted would win.

Even if a group collaborates to generate suggestions, leadership is needed to test bold ideas.

Win with Confidence

One tempting solution to complete tests more quickly is to accept a lower confidence level. You may be comfortable accepting an 80 or 90 percent statistical confidence level or, like WiderFunnel, aim for a 95 percent confidence level with every test result.

Whatever you decide as a business, don't be tempted to read too much into the early results of a test before it hits your confidence threshold. Small numbers can seem more important than they really are. They can easily be based on pure random chance and statistical clumping. Statistics are misleading when misread or interpreted too early. Understand what your testing tool's reports mean before you interpret results.

Maintain Your Control

Repeat after me: "I will not change my control page—not even a little bit—until the test is complete."

This is a fundamental principle of controlled, scientific testing. Any change to the control or challenger variations during the test invalidates the test result. It becomes useless, pointless, worthless. (As you may be able to tell, I'm passionate about this point. It's a common temptation for companies that are new to testing.)

Just don't change it.

The exception to this rule is for dynamic pages or changing offers. If you're testing on a template with changing content, the variable content on all challengers should change to match. That's okay, as long as the components you're testing remain consistent, which in this case is probably the layout template or value-proposition messaging.

Use Testing Expertise

Many people start their search for conversion optimization by looking for a tool first. This is a mistake of the "tail wagging the dog" variety. The tool should follow the strategy. Begin by bringing in the expertise you need to develop a strategy, and then find the tools that best support it.

Another common mistake people make when starting with testing is to use their testing software vendor to develop test plans. Software vendors generally provide excellent service for the technical aspects of setting up tests, but not the best testing strategy. Every company has its primary expertise area. Software developers are best at developing software, and services agencies provide the best strategy and test execution.

Depending on your situation, bringing in the expertise of a specialist conversion-optimization agency could be a good option for you. There are many reasons you may want to consider hiring a conversion-optimization agency. Here are a few that I often hear:

- A specialist conversion-optimization agency brings a proven process for developing powerful hypotheses that get results more quickly.

- The agency has trained and experienced team members with all the important skill sets you need: strategists, designers, copywriters, developers, and account managers.

- Dedicated resources at an agency can get tests running faster than doing it on your own or with constrained internal resources.

- You get access to the learning from tests on many other websites.

- You'll avoid the common mistakes and get quick early wins to cement organizational support.

- The expert perspective from outside the company can help persuade the website's stakeholders to test new ideas.

- You can be more confident that you're interpreting the results of the tests properly and maximizing your marketing insights.

- An arms-length agency can give you unbiased advice about the right software to select.

The agency option isn't for everyone, and I recommend you start with an ROI calculation to help with the decision. If those benefits would be helpful for you, I humbly suggest that you consider WiderFunnel as an option to help improve your conversion rates.

 Note: Do you have tips for getting the best test results? Check out YouShouldTestThat.com/ Test-Your-Hypotheses to contribute your ideas and join the discussion.

Continue reading to Chapter 12, "Analyze Your Test Results," to learn how to glean insights from the results of your tests.

12

Analyze Your Test Results

*It is a capital mistake to theorize before one has data.
Insensibly one begins to twist facts to suit theories,
instead of theories to suit facts.*

—Sherlock Holmes

In 2005, the people of Italy were presented with a unique statistics opportunity. The number 53 had not been drawn in the national lottery for the preceding two years. This became the talk of the country, with many strategizing the best way to take advantage of it. It became clear to many people that 53 had an increasing chance of being drawn as each week passed.

Many Italians bet huge sums on the number 53. As *The Guardian* reported:

> *In a frenzy that even lottery-mad Italy has rarely seen, some 53 addicts ran up debts, went bankrupt, and lost their homes to the bailiffs.*
>
> *Four died in 53-related incidents. A woman drowned herself in the sea off Tuscany leaving a note admitting that she had spent her family's savings on the number. A man from Signa near Florence shot his wife and son before killing himself. A man was arrested in Sicily this week for beating his wife out of frustration at debts incurred by his 53 habit.*
>
> *In all, more than €3.5bn (£2.4bn) was spent on 53, an average of €227 for each family.*

Statistics can be confusing for even the most analytical people. As pattern-seeking creatures, we have a tendency to see repetition and trends where none exist. Pairing that with our aversion to ambiguity gives us a strong desire to interpret meaning. We want things to make sense and will make sense even when it's nonsense.

Consider this scenario: I have a coin and challenge you to a game of heads or tails. The coin is perfectly weighted so the probability of landing on either side is 0.5. Now think about these questions for a moment, and write down your answers before reading on:

- I flip the coin, and it lands on heads. What is the chance of landing on heads again?
- I flip the coin, and it land on tails. What is the chance of landing on heads?
- I have flipped the coin and gotten tails four times in a row. What is the chance of flipping tails again?

Contrary to what many people believe, the probability in each scenario is still 0.5. This tendency to misjudge randomness is known as the *Gambler's Fallacy*, and it's just one example of how we misperceive statistics.

Interpreting statistical results is one of the most important, and most neglected, skills for conversion optimization. Although this chapter will by no means turn you into a full-fledged data analyst, you'll learn the most important principles for monitoring your test, evaluating the results, and then moving on to the next test with intelligence.

Reading the Tea Leaves

The scientific marketing process requires a rigor that most aren't accustomed to. People find it difficult to say, "I don't know," or "That theory will take more testing." Everyone wants the expert opinion, the fast answer, the conclusive finding.

Before you begin testing, your colleagues know that you're working from imperfect data. The risks of misleading each other are slim because you've all got the same data—none.

Once you start testing, however, people will start looking to you for the answers. They'll want to know the principles you've discovered:

- Should we put images of people on our landing pages?
- Should our offers promote discounts, premiums, bundles, or product value?
- Should we direct traffic to long-copy landing pages, short teasers, or internal web pages?

The only thing worse than not testing at all is misinterpreting your test results. Consequently, the first requirement to analyze your test results is to have a pure heart.

At this point, you may think I've been dipping into the sauce or channeling Master Yoda, but I'm quite serious. Those with distorted motives can contort statistics to say many different things.

If your intention is to prove that your favorite idea is a winner, you can probably find some data to support that conclusion. Maybe your challenger has a lower bounce rate, higher average order value, or more "Likes." The real question should be, "Which challenger drives more business goal conversions and revenue?"

Follow the Scottish poet Andrew Lang's advice to avoid using statistics "as a drunken man uses lamp posts—for support rather than for illumination."

Your first opportunity to make decisions that affect your test outcome is while the test is running.

Monitoring Your Tests

Even before your test is complete, you can make tactical moves to help get the best result. You'll need to understand when you've achieved statistical significance, and decide when to remove under-performers and when to stop the test.

Wait for Statistical Significance

Once you've launched your test, do yourself a favor and take a break from watching the results for a few days. You're not going to make it finish any faster by watching it, and you may be too tempted to draw early conclusions.

You should set a minimum time period for your test as well as a statistical significance threshold. As a minimum time period, I recommend running most tests for at least 10 days over two weekends to iron out any day-of-week seasonality that may be influencing the results.

Various organizations have different comfort levels with decision-making uncertainty. Some of WiderFunnel's clients have decided that an 80 percent statistical significance level is sufficient for them to move on to the next test, whereas others want to stick with our 95 percent benchmark and even run follow-up confirmation tests to be even more certain they've picked the right winner. This isn't a matter of a right or wrong answer.

Each approach has pros and cons. A lower decision threshold allows you to run more tests quickly but gives you a higher chance of errors. A higher threshold produces more confident decisions with more data but can slow down your iteration.

You should decide what your success threshold will be at the beginning of your conversion-optimization strategy and stick with it. Especially in larger organizations, these decisions should be understood by colleagues and stakeholders up front. You'll find more tips for getting buy-in in Chapter 13, "Strategic Marketing Optimization." Whatever decision threshold you decide on, find out from your software vendor or conversion consultant how to read the tool's reports properly. Each tool has different ways of displaying statistical significance, and some can be confusing.

Remove Under-Performers

If challengers are under-performing the control page during your tests, you can remove them without stopping the entire test. This allows you to keep your test running while minimizing the temporary reduction in conversion rate from low performers.

But don't make that decision too hastily. Early test results before hitting statistical significance are often different than the end result. If you remove an under-performer before it has a chance to prove its worth, you may kill a potential winner.

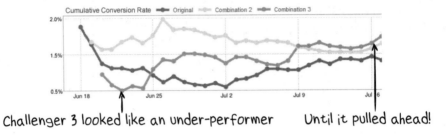

Challenger 3 looked like an under-performer   Until it pulled ahead!

You should set minimum significance and performance thresholds to avoid removing potential winners too early.

Don't Give Up Too Early

Another common temptation is to give up on tests prematurely. Occasionally, the performance of all test variations converges during the early stages of a test, and the test may seem like a waste of time to continue. It can be frustrating, especially if you watch the results daily, to see the performance of the variations enmesh into an undifferentiated mass.

But, don't despair too soon! Many times, I have seen challengers separate after converging.

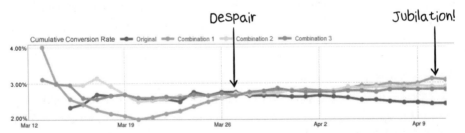

There are many reasons why a test may separate and become more accurate with time. With a lower number of conversions, statistical clumping has a greater effect.

This pattern is more common for campaigns where the conversion isn't immediate. If the conversion decision cycle is longer than one or two days, you need to keep the test running long enough to take those longer conversions into account.

Evaluating Results

At WiderFunnel, we often see tests with interesting and conflicting test results. One challenger may have more online chat or lead-form conversions, whereas another has higher e-commerce purchase conversions, and yet another may have higher average order value. Which one should be the winner?

You'll know if you followed the steps in Chapter 11, "Test Your Hypotheses," for setting a clear goal at the beginning of your tests. When your success criterion is clear at the beginning, the debates during results analysis are minimized.

The first thing to understand is...

How Accurate Are Your Results?

Some people are disappointed when they learn that their split test results aren't 100 percent precise. I have to admit that I hesitate to write this section, because I know it can create unnecessary disillusionment. If you think statistics are infallible, you may be shaken to learn that they aren't as predictable as you thought. Scientific testing, however, is still the best method for marketing optimization. Questions of accuracy and precision are common and important to understand.

At a statistically significant confidence level of 95 percent, the result you see is expected to be consistent 19 times out of 20. That means you can be 95 percent confident in the result.

"Sure, the conversion rates are accurate to within a fraction of a percent, 19 times out of 20," some say, "But I want it *exact!*"

Let's take a step back to find out if that's what you really want. Ask yourself why you're running conversion-optimization tests. You probably want to make the best decision you can about your marketing, right?

But you know you can't always make the best decision, because you don't have enough information. You're expected to make the right decisions without the benefit of hindsight. I empathize with your situation. That's a lot of pressure, and it's understandable that you want some relief.

That's where testing comes in. Testing offers a respite from the decision-guessing pressure. Instead of guessing, you can *test* to find out what works better, and the information you get from testing is statistically significant.

But your test results may not be telling you what you think they are. I'm going to share a little secret that may surprise you: statistics tell you about confidence, but they don't tell you the "right" answer.

Let's say you get a test result showing a 16.5 percent conversion-rate lift at a 95 percent confidence level. Great! You should be happy about that. That's a great result from a single test!

Here's the secret: that result doesn't necessarily mean that you'll get a 16.5 percent lift on an ongoing basis. You may get more. Or less. But there's a very good chance (a statistically significant one, in fact) that you'll experience a conversion-rate lift.

Take a look at one of WiderFunnel's recent test results. Challengers 1 and 2 both achieved 95 percent statistical significance. The bar chart shows that the significance bars have cleared the control bar. Those bars represent the range of conversion rates for each variation, and when they no longer overlap, the variations have a statistically significance difference.

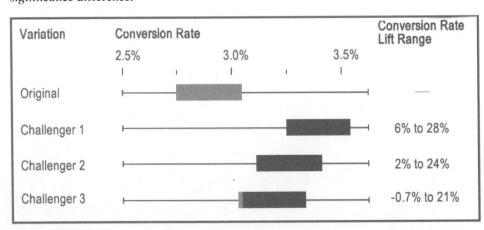

According to statistics, the exact amount of the conversion-rate lift can't be known with the amount of data available. For Challenger 1, statistics tells us we can be confident that it will be in the range of between 6 and 28 percent.

Challenger	Conversion Rate	Low	High	Observed Conversion-Rate Improvement	Conversion-Rate Lift Range
Control	2.91% ± 0.15	2.76%	3.06%	—	—
Challenger 1	3.39% ± 0.15	3.24%	3.54%	16.5%	6% to 28%
Challenger 2	3.26% ± 0.15	3.11%	3.41%	12.0%	2% to 24%
Challenger 3	3.19% ± 0.15	3.04%	3.34%	9.6%	-0.7% to 21%

"Wait a minute!" you say, "That's a big range! Isn't that inaccurate?" Actually, *this result is very accurate* for the question we asked: "Will it lift conversion rates?"

The answer is, "Yes, it will (and I'm 95 percent confident)." As a business rule for decision-making, a 95 percent confidence level is a very high hurdle to clear.

If your question is, "By how much will it lift conversion rates?" then the answer requires a higher level of precision and more data. If that's your question, you have a cost-benefit business decision to make: how much time is that extra precision worth?

You can keep the test running longer to collect that data, but doing so has an opportunity cost. You could use that time and traffic to run another test and have a shot at even more conversion-rate improvement.

Incidentally, Challenger 3 in this example is also likely to beat out the control, but it hasn't proven itself yet. Its minimum statistical value within the Conversion-Rate Lift Range (see column) is still slightly negative, so we don't call it a winner yet.

But here's another statistical secret: there is no "real" conversion rate other than the conversion rate you track and observe. Statistical analysis doesn't attempt to reveal your "real" conversion rate. It tries to give you a level of confidence in the result. With more data, statistics tell you that you can be more confident in the observed conversion rate.

Whereas statistics are concerned with probabilities and confidence, business is about making good decisions. The most accurate conversion rate you have at any time is the one you have observed. In other words, the "real" conversion-rate lift is the observed conversion-rate lift we've tracked in the test: 16.5 percent.

After all this, you may be wondering if you should make decisions based on split test data. I believe you should accept the accuracy of a controlled test any day of the week. In the end, you can either take the winning result, which is likely to give a 16.5 percent (plus or minus) conversion-rate lift, or keep the control page, which probably wasn't tested in the first place! Which would you rather bank on?

Multiple Goals

If you've set up your test to track multiple conversion goals, you'll need to evaluate the results differently than for single goals. That is, unless you assume each type of conversion has the same value. In that case, the analysis is easy.

Different types of conversions usually have different values. In a B2B setting, whitepaper downloads usually have lower value than quote requests or live chat sessions, for example. To analyze multiple goals, you need to consider the relative contribution from each type with weighted conversion goals.

Consider a simple scenario with two goals that have a $10 and $75 value, respectively. If you track four challenger variations with the conversions shown next, you can see how the weighted value influences the result.

Challenger A had the highest number of conversions, but Challenger C ended up with the highest contribution value because it gained a much higher proportion of Goal 2 conversions.

Weighted Value of Conversions

Challenger	Goal 1 Conversions	Goal 1 Contribution @ $10 each	Goal 2 Conversions	Goal 2 Contribution @ $75 each	Total Conversion Count	Total Contribution	Revenue Lift %
Control	105	$1,050	49	$3,675	154	$4,725	—
A	230	$2,300	61	$4,575	291	$6,875	45.5%
B	118	$1,180	65	$4,875	183	$6,055	28.1%
C	96	$960	92	$6,900	188	$7,860	66.3%

Often, the weighted values of conversions reveal interesting findings. We often see that some challengers can shift prospects toward increasing their commitment and taking higher-value actions.

A special case of multiple goals is when you have direct revenue to analyze along with other conversions.

Revenue Results

The ultimate goal of conversion optimization is to maximize revenue. You should optimize for the challenger that produces the most overall revenue per variation. That's one reason I tend to downplay the term conversion-*rate* optimization in favor of conversion optimization or, even better, marketing optimization. In many cases, there's a lot more potential to optimize than a single conversion rate.

As you saw in Chapter 2, "What Is Conversion Optimization," when direct revenue isn't available to measure, you can create revenue estimates. Working to create more accurate estimates is helpful in feeling more confident in your decisions. Even if it's a work in progress, start with what you're able to track and view it as a work in progress.

As you'll see in the following case study, a challenger may contribute a much larger revenue lift than its conversion-rate lift would indicate.

Case Study: 41 Percent Lift in Revenue per Visitor for Wine Retailer

WineExpress.com is the exclusive wine shop partner of Wine Enthusiast catalog and website, which has been providing quality wine accessories and storage for more than 30 years. WineExpress.com adheres to a strict philosophy of offering only the finest, best-value wines. And, like Wine Enthusiast, the company differentiates itself by delivering unsurpassed customer service and expertise to its growing clientele.

WineExpress.com®

The Business Need

The WineExpress.com management team was familiar with A/B/*n* split testing techniques and had already conducted a number of tests on their sister website, www.wineenthusiast.com, to boost sales conversions. The group had also run extensive testing on their email campaigns, which represented a significant portion of the WineExpress.com retention efforts.

Now the team was turning their attention to one of the most-visited pages of the WineExpress.com website—the Wine of the Day page—and was looking for ways to further stimulate sales conversions.

To drive traffic to the page, each day, management sends an email to its significant opt-in email list promoting a different wine selection, with a shipping charge of just 99 cents. The landing page's central focus, aside from the featured product, is a virtual wine-tasting video featuring the company's highly regarded wine director.

The Challenges

The Wine of the Day page at WineExpress.com enjoys an exceptionally high sales conversion rate. The opt-in, in-house email list ensures quality traffic. The page's strong persuasive power stems very likely from the wine director's credibility and the compelling nature of the video tastings. So the first challenge for WineExpress.com was to optimize a page that already converted well.

Continues

Case Study: 41 Percent Lift in Revenue per Visitor for Wine Retailer *(Continued)*

The control landing page

Additionally, as with all e-commerce sites, WineExpress.com faced the challenge of finding equilibrium between optimizing sales transactions and optimizing overall revenues. Focusing solely on the number of sales conversions could end up having a negative impact on the WineExpress.com bottom line if average order value was deflated in the process.

The Solution

WiderFunnel came in to develop and execute a conversion-optimization strategy for the WineExpress.com Wine of the Day page. The team designed the test and tracked conversions and revenue.

WiderFunnel developed and tested three design challenger variations, aiming at testing different layout approaches.

Variation A: "CTA Right"

This challenger brought forward product information, video, and customer reviews while displacing distracting elements. The following changes were made:

- Removed the top navigation

- Streamlined the top banner
- Added a countdown offer to the top
- Moved the product description up
- Moved the video above the fold
- Increased the prominence of customer reviews
- Decreased the prominence of "you may also like" items
- Widened the page

Variation B: "New CTA Right"

This challenger was essentially the same as Variation A, "CTA Right," except that the call-to-action area was enlarged, pushing the video to the fold line.

Variation C: "New CTA Left"

This was a mirror image of Variation B, "New CTA Right," moving the CTA and video feature to the left while product info and customer reviews went into the right column.

The Results: 41 Percent Increase in Revenue per Visitor

Two of the three challengers outperformed the original page in terms of purchase conversions and revenue per visitor. The winner, "CTA Right," lifted the sales-conversion rate by 5 percent and revenue per visitor by 41 percent!

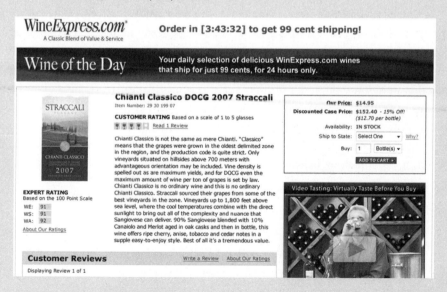

Winning Challenger page

Continues

Key learnings for the WineExpress.com team were as follows:

- The need to optimize for and track revenues, not just conversions
- The impact of the fold
- The importance of eyeflow and placement of design elements

With a solid success in hand, the WineExpress.com team plans to further refine the layout of the Wine of the Day page with additional conversion testing.

This WineExpress.com results analysis showed findings similar to the case of AllPopArt's product page, which you saw in Chapter 8, "Optimize for Anxiety." The conversion-rate lift in both cases was significant, but the total revenue lift was even greater. In both cases, the increase in average order value and, consequently, revenue per visitor showed the most important gains for these businesses.

Once you've determined the winning challengers based on conversions and revenue, you can identify the impact of the test's isolations.

Compare Isolations

Although every test has the potential to improve conversions and revenue, tests with strategic isolations can also teach you about your target audience. Isolations are where you gain learning and insights.

Learning can come from a single test, but true insights are only developed through a series of strategic isolations. From a single test you may learn that your customers respond better to a page with a product image versus an image of a smiling person, for example. It would be a mistake to take that one finding and assume it's a general customer insight about product versus people images. That particular person image may not have worked as well as another, or the offer and value proposition on that page may have resonated with the product image.

This is a common mistake when analyzing test results. Many people are publicly promoting the following beliefs:

- Videos increase landing-page conversion rates.
- Videos don't work as well as still images.
- Benefits work better than features.
- You should emphasize features rather than benefits.
- Smiling people increase conversion rates.
- People are distracting and should be removed.
- You should emphasize trust seals.
- Testimonials should be prominent on landing pages.

- Product page order buttons should be on the right side of the page.
- You should reduce the number of steps in your conversion funnel.

At best, claims like these may be based on the results of one or two tests—not nearly enough to produce a general insight. Be careful to understand your test isolations and take the findings as *potential* insights that need further testing.

What to Test Next?

The most important principle of conversion optimization is that it's a continuous improvement process. One test doesn't create an optimized page. The word *optimization* itself can be misleading because the goal isn't to achieve or discover the perfect optimized page. Even if the perfect page were achieved, it would be a temporary achievement, because the tastes, needs, and expectations of your audience change. The journey of continuous learning, insights, and improvement will never be complete.

Re-Prioritize Your Priorities

After each test, you can move on to the next test priority. If you've developed a conversion-optimization strategy, your next priority will be laid out in advance. However, you should also frequently reevaluate the test priorities based on your findings.

Your conversion-optimization strategy should always be considered a work in progress. After each test, evaluate the new information you gather from the test results to determine how it affects your priorities.

If you've had a big lift, this could indicate that the page has even more potential for improvement. Your results analysis may have revealed potential marketing insights or new hypotheses to build on in follow-up test rounds. Surprising results are the most interesting, especially when they provide ideas for new experiment hypotheses.

Or you may have already achieved most of the gains in that single test. You won't know without testing on the page at least two or three times with different approaches.

If there isn't much movement in the conversion rate or revenue, you may have either found that there's low elasticity on that page or tested the wrong things. In either case, you'll have new hypotheses to test and should consider whether that priority page warrants another test round or if you should move the page down the list and test on the next priority.

Beat the Dreaded Inconclusive Test

Fear of failure is a natural part of being human and was a beneficial part of our psyche when the dangers were more related to sabre-toothed tigers than website conversion rates. Fear of failure isn't as helpful for conversion optimization.

Occasionally a test round doesn't produce a new champion page. The control page sometimes wins, or the test may prove to be inconclusive over an extended time. This is a natural part of testing and doesn't have to lead to frustration. You have learned something from the test, even if there isn't a winner. If nothing else, you've learned what *not* to test again. And there's even more hidden potential. You can glean potential insights from losing or inconclusive tests. If you've isolated a single variable, such as a headline or image, you may have some new data about the types of messaging that don't work for your audience.

At WiderFunnel, we often find that building on the learning from early test isolations gives us insights that contribute to bigger successes in following tests, even if the first test rounds don't give us the home-run results we all want to see. I'll show you two examples from WiderFunnel conversion-optimization strategy clients. In both, the results from the first test round gave our strategists potential learning that helped us develop better hypotheses in the following test rounds.

Variation	Estimated Conversion Rate	Observed Improvement
Original		—
Combination 3		-11.2%
Combination 2		-12.5%
Combination 1		-19.6%

We compared and hypothesized

Variation	Estimated Conversion Rate	Observed Improvement
Original		—
☆ Top high-confidence winners.		
Combination 1		16.1%

And the next test won!

Variation	Estimated Conversion Rate	Observed Improvement
Original		—
Combination 2		4.03%
Combination 3		1.24%
Combination 1		-4.28%

We analyzed for learning

Variation	Estimated Conversion Rate	Observed Improvement
Original		—
☆ Top high-confidence winners.		
Combination 3		134%
Combination 1		69.8%
Combination 2		31.9%

And the next test—Shazam!

As you can see, there is an art to conversion-rate optimization, and over time you'll gain the instinct of an experienced conversion strategist that will help you build on insights by testing the right hypotheses on the right pages and for the right time.

Most important, every test you run contributes to the experience that will make you a better conversion-optimization expert. Becoming a conversion-rate optimization expert takes practice running many types of tests in a variety of scenarios. WiderFunnel's strategists, for example, develop their expertise through their exposure to many hundreds of tests in all types of website scenarios.

 Note: Do you have tips for getting the best test results? Check out YouShouldTestThat.com/AnalyzeResults to contribute your ideas and join the discussion.

Continue reading for the advanced discussion in Chapter 13, "Strategic Marketing Optimization." You'll learn how to become a champion for SMO and maximize your personal and business value from conversion optimization.

13 Strategic Marketing Optimization

An ounce of practice is worth more than tons of preaching.

—*Mahatma Gandhi*

The term *conversion-rate optimization* is a misnomer. It implies that conversion-rate improvement should be the sole goal of your testing work. That's a limited view.

Although conversion-rate lift is important and should be a goal for individual tests, the result of a testing strategy produces much more. As you've seen from the case studies in this book, test results can produce massive revenue improvement, learning, and customer insights. Forward-thinking CMOs and business leaders use these quantitatively tested insights to create a positive feedback loop into their marketing and business strategies.

Beyond even those outcomes, testing produces an organizational culture shift toward data-driven decision-making. In a scientific marketing organization, data is valued over personality, experimental methods are structured and refined, and tested learning is disseminated throughout the organization.

When you begin to leverage the ongoing learning and insights from conversion-rate optimization, you'll have progressed to a state I'll call *strategic marketing optimization (SMO)*.

Through the ideas presented in this book, I hope to inspire more than just conversion-rate optimization. I hope you'll take up the challenge of building a culture of ongoing SMO.

Aim for Marketing Insights

Despite how much attention conversion optimization is getting today, it's still being undervalued. Most marketers don't appreciate its potential.

Think about it this way: you have thousands of visitors to your website every month. From those visitors, you have the ability to gain insights with scientific certainty. Yet the predominant talk about conversion optimization views it as a method for eking out small conversion-rate bumps on landing pages.

This is tragic!

Those of us who do the most testing understand the power of all the beautiful traffic arriving on your website. Not only are these prospective customers looking for an opportunity to buy from you, but they're also willing to (unknowingly) tell you the types of messages and experiences that are most effective.

Consider the far-reaching effect of testing your value proposition, for example. By running controlled tests of your messaging approaches, you can gain statistically significant learning about which messages move the most customers to action. Yes, those tests can give dramatic lifts in leads, sales, and revenue. But beyond that, the insights can lead to even greater changes in your marketing and business strategy.

As marketers realize the potential for gaining marketing insights, the conversion-optimization industry is evolving. We're no longer just tweaking and tuning button designs and headline colors. We're no longer just boosting conversion rates on landing pages. We're fostering a culture of data-driven decision-making. I hope you'll join us in adopting the Optimization Manifesto, which encapsulates this culture of continuous testing and optimization.

The Optimization Manifesto

We listen to our gut, and then test what it says.
We gather marketing research, and then test it.
We create best practices, and then test them.
We listen to opinions, and then test them.
We hear the advice of experts, and then test it.
We believe in art and science,
Creativity and discipline,
Intuition and evidence,
And continuous improvement.
We aim for marketing insights.
We aim to improve business results.
We test because it works.
Scientific testing is our crucible for decision-making.

Come with me as we push the boundaries of conversion optimization toward SMO. For a full-size printable graphic version of the manifesto, visit YouShouldTestThat.com/SMO.

Be a Marketing-Optimization Champion

Your organization needs a marketing-optimization champion. The challenges of developing a data-driven culture may be great. Some will resist the rigorous discipline of a testing strategy. Those who have spent their lives following their intuition alone are unaccustomed to asking the data for direction.

If you're a data-driven decision-maker, this may be frustrating for you. Why would any company willingly reject conversion optimization when so much revenue could be within easy grasp? Sometimes decision rationale doesn't make sense.

Your organization's culture and norms determine how decisions are made. The company may be accustomed to following the strongest personalities, or letting the HiPPO dictate direction, or following the whims of the Black Turtleneck (See Chapter 1, "Why You Should Test That"). Creating a data-driven culture can take time and effort. Persuading people to adopt a marketing-optimization strategy requires an organizational champion.

Your company needs you to step up and be an influence for marketing testing. Fortunately, being your organization's champion is very rewarding. Marketing testing is one of the most easily provable strategies, and the rationale for it is unassailable. When you stand as an advocate of the data-driven approach, you'll reap the rewards in your career. Data advocates inevitably rise to positions of influence.

Here are some tips for creating a data-driven culture:

Get Senior-Level Buy-in for Testing   No matter how strong your project results are, you'll face an uphill battle without senior management support. Many of your colleagues look for cues from HiPPOs when deciding what to support, and senior managers probably allocate funding. Suffice it to say, your job will be much easier with their backing.

What is success for your senior decision-makers? Start by finding out how they're incentivized so you can show how optimization will help them reach their goals. If you can help them look (and get paid) like rock stars, they'll support your projects and reward you in return.

You can also appeal to the rational support they need by building a business case for testing. With directly measurable results, the case for testing is easy to make. Show the conversion-rate lift that other organizations are getting, and estimate the return on investment (ROI) for a testing strategy. You can download ROI calculators from YouShouldTestThat.com/SMO.

Create a Tangible Opportunity   Get support for testing by creating a tangible problem that testing solves. Bring in a conversion-optimization expert to tell decision-makers how your website needs to improve. The credibility of a third party like WiderFunnel can carry more weight than internal voices.

You can also record feedback from real customers. Videos of customer frustration can be powerful motivators.

Sharing case-study examples of companies can be a source of inspiration and motivation, too. You can download case studies of conversion-optimization tests at www.ConversionSkills.com.

Conduct Skunkworks Tests   If you don't have senior support at the beginning, you could try an under-the-radar approach. Pick a few target pages with low political visibility to gain some quick wins. Landing pages outside the main website can be good candidates for this. Then, use the winning results from those tests as ammunition in your campaign for support to move on to more important optimization areas.

Involve Other Departments   You'll need the support of others to get your tests running: IT, finance, marketing, branding, and more may present barriers. Save yourself surprises by involving them early.

Tie Results to Revenue   When you present results, don't just show the improvement in conversion rate or KPIs. Tie the results to revenue to show real cash impact. Percentages are intangible, but everyone relates to cash. What would you rather get: a *10 percent* conversion-rate lift, or *$500,000* greater profit?

Note: Look for the WIIFM When you're presenting results to an individual stakeholder or decision-maker, tie the result to their personal performance measurement or bonus. They're subconsciously asking, "What's in it for me?" so make sure you answer that question. If you can relate your work to their personal benefit, you'll create an ally.

Share Results Far and Wide   Many of WiderFunnel's clients have used our results-analysis presentations to create an internal event in the organization. The champion invites members from throughout the company to see the results of tests, guess the winners, and discuss what was learned. The presentations are a lot of fun, especially for those departments that aren't normally involved in external communications. Make sure to invite people from all functional areas.

You'll see several benefits from these meetings. Positive results with statistical certainty are exciting for everyone and create momentum. They educate your colleagues about the process of testing and inspire the organization to support your projects. You'll be positioned as a leader with ideas that deliver results.

When WiderFunnel runs tests, we hold a vote with everyone involved to guess which one will win. The results presentation could be a good time to award prizes and boost the fun factor.

Be a Leader   You have a decision to make about what you stand for in your career. Every idea you want to sell depends on the influence you have with colleagues, friends, and clients. The foundation of that influence will be based on what I'll call *soft* or *hard* credibility. Soft credibility is based on your personality, charisma, and personal connections, whereas hard credibility is the data, evidence, and goal alignment that you bring.

Become a thought-leader by reading more and sharing more knowledge with your colleagues. Take opportunities to conduct group discussions, distribute summaries of your learning, have lunch with unconvinced team members, and go to conferences.

Never Give Up   As Winston Churchill said in a famous speech, "Never, never, never, never give up." Testing and optimization are not one-time events. You'll face opposition, confusing results, and disappointments, but they will melt away when you experience big wins.

The biggest threat to your success is what I call *the shiny new thing*. There will always be new tools, tactics, and opinions that will tempt you to abandon your testing discipline.

As Chet Holmes said in his book *The Ultimate Sales Machine: Turbocharge Your Business with Relentless Focus on 12 Key Strategies* (Portfolio Trade, 2008), his "pigheaded discipline and determination" are key to his results. As he says, "Implementation, not ideas, is the key to real success."

Some organizations will never adopt marketing optimization. The culture may be too entrenched in old ways. I cringe when I see companies start on the path of testing and then turn around and redesign their website wholesale without considering the progress and learning they've already made. If you don't see progress in your data advocacy, you should move on to a company that values it. Companies that don't test will eventually yield to competitors that do. Life is too short to battle for years as a cultural misfit at companies with outdated thinking.

My goal for this book has been to make the case for why conversion optimization is important for gaining business improvement *and* marketing insight. I've also given you many tips, frameworks, and insights to get the best results.

I hope I've convinced you that there's a better way to handle expert and colleague opinions and recommendations. I hope the next time you come across a good idea, your instinct will be to say, "You Should Test That!"

Index

Note to the reader: Throughout this index **boldfaced** page numbers indicate primary discussions of a topic. *Italicized* page numbers indicate illustrations.

Symbols and Numerals

A

B

Y

Yahoo, 2
    page-load times and site usage, 218
Yantis, Steven, 100

Z

Zappos, *217*, 217
    free shipping offers, *141*
zoom-in functions, for images, 186